The Minimalist Photographer

Steve Johnson

The Minimalist Photographer

rockynook

Steve Johnson, minimalistphotography101.com

Editor: Joan Dixon
Copyeditor: Jeanne Hansen
Layout: Petra Strauch
Cover Design: Helmut Kraus, www.exclam.de
Printer: Friesens Corporation
Printed in Canada

ISBN 978-1-937538-09-5

1st Edition 2013

Rocky Nook, Inc.
802 E. Cota Street, 3rd Floor
Santa Barbara, CA 93103

www.rockynook.com

Library of Congress Cataloging-in-Publication Data

Johnson, Steve, 1960 June 14-
The minimalist photographer / by Steve Johnson. -- 1st edition.
pages cm
ISBN 978-1-937538-09-5 (softcover : alk. paper)
1. Photography. I. Title.
TR146.J5725 2013
770--dc23
2012036210

Distributed by O'Reilly Media
1005 Gravenstein Highway North
Sebastopol, CA 95472

This book is printed on acid-free paper.

For Meg
She was right.

Table of Contents

Introduction

A short while after I first became interested in photography I came up against a problem that almost made me put my camera away forever. I have come to realize through countless discussions with many others that I am far from unique in having this problem and that it is very common among those who took or want to take photography seriously. The problem can be summed up in two words: "What now?" Although I knew that I wanted to make images, and the camera seemed like the ideal tool, I could not generate any real enthusiasm.

To find photographic fulfillment, I bought camera equipment and photography magazines, read technical discussions by famous photographers, and attended every photography exhibition within a fifty-mile radius of wherever I was at the time. This did little more than fill up my camera bag and bookshelf and deplete my wallet. None of this advanced my photography in any meaningful way.

After becoming competent with a new lens or learning a new technique, I always found myself returning to the question, "What now?" I gradually came to realize that the answer did not lie in acquiring more equipment or knowledge but rather in rethinking my relationship with photography. To cut a long story short, I realized that I needed to bring a philosophy to my photography rather than approach it as a blank slate.

This is where minimalism comes in. There are many definitions of minimalism, all revolving around the idea of simplification and how best to achieve it. This is true whether the subject being discussed is fine art, lifestyle, or just about anything else. All these have one thing in common, though, and that is that the process is not random, or simply a matter of getting rid of a certain percentage of something and hoping for a worthwhile result. The objective is always to remove the non-essential in order to get to what is essential.

It is easy to see how a minimalist philosophy can be applied to an area such as composition as it dovetails perfectly with the idea that visual clutter should always be reduced as far as possible. Less obvious areas where a minimalist approach would serve the photographer well are equipment choices, an understanding of the history of photography, and even the possible future of photography. I do not think that there is any aspect of photography or the development of the photographer that does not benefit from this reductionist approach.

The upshot of this approach is that, for me, "What now?" has been replaced by a different question, "What next?" I now have a half dozen photography projects that I am enthusiastically tackling at any given time. The realization that I had to bring a philosophy and a belief system to photography, and that the best philosophy was minimalism, underpins this book, and it is that idea I am excited to be able to share with you.

At the end of each chapter you will find a small gallery of images. Each gallery is based on a theme that is intended to teach, to inspire, and, last but not least, to simply be enjoyed.

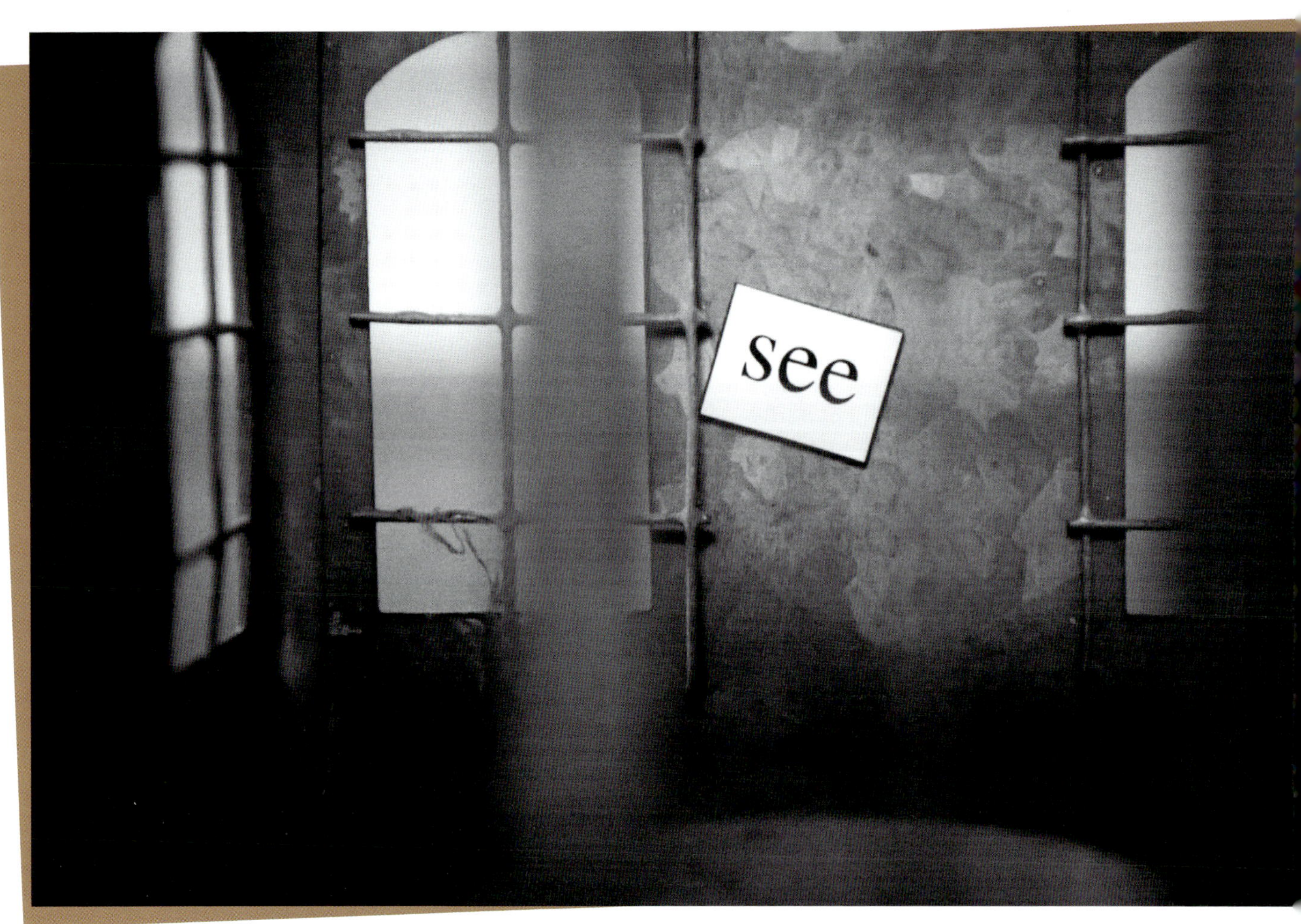
see

Chapter 1
You

The more you know about yourself as a photographer—your preferences, your motivations, and your goals—the better your photography will be. Here we will take a look at these issues so that you can see the importance of defining them for yourself.

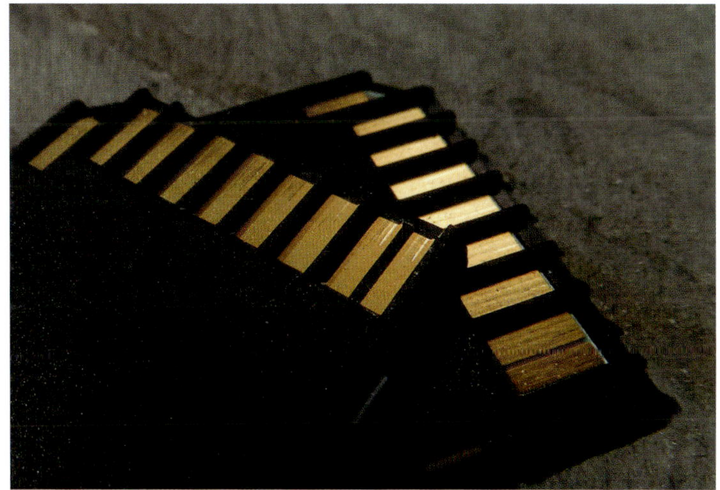

Memory cards

So You Want to Take Better Photographs

By far, the most profound change that occurred over the past 20 years was the shift from film to digital. The appearance of the first consumer-level digital cameras in the mid-1990s really did change everything. Producing photographs went from being an expensive pastime to something that was basically free after the initial equipment was purchased. The cost of early digital cameras was very high, and the image quality was low when compared with film cameras, but this is no longer the case.

I now take for granted that I can take 50 or 500 shots of a subject, whereas with film I may have limited myself two or three at most. The extra cost is nothing more than a miniscule amount of depreciation on the camera and on the rechargeable battery—a couple of cents against tens or even hundreds of dollars. This reduced cost of digital photography has made it much easier to experiment with the medium and has allowed many people to produce images who could not have afforded to do so with film. Another big technological advance is the modern-day ability to instantly see the result of a shot on the camera's LCD screen, rather than having to wait for it to be returned from the photo lab. Adjustments to an exposure, and other on-the-spot modifications based on viewing the original, can now be implemented without an intervening period of days or weeks.

Since the cost of producing a perfectly serviceable photograph is only a fraction of what it used to be, and experimentation is now within reach of just about everyone, there are a lot of people taking photographs who otherwise would not have been. This includes, among other loosely defined groups, thousands of people taking photographs of their daily lives as well as visual artists who can now afford to use a camera for something other than simply recording the work they produced in other mediums. For the first time, photography has become a serious medium for those whose background is not primarily photography.

Of course, the digital revolution has influenced more than just camera technology. The computer has now replaced the darkroom. What used to require a small room, lots of chemicals, and lots of waiting for stuff to happen can now be accomplished on the same machine that most of us use for our taxes and letter writing: the computer. Of course, specialized software is required, but this can be had for free. Now on a computer, anyone can do much more to an image than was ever possible in even the best-equipped darkroom. Even more amazing is the fact that this often involves no extra financial outlay. It is easily possible for one to have purchased a smartphone and a computer without even a thought about photography, yet they will have all the tools required to produce stunning images. Anyone can make a photograph, from choosing the subject to shoot to doing the final editing. Sometimes it is easy to forget just how far things have come.

Any effort you put into answering the 'why' question at any time during your photographic career will pay for itself many times over.

In the days of film, one of two things was likely to happen: a print would end up in an album and be shown to a couple of dozen people. Or the print might be placed in a shoe box, or possibly an old box file, and it would be lucky to ever see the light of day again. Today, websites like Facebook, Flickr, Twitter, and more recently Google+ provide virtual spaces where anyone can publish their images and receive feedback from photographers and non-photographers alike.

Historically, for a photograph to have appeared in a print publication, other than in rare cases, it had to be approved by someone, probably a picture editor. The Internet dynamic is completely different—photographers decide for themselves what they publish and exactly how they publish it. With a little self-promotion, it is possible for unknown photographers with something interesting to share and a feel for the Internet as a medium to have thousands, or even tens of thousands, of people viewing their work on a regular basis.

The importance of this change from a virtual dictatorship to a democracy cannot be overstated. Photographers can publish what they want, and others can decide whether it has merit or not. This situation may pass the test of time, but I'm not overly optimistic. I suspect that a new class of gatekeepers will emerge, albeit a less rigid one than in the pre-digital days. At this moment in photography history, though, things could not be better for the photographer who wants to find and connect with an audience. The other thing that this democratization of photography has led to is an explosion of styles and approaches. If you have something different to communicate, there has never been a better time to do it, because photography is no longer the backward-looking sibling of the other, more enlightened, visual arts. This really is the best time to be a photographer.

Why Do You Want to Take Photographs?

At first, this may seem like a question with an obvious answer, rather like asking someone why they want to drink coffee. But this is one of those questions that seems to get harder the more it is grappled with. Let's return to the coffee example for a second. There are several possible, easily defined reasons why someone may want to drink coffee. These reasons include taste, stimulative effect, and possibly social contact. Now try answering, with some level of clarity, the question of why you want to take photographs, and then write down your answers. The good news is that any effort you put into answering this question at any time during your photographic career will pay for itself many times over.

This is my most recent attempt to answer the question: I am obsessed with aesthetics and composition. The camera and digital editing tools provide a means to capture and manipulate lines, tones, colors, and shapes very quickly and relatively easily. Photography allows me to cover much more ground than any other visual medium. I am interested in showing the connection between the photograph and human emotion. More specifically, I want to experiment with how much information can be removed from an image before it loses emotional impact. Allied to this, I want to study why contrast seems to be the most important quality when it comes to eliciting an emotional response. I enjoy exploring the relationship between the logical and the emotional, and the camera is the best tool for this process.

The less generic and more personal the response, the more useful it is likely to be. I have no desire to go all Zen at this point, but the answers should come from within and should be *your* answers. While you work on answering this question, forget my opinions and the opinions of writers and photographers that you admire. For the moment, it really is all about you.

One other bit of advice is to make your answers as open, as opposed to closed, as possible. Think in terms of exploration, not being the best or getting to some imaginary winning post.

If I had taken the time to ask this question of myself when I first started out, the answer would have been along these lines: I want to find the most beautiful scenes, people, and objects and produce the best possible two-dimensional representations of them.

This answer is a lot less open ended than my current working one, and consequently it would be a lot less useful. It is also much more generic, and while it would be better than nothing, it is nowhere near as useful as my current answer.

Of course there are many possible answers; the important thing is to be honest. The worst trap to fall into is writing something down because you think it is more worthy than what you really want to use the camera for.

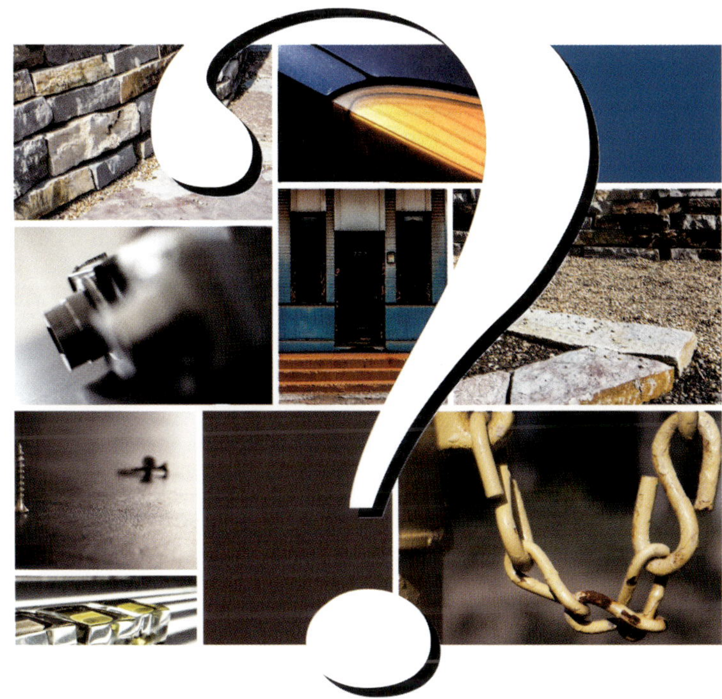

Here are just a few possible reasons for wanting to pick up a camera:

- Record family life
- Record another interest, such as a sport
- Sell stuff on an auction website
- Build a record of beautiful things
- Understand visual language
- Explore artistic concepts
- Expand personal horizons
- Supply images for a website or social media page
- Spend time with your photographer friends

Ideally, the question of why you want to take photographs should be a fundamental part of your ongoing internal dialog about photography. Every image you make changes you, usually by a tiny amount, but occasionally by a massive amount. These changes accumulate and will cause you to periodically revise how you think about your own photography.

The question of why you want to take photographs should be a fundamental part of your ongoing internal dialog about photography.

However dedicated you are to photography—or even if you're obsessed with it—there will be times when pointing a camera at stuff no longer excites you and editing your images becomes more of a chore than an exercise in discovery. We all have days like this, but if these days start to stretch into weeks or months, then it is a fair bet that you need to take another look at your reason for taking pictures. If it's just for a day or two, though, do something other than photography if at all possible. We all get jaded from time to time.

If this whole approach seems a bit daunting, another exercise to try is to look at images on the Internet, or in books, museums, and galleries; find photographs that appeal to you and then find out a little about the photographer and his or her motivations. In addition, you can look for common features in photographs that appeal to you. A quick indication of your artistic preferences can be gleaned by determining whether it is the subject matter that appeals to you or the use of color, strong lines, or other compositional elements. This exercise will aid you toward expressing why you want to take photographs. It may take a little time, but that is perfectly okay; this is not a race.

I suspect that most people who buy a camera and then leave it at the back of a drawer or let it gather dust after taking a few dozen photographs do so because they don't take time to address this fundamental question.

What Type of Photographer Are You Now?

What was the first thing that came to mind when you read this question? At the risk of stating the obvious, if you like to photograph landscapes, you would probably have answered that you are a landscape or possibly a nature photographer, and if you enjoy making images of people, then you might have answered that you are a portrait photographer. The problem with this type of labeling is that it can be self-limiting. If you think of yourself as a nature photographer, for instance, you might stop yourself from seeing the slightly less obvious beauty of urban and industrial environments.

A better approach is to categorize the type of photographer you are in a way that doesn't restrict the subject matter. Professional photographers often prefer to use terms such as *fine art photographer, stock photographer,* or other terms that define the market they are selling to.

Another way photographers define themselves that is less common is by using a philosophical or artistic label. Minimalist, experimental, and even abstract are among the more obvious examples. Whereas more commercial photographers are likely to use market-based terminology, more academic-minded or, for that matter, hobbyist photographers are better served by using the philosophical approach. The reason is simple—this method of labeling provides a lens through which just about anything in the visual world can be understood.

I call myself a minimalist photographer for several reasons, but the main reason is that it forces me to focus on the essential and find ways to either lose, or at least minimize, everything else. The label helps me achieve what I want to achieve. If I am struggling with an assignment, it is because of a lack of clarity. I solve the problem just by the act of thinking about what type of photographer I am. If I called myself a portrait photographer and was having trouble with a shoot, say, of street photography, reminding myself that I was a portrait photographer wouldn't help me nearly as much.

It may seem that I have belabored this point, but it is important, and as much as we may have problems with labels, they are important. A label communicates a lot of information in shorthand form to other photographers, viewers, and clients, but most important, to ourselves. Give yourself the wrong label, and you could be fighting it for the rest of your photographic life. Choose a label that expands your horizons and provides clarity, and it can be one of your biggest assets.

What Type of Photographer Will You Become?

The short answer to this question is that no one knows, and other than in rare cases, that includes you. That said, certain changes and shifts on your photographic journey are likely. You will see things very differently after spending time with a camera. This is a continual process; it never stops. Photographers who have worked for half a century still discover new things regarding their relationship to the art.

I know that in a year's time I will see differently than I do now. The change may be a massive, fundamental one, or it may be of a smaller, more incremental nature. I know this much based on past experience: A year has not gone by in which my photography has remained static. The thing that keeps me going day after day is not knowing where this journey will end up. If I knew, there would be little point to continuing with it.

Photography writing tends to treat the art as a top–down process. The assumption is that there is this finite amount of technical and artistic knowledge required, and when you have this knowledge, you are a master. You can then call yourself a photographer and charge money for your services, with no need to do more than keep up-to-date with equipment advances. This approach is fundamentally wrong. Photography is a bottom–up process; it is about learning from the past, experimenting, making mistakes, and heading toward an unmapped future. This approach produces great photographers.

Temperament will play a huge part in determining your photographic future. Possibly the hardest work that you will have to do as a photographer is to mesh your art with your own nature. If you are easily bored and always looking for novelty in other parts of your life, then traditional landscape photography, for example, may not be for you, because it requires a high level of patience. For this type of person, the sheer unpredictability of street photography may be a much better fit. I may be stating the obvious,

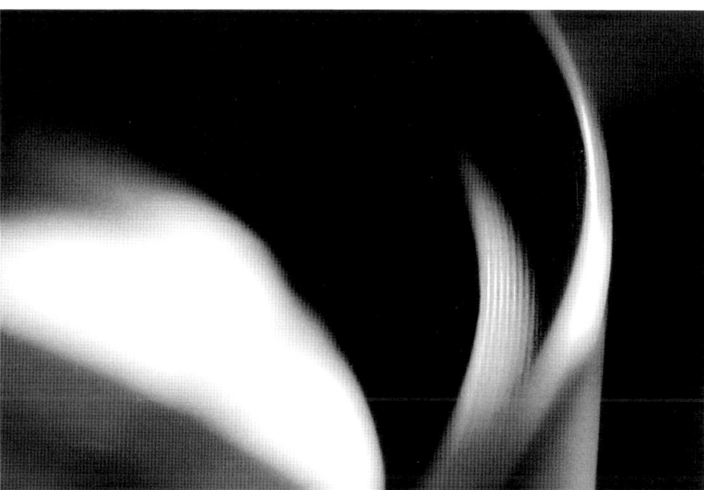

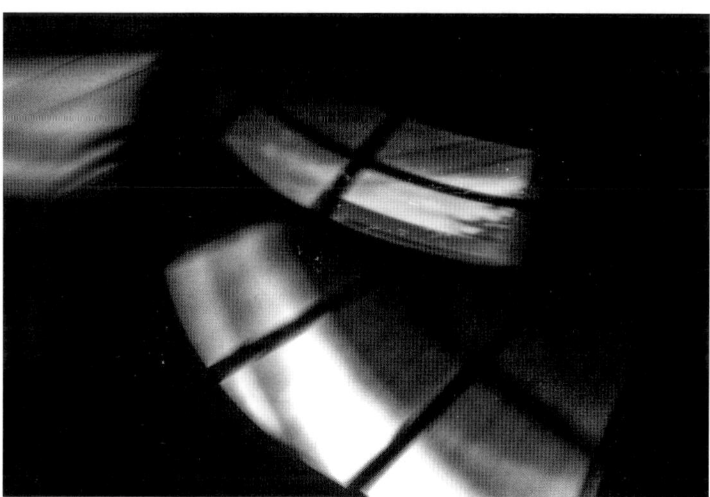

Abstract monochromes. The objects' identities are completely immaterial in these two images—it is all about the relationship between the light and dark areas. It is this type of work that defines my own chosen label.

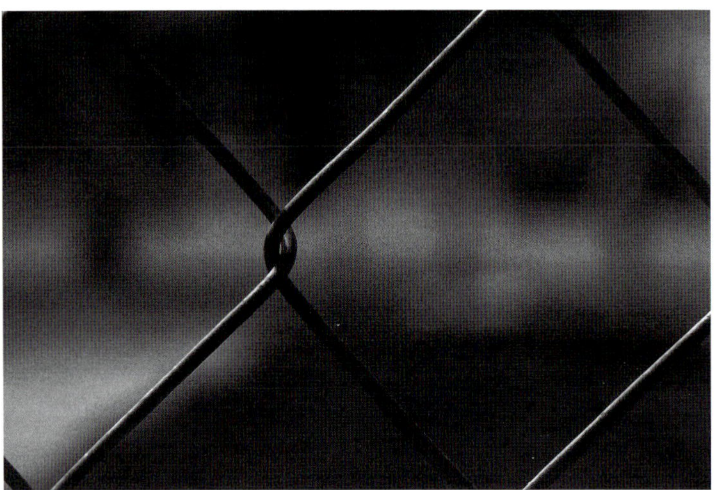

I am drawn to fences and ambiguity. Abstracting what lies beyond the fence (using depth of field) is also a metaphor for something that is unobtainable. I think that I will move toward more conceptual work in the future, but it is impossible to be definite about this.

but the fact that many photography courses and instruction books leave the photographer's temperament out of the equation never ceases to amaze me.

I do feel that photographers should explore as many different avenues as their temperament allows and I generally am opposed to the idea that specialization is a good thing. In fact, I think that specialization should be avoided for as long as possible, or failing that, the photographer should switch genres regularly to keep the eye and the mind fresh. Becoming a photographer is about developing a way of seeing. Ultimately, this way of seeing is something that should be applicable to just about anything in the visual world.

The rush to specialization is largely driven by the mistaken belief that specialization and style are intimately connected. Photographers are often told that they have to develop a style and that the developed style comes as a result of specialization. This is false. A style develops organically through constant practice and not through the adoption of a photographic niche.

Great painters, for example, all have a recognizable style. If we are looking at a particular painting of a flower, a person, or a night sky, we do not have to read the signature to know that it is a Van Gogh. Painters do not set out to develop a style, they set out to paint. Throughout their careers, their styles evolve and mature independently of intent. As a photographer, my greatest satisfaction comes from someone recognizing one of my photographs, regardless of subject matter, as mine without any clues other than the image itself.

Although there is no way of knowing where the journey will take you, it is worth keeping a few things in mind:

- By and large, do things photographically that work with your own fundamental nature
- Do not specialize too soon; instead, build a broad foundation
- If you practice enough photography with these points in mind, a recognizable style may emerge

A note about the use of the term style*: for the purposes of this book, style is something that develops through constant practice and is not something deliberately aimed for. It happens organically.*

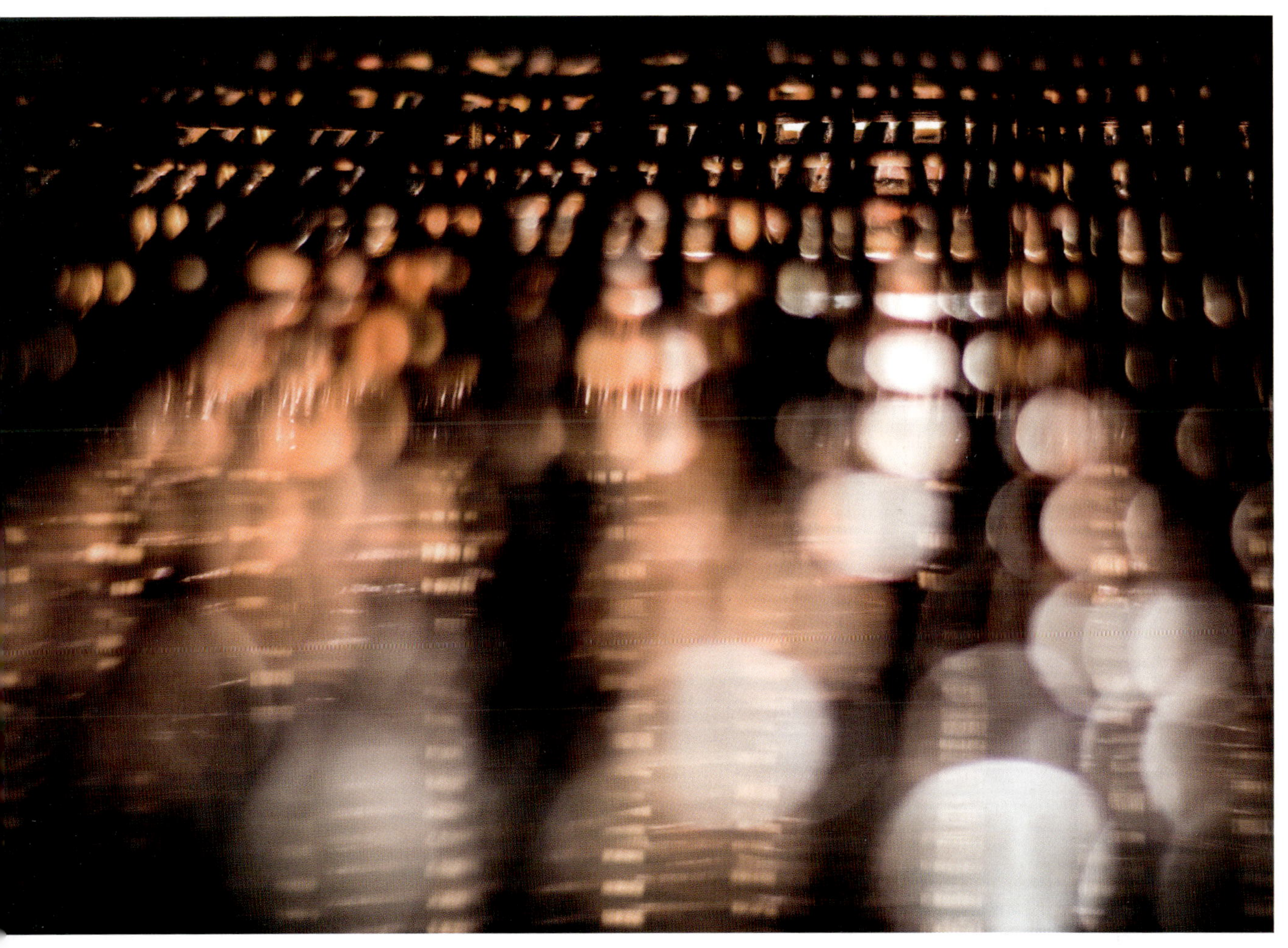

This effect was achieved by placing a strobe in a laundry basket

Gallery 1: Only the Essential

Losing background clutter is an essential photography skill. A minimal aesthetic takes this as far as possible without losing the essence of the image.

A texture layer has been added to this photograph to heighten the mood

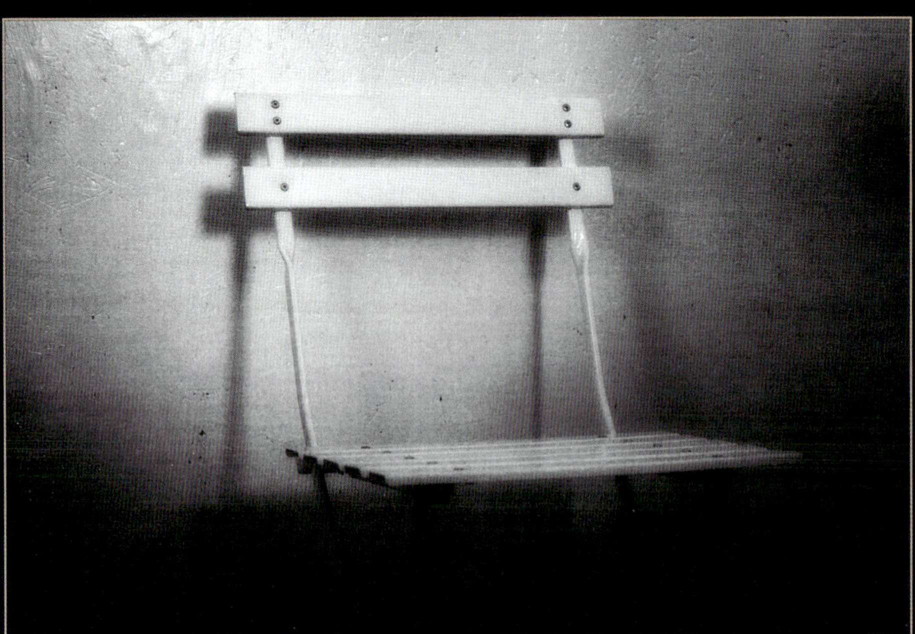

Repetition and strong shadows make this image interesting

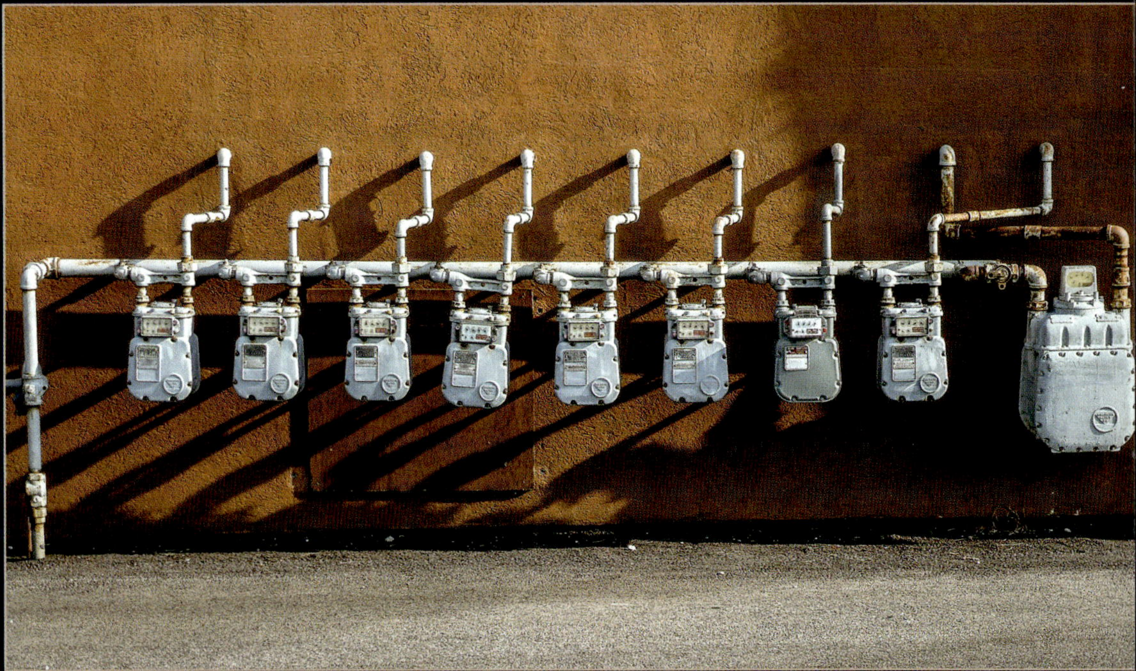

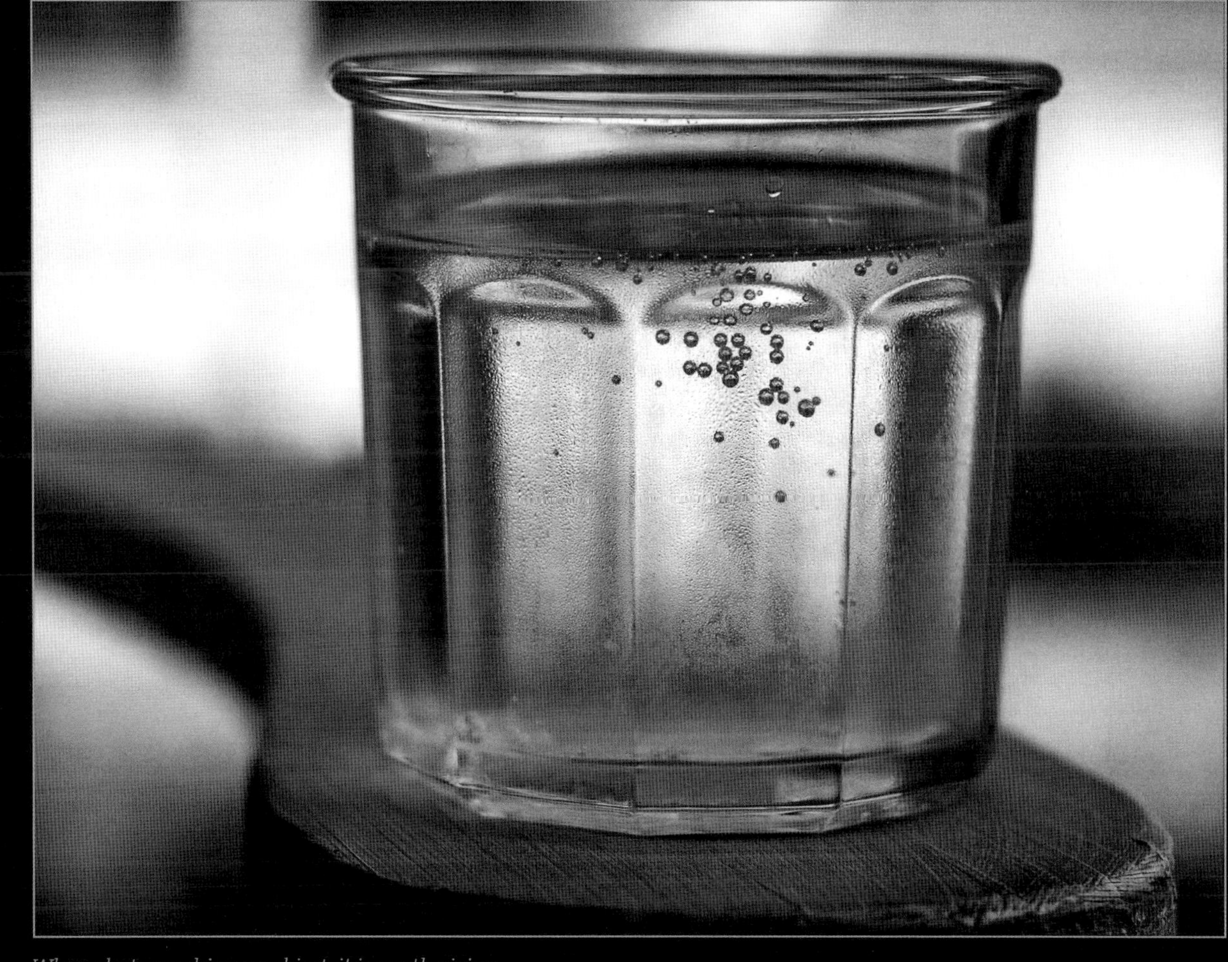

When photographing an object, it is worth giving some thought to the supporting surface. In this case, the glass of water is on the arm of an Adirondack chair.

Early morning sunlight on stacked chairs and tables. Getting the framing right was critical with this shot.

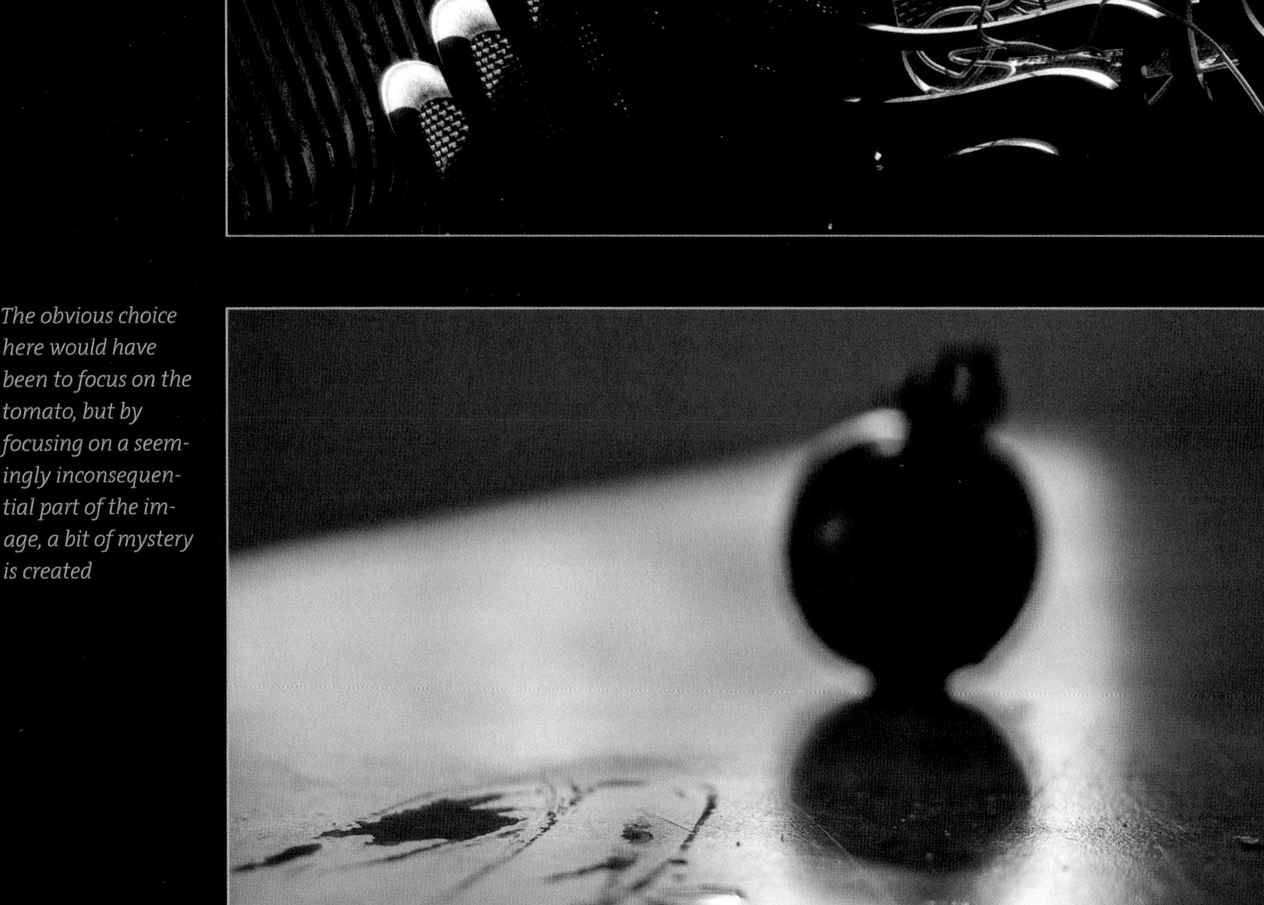

The obvious choice here would have been to focus on the tomato, but by focusing on a seemingly inconsequential part of the image, a bit of mystery is created

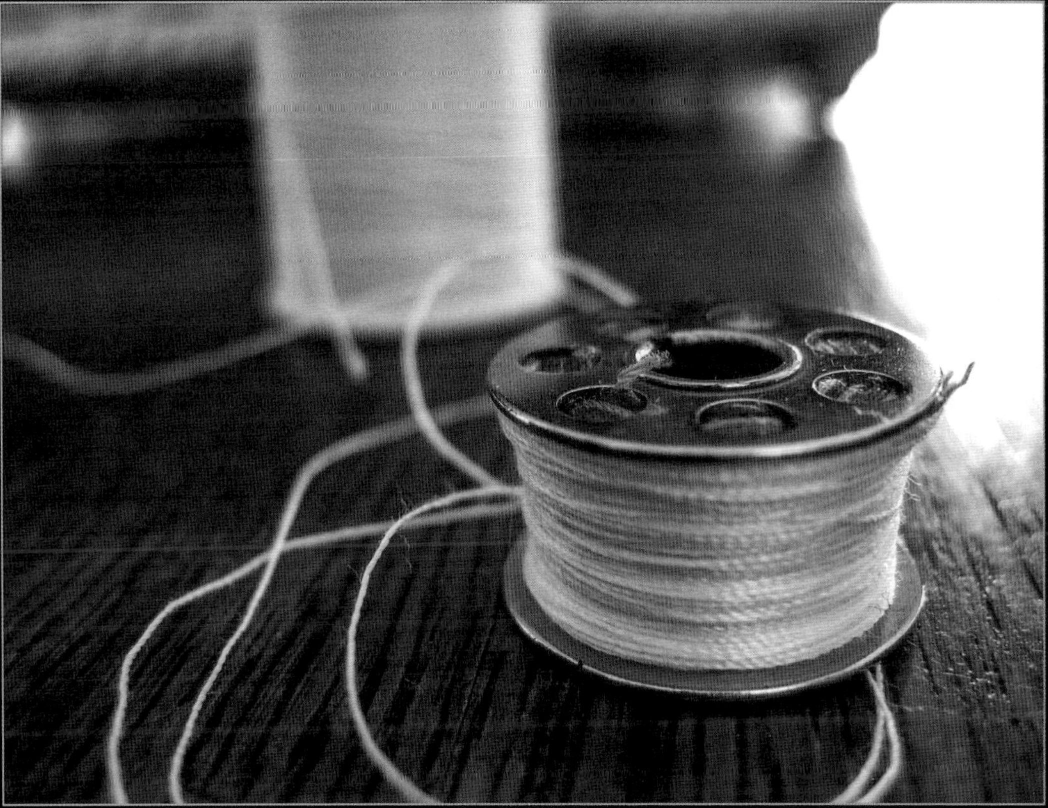

This image appears to be about the cotton spool, but the wood grain is an important part of the composition because it draws the eye into the image

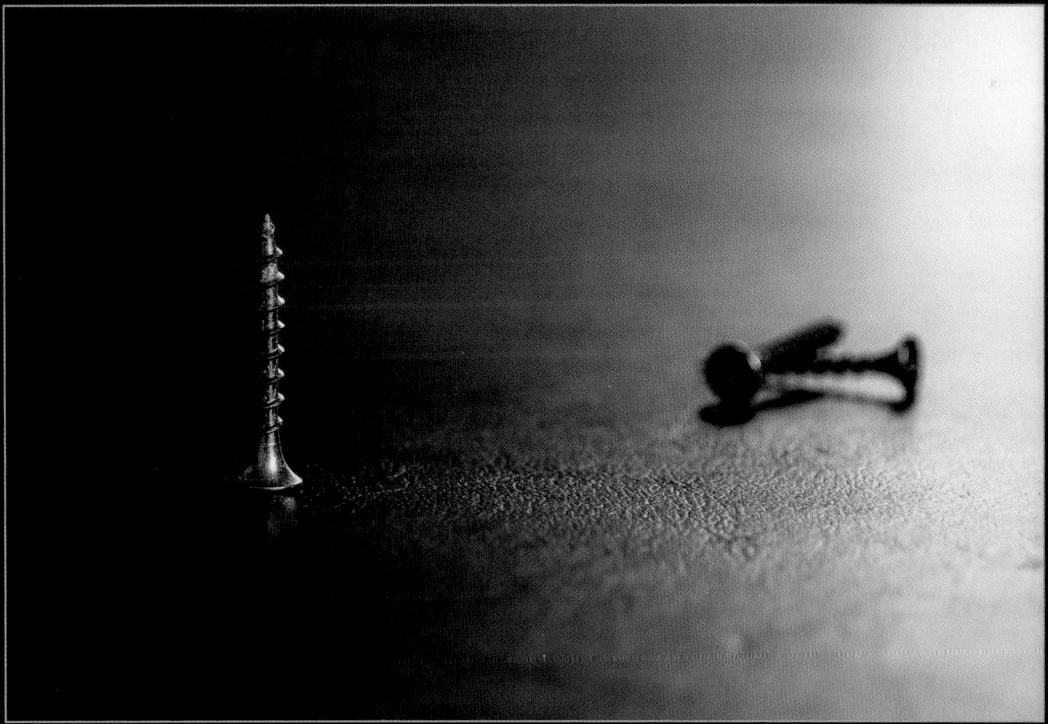

A composition to focus the viewer's attention on the upright screw

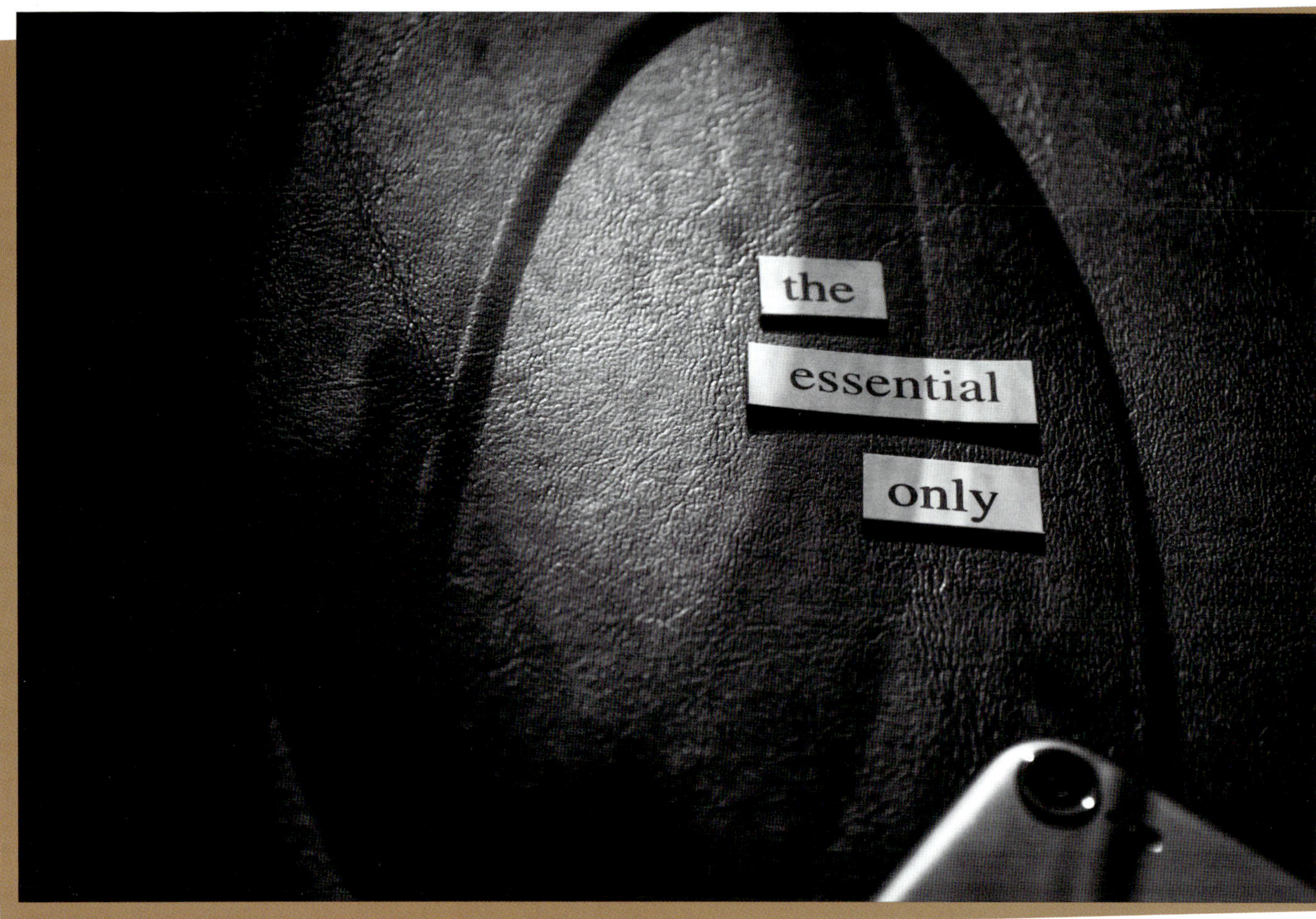
the
essential
only

Chapter 2
A Minimalist Approach

The following areas of photography can benefit from a minimalist approach: Equipment should be purchased according to need, the workflow should not increase the size of the task at hand, and a composition should never be cluttered. Let's take a deeper look at each of these elements.

Equipment

In the past, a photographer would simply buy the best equipment that he or she could afford. Things have changed a lot over the past few decades, though, and this cash-driven approach is no longer the only approach, or even the best approach. Under the old model, two things were regarded as absolutely key, both concerning lenses. First was the speed of the lens, or if it was fast enough for a correct exposure. Second was the quality of the components that made up the lens. This second factor determined the sharpness of the image. Faster and sharper lenses cost much more than the slower, slightly less sharp counterparts.

A fast lens makes it possible to work in darker conditions than would otherwise be possible, at least without a tripod or supplemental lighting. In other words, it enables photographs that would not otherwise happen. Sharpness, on the other hand, is an incremental thing. A less than perfect lens will not stop the photograph from happening; it will just make it slightly softer. It does not take a conspiracy theorist to see that the photography industry's interests are best served by pushing the importance of speed and sharpness, because this is where the greatest profits lie.

I think the emphasis on speed is justified, but the obsession with sharpness is overdone. Just think of some of the photographs that have really affected you and try to remember whether they are tack sharp, moderately sharp, or not very sharp at all. I have my own favorite images by other photographers and cannot remember which, if any, are super sharp. The truth is that sharpness doesn't have the same influence on emotional and art-appreciating centers of the brain as contrast does. While absolute sharpness can be achieved at a cost, contrast can be optimized using relatively cheap or even free software tools. An impression of sharpness can also be created by judicious use of contrast, especially local contrast, but that is a discussion for a later chapter.

One thing needs to be clear: I am not making an argument for buying and using only cheap equipment, but rather I am making the case for not spending a fortune that you do not need to spend. If your images are going to be used as fine art prints, 300 dots per inch (dpi) at three feet per side, then get ready to spend some money. You will need a top-quality lens, a camera body with a large sensor, and some expensive software. Not many of us are producing such large, high-quality prints, though, so a considerable amount of money can be saved by not paying for incremental improvements that will be unnoticeable in our final output. The bigger and more expensive approach may be flawed, but there is something at the other end of the scale that is just as wrongheaded. This is the recent trend toward self-imposed limits on equipment. New websites and publications are appearing all the time where the owner seeks to showcase work done with basic gear. Some of these websites show only photographs taken with point-and-shoots, while others go even further and only show work from smartphones. Artificial limits on technology encourage serious exploration of the equipment at hand, but there are times when a different type of camera really would be better suited for the task.

The type of photography you want to do should guide your choice in equipment, as opposed to the industry-approved approach of setting a budget then spending up to your limit. There are times when cheaper equipment may actually outperform a more expensive kit. If you want to take photographs to appear with blog posts or to sell products on eBay, then a budget compact camera may be more useful than a DSLR. The compact camera will give a larger depth of field, be easier to handle, and the picture quality will be sufficient for output to a computer screen.

Workflow

Workflow encompasses everything from pressing the shutter-release button to the final resting place of the photograph, be it a print, on a website, or as fodder for a graphic artist or designer. A good workflow saves time and minimizes frustration, while a bad, elaborate, or nonexistent workflow does the complete opposite. A minimalist workflow does exactly enough.

For someone who takes photographs occasionally, workflow is a minor issue. It is only when dozens of images need to be edited, sorted, and stored on a regular basis that a system needs to be put in place. The system should be tailored to suit the individual photographer, not the other way around. The photographer should always work in a way that suits his or her own temperament, not in a way that others say is ideal. This means the process should be an organic one, arrived at by trial and error.

Think minimalism when creating your workflow, and try to keep things as simple as possible. The fewer required actions, the more likely you'll adhere to the process and reap the benefits.

Other than the photographer's temperament, the final output will influence workflow the most. If your photography is the starting point for an intensive graphic design or fine art project, then your workflow will be different than that of a photographer who deals with a lot of finished images but doesn't want the photographs to look very different than when they were originally shot.

As I mentioned in chapter 1, the biggest change over the past couple of decades was the shift from film to digital photography. Computers have replaced the darkroom, and any time invested in learning how to use the newest technology will more than pay for itself. Working knowledge of a decent photo-editing software package will add another dimension to your work.

While we're on the subject of computers and photo-editing software, I would like to throw in one piece of advice: if you haven't already, do not go out and purchase Adobe Photoshop—at least not yet. Unfortunately, we have been influenced to think that being taken seriously as a photographer means having to own a full copy of this package. It is an excellent software package, but it is not necessarily the right one for the majority of photographers. Despite its name, it is much better suited to graphic designers and digital artists.

If you feel the need to invest in software right now, I recommend Adobe Lightroom. It is much more affordable, much faster, and the structure of the application is a lot more intuitive than Photoshop.

My Workflow

What follows is an outline of my workflow, along with my rationale and some other thoughts. Bear in mind the bit about finding what works for you. If you can adapt some of this to your own needs, or gain a better understanding of the workflow concept, then this discussion has been a successful one; however, it is definitely not a tutorial in any way.

I use two cameras, a compact point-and-shoot and a DSLR. The compact shoots only JPEG images, and the DSLR offers the standard choice of RAW or JPEG. Many photographers advocate always using RAW if the option is available because it allows for greater flexibility in editing. I use RAW for mission-critical work, if possible, and JPEG for other things (such as blog posts). The much smaller file sizes of the latter format give a speed advantage that, to me, is worth the loss of flexibility. You may well think that losing editing possibilities and some quality is a strict no-no under all circumstances. There is really no right or wrong answer. This applies to just about everything in a workflow.

As a rule of thumb, the earlier in the workflow process that any decision can be made, the better. I like to delete unwanted images as I go, while the pictures are still in the camera. By and large, I'll know quickly if a photograph has potential or if it is likely to just take up space on my hard drive for years to come. I delete the unwanted images before they ever get to the hard drive. This probably cuts my processing time in half because it is easier to hit the delete button twice on my camera than to later separate 20 or so keepers from a group of 200 images on the computer. I find the thought of whittling down images from hundreds to a couple dozen to be overwhelming.

The next job is to transfer the images from the memory card to the computer. Since I diligently delete as I go, there are only a few images to import. I use Adobe Lightroom for this. Lightroom is set up to automatically detect a memory card and import files into a folder. I rename the folder to something meaningful. I then do a second transfer of the files from the memory card to an external hard drive using the computer operating system. This means I have a working set of images within Lightroom plus a backup set on a hard drive that I can attach to any computer and work on in case of emergency. I do not delete the images from my memory card at this stage because space is not critical, and leaving them alone provides a third, albeit temporary, backup. Again, this is a matter of choice; many photographers prefer to work with a clean card every time they get their camera out. In fact, memory cards have come down in price so much that some photographers use them just once and then store them with the client's file after transferring the images. If I were a wedding photographer, I would definitely go this route.

I always want to be sure that I am not working on an original copy of a photograph because there is nothing worse than editing a photograph and then deciding to reject the edit, only to find that you have destroyed the original. Making a separate backup as previously described ensures that you have an intact original, but with Lightroom you have another fail-safe: nondestructive editing. This means that whatever you do in Lightroom, or in another application that can be opened via Lightroom, it is always possible to retrieve the original photograph. One benefit of shooting in RAW format is that it's impossible to edit over the original—work is always done on a copy. When it comes to your original images, redundancy is never a bad thing.

So far I have described importing the photographs and backing up, the boring but essential

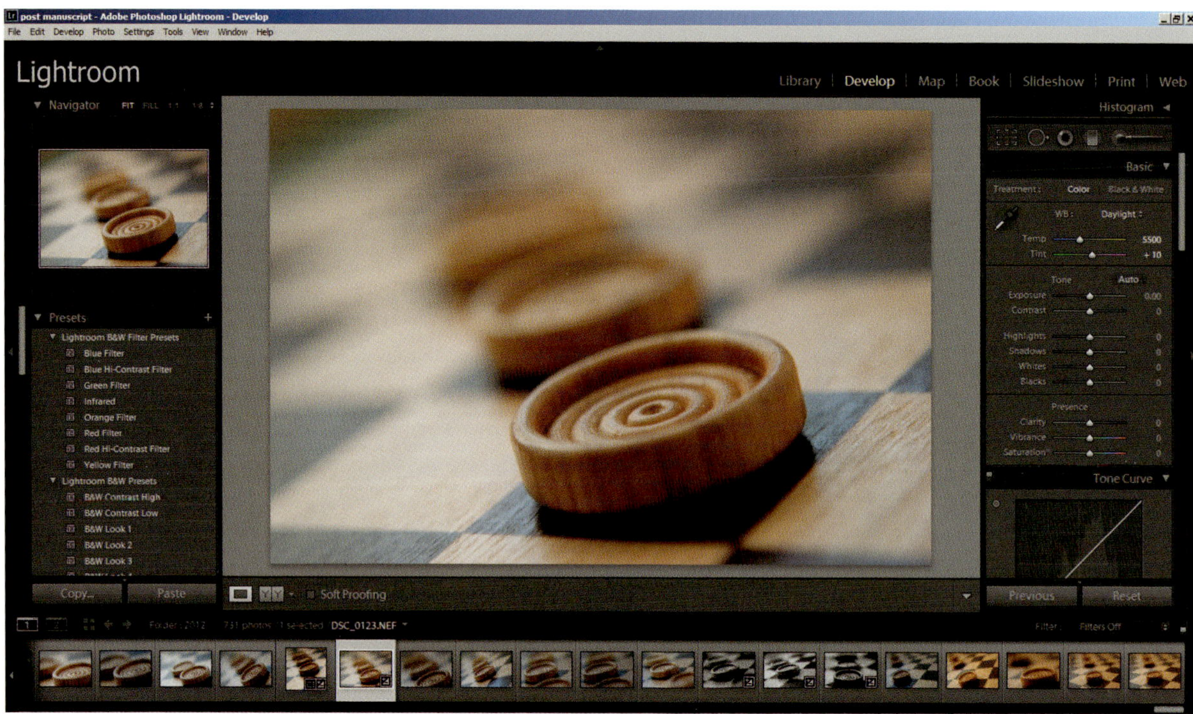

Adobe Lightroom. A major advantage of this type of software is the nonlinear workflow. Any image can be worked on by highlighting the bottom strip and adjusting the settings to the right. The software will remember whatever changes have been made, so no saving is required. This makes it very easy to move quickly between images.

parts of the process. Now is the fun part, which is making the most of the images. Before starting to edit, I do one more pass to reject any shots that I thought might be okay when I saw them on the camera's LCD screen, but that do not work as well when viewed on a larger monitor. I reject about a quarter of the remaining images at this stage, which leaves me about 10–15 keepers from an average shoot.

This is the point at which I start to think about the end use of the image. Certain types of shots may suit my blog or social networking projects, while others may have potential as stock photographs or even prints.

Now I start to edit the individual photographs. The main advantage of a nonlinear editor such as Lightroom is speed, especially when applying changes to more than one photograph. If, say, I'd set my exposure slightly low during the shoot, it would take only a few seconds to compensate for this across the entire set of images. Even if I were editing 200 photographs at the same time, it would not take longer. It is also very easy to generate multiple copies of a photograph, so if both a monochrome and a color version were required, a couple of mouse clicks would do the trick. Saving files can be done individually or in bulk, with all of the parameters, such as size, sharpening, output folder, and so forth, preset. Saving 15 or 200 edited files takes little more than a few seconds.

As far as editing options go, I rarely need anything that isn't doable in Lightroom because it covers all of the basic editing functions to

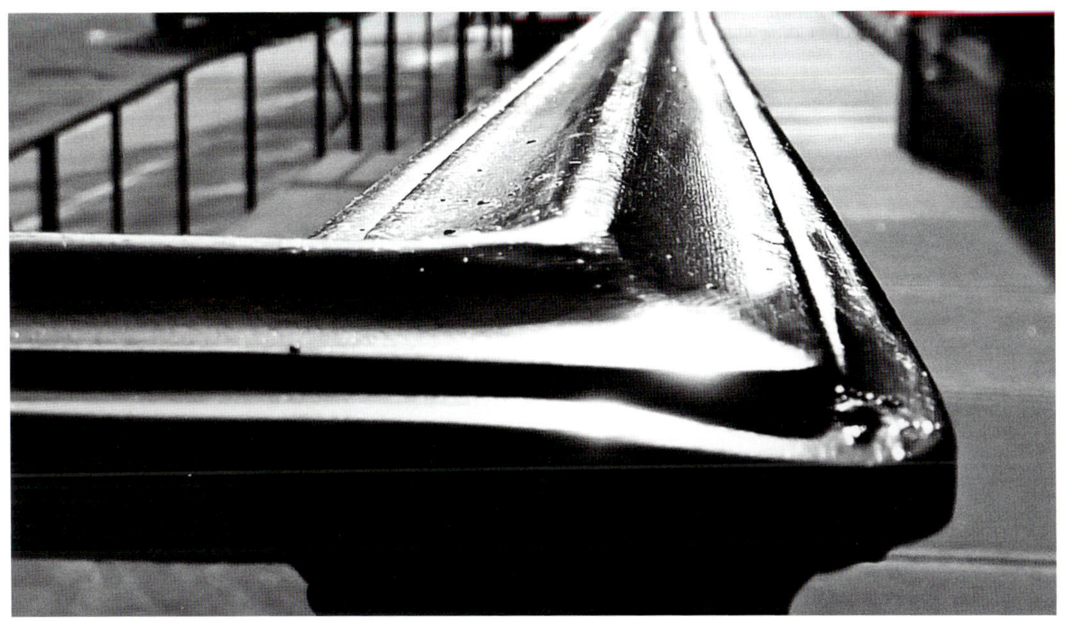

A handrail from an unusual perspective makes for a simple composition. The photograph was shot in color and reduced to black-and-white in Lightroom.

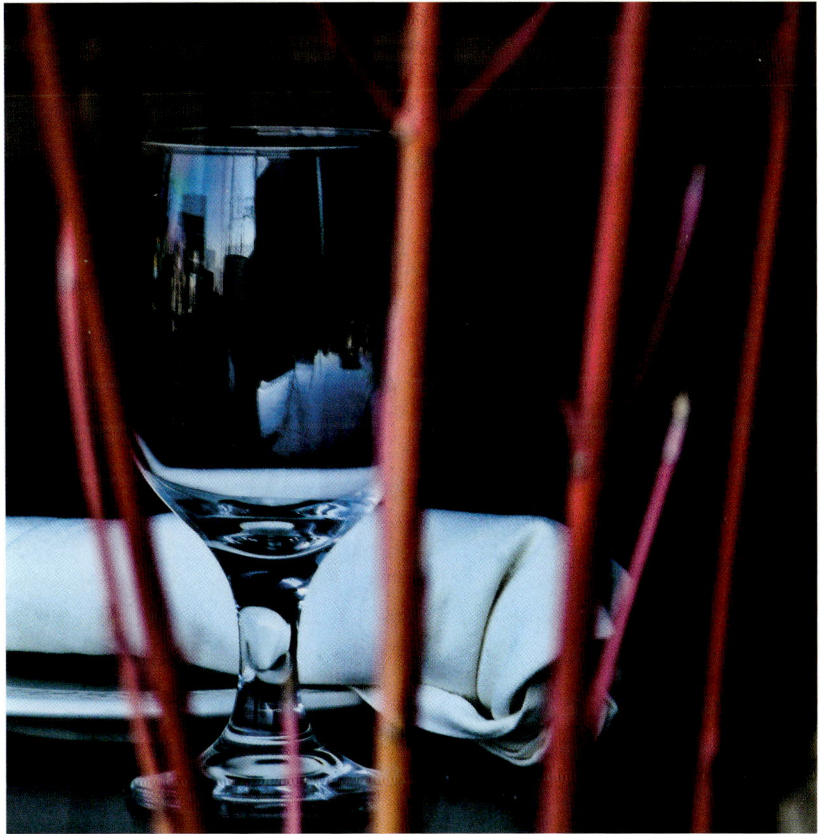

An image does not have to be perfect to have impact. Technical perfection and impact often have to be balanced.

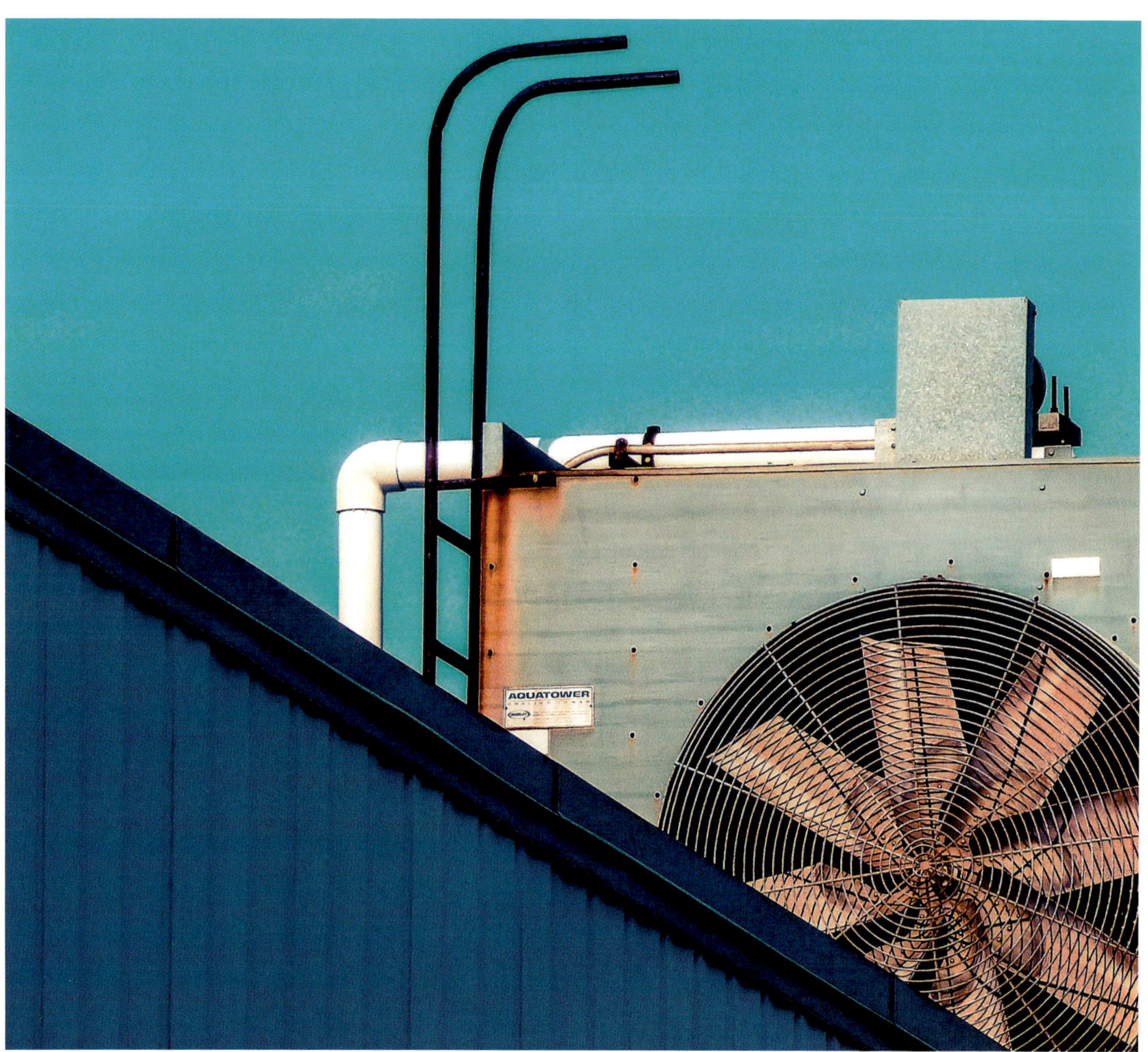

Split- or dual-toning has been applied to this image in Lightroom. Dual tone is a process where dark tones and light tones are given different colors. The process is usually applied over a monochrome image, but in this case a little of the original color was left in.

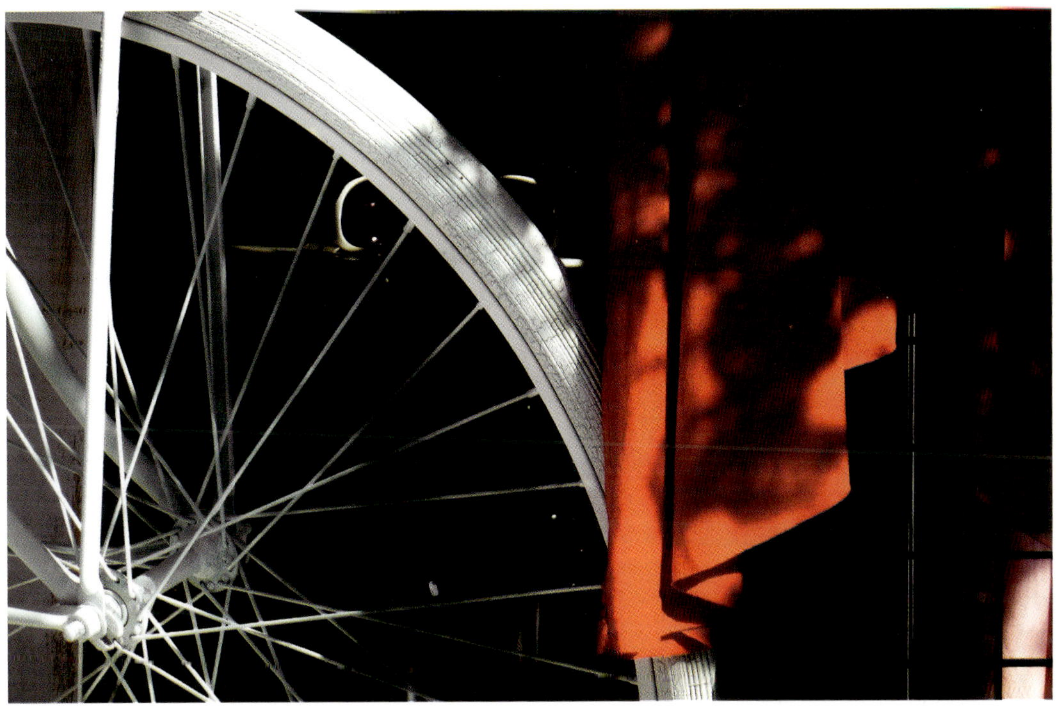

This image has been edited to make the darker tones black. This technique reduces visual clutter and is a simple task with plenty of flexibility when done in Lightroom.

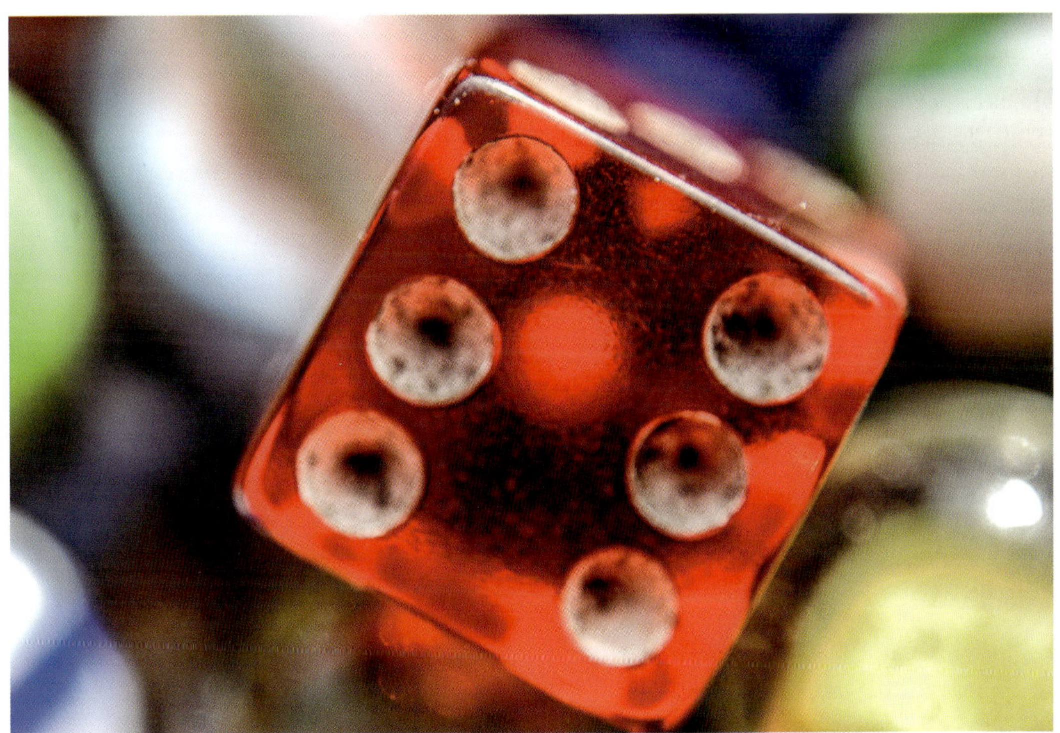

To highlight the die's transparency, the local contrast was boosted. When you're editing, a proactive approach works best. It is always good to know which characteristics you want to emphasize.

Photography is about seeing, and that cannot be emphasized enough.

a professional standard. Contrast, saturation, sharpening, noise reduction, cropping, spot removal, and curves, along with some more creative options such as vignetting and split toning, are available. Sometimes I need to do something that is beyond Lightroom's scope, and setting up other editors (including Adobe Photoshop) for round-tripping is straightforward. Occasionally, I use some other software for adding a border or for more esoteric artistic effects, but the end result is always returned to Lightroom, where images can be exported along with the rest of the edits.

There are some good free workflow tools out there, the best of which is probably Picasa. This application, owned by Google, has come a long way and now offers high-quality editing and cataloging. Editing is faster and more flexible in Lightroom, but Picasa will provide more than enough tools and options for most users, and the results are very good. However, if you intend to output a lot of images to print, Lightroom (ideally along with Photoshop) is the way to go.

The most important thing about your workflow is that it has to suit you. This probably seems like stating the obvious, but the Internet is full of articles whose authors think they have the only solution. If you find a method that suits you and provides the results you like, stay with it and don't feel obliged to follow someone else's lead. The only thing that is non-negotiable, as far as I am concerned, is backing up the original files from the camera and keeping them safe, preferably on two different drives. Regard your native image files as you would negatives, if film were the medium, and protect them by backing up.

There is a difference between looking and seeing. *We look at things whenever our eyes are open, but we only really* see *things when we make a conscious effort to do so.*

Subject Matter and Composition

One of the greatest advantages of a minimalist approach is that the most seemingly banal subjects can make the most interesting photographs. While traditional photographers may have to drive a hundred miles, setting out at four o'clock in the morning to capture the perfect sunrise over the perfect landscape, or invest in a studio full of incredibly expensive equipment to practice their art, you can give minimalist photographers a basic camera and an object, and they are good to go. I have spent a whole day working with a jar of screws and a hundred dollar point-and-shoot. Some of the images from these low-budget shoots are among my best sellers.

Seeing

Photography is about seeing, and that cannot be emphasized enough. We all know what a screw looks like, that it has a thread and a head, but how many people have really looked hard at a screw? A closer look reveals so much more, especially if it is old and used—with metal shavings, dents, pits, and possibly flecks of old paint. The head design could be one of a hundred variations, and it could be anything from pristine to unusable due to the slot or slots being worn beyond recognition.

Light is, of course, an important factor. It can be hard, highlighting the metallic nature of the screw with its sharp tonal changes, or it can be soft, giving very smooth tonal gradients. The same screw framed in different ways will lead to photographs with different visual results. The negative space around the screw becomes as important as the screw itself.

These suggestions demonstrate the difference between looking and *seeing*. We look at things whenever our eyes are open, but we only really *see* things when we make a conscious effort to do so. Seeing takes practice. When we learn to see, just about anything can be the subject for a potentially good photograph. If the camera records what we really see, the photograph stands a chance of being a good one, but if it merely records what we look at, the image

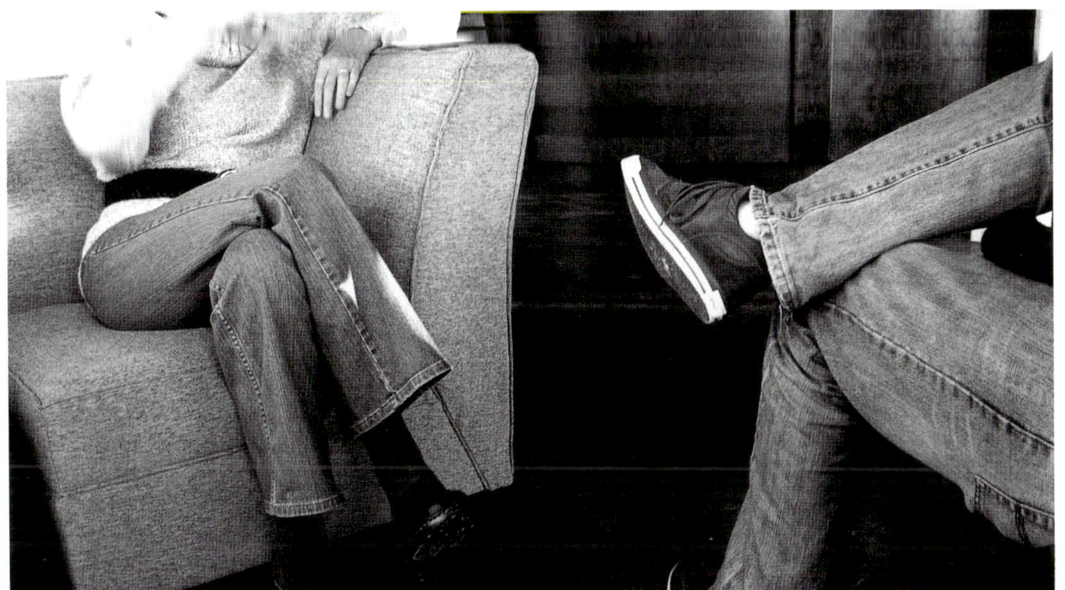

Minimalism is about getting to the essence of something. With this image, the essence is in the relative positions of the limbs.

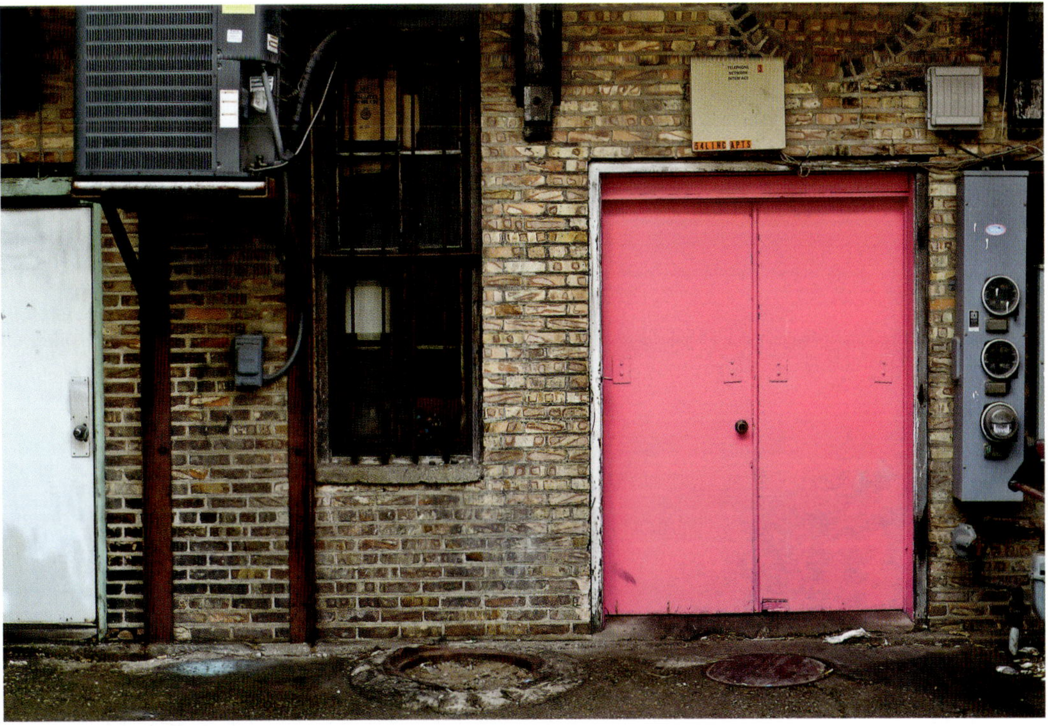

Something simple in the middle of an urban scene, in this case a shocking pink door, can provide an interesting contrast

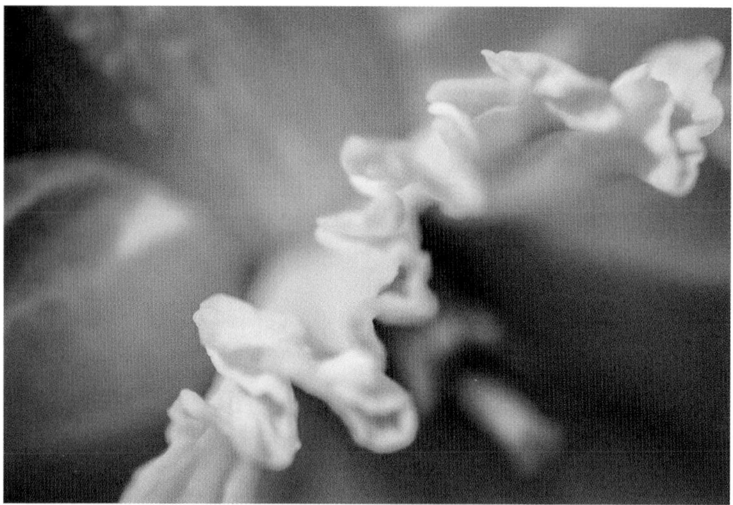

A daffodil photographed to emphasize the delicacy of the flower. The fact that it is hardly recognizable forces the viewer to see the attribute as opposed to the object.

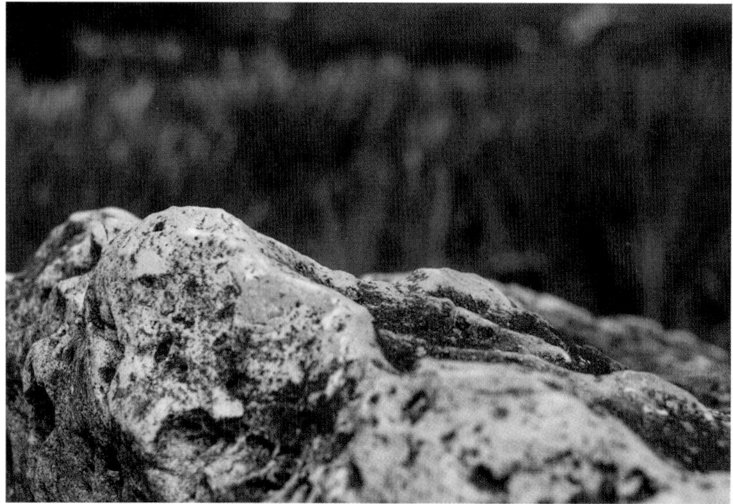

A minimal landscape that is very different than a traditional landscape because there are no leading lines and no focal point. The image instead relies on texture and a very simple, flat composition.

will never be more than a snapshot. After I have really seen something, the photograph comes easily, and if I haven't seen it, the photograph will never come.

Of course, the subject does not have to be as small or even as simple as a screw. With larger objects, framing makes or breaks the photograph. There is no rule that says the whole object has to be in view, or that it must fill the frame. Cropping an object is a great way to practice seeing because it forces you to see in terms of lines, shapes, tones, and contrast. This is the first step toward abstraction because the identity of the object becomes less obvious. It is impossible to be a good photographer, let alone a minimalist photographer, without an understanding of abstraction.

Going in the other direction, making an object appear very small in the frame can have a similar effect. If you shrink an object enough, it becomes, essentially, a point. Points and lines are extremely important elements in abstraction and minimalism. An object can be large enough to be recognizable yet still work as a point in a composition. A common example is a few seagulls over a calm sea under a clear sky. The seagulls, though recognizable, serve as points in the composition, and are often balanced by the single line in the image, or the horizon.

Framing

Framing, done well, can make an image more abstract and less literal. Good framing forces the viewer's brain to see the photograph with fresh eyes. When we see a chair presented normally and in a common context (all of it in the frame in a sitting room), the brain recognizes it for what it is, decides that there is nothing of interest going on, and stops working on the image. Now, show only a part of the seat, or change the context to a distant shot of an armchair on a beach. The viewer's brain wakes up and *sees* the image because it had to work to build context. Novelty for novelty's sake is usually a bad idea photographically, but novelty coupled with something genuinely interesting will always make a strong image.

Any photographer should aim to make composition an instinctive skill. The ideal is to be able to size up a scene, frame it, and shoot, knowing that a reasonable photograph will result. When I see photographers who advise others to have the tic-tac-toe grid on their viewfinders so they can use the rule of thirds to compose an image, I want to punch walls. The only possible use for this grid is after the fact. If an image works much better than expected, or if it fails to work despite the photographer's best attempts, the grid may—just may—be a good way of finding out something interesting. As a photographer, you need to be surprised; if you turn photography into math, this is not going to happen. The resulting work will be workmanlike at best, but more likely it will be static and devoid of interest.

This is not an argument for not knowing theory, though, and I recommend understanding the basics, such as the rule of thirds, tone, color, and so forth. I do cover these topics later on in the book. If you are truly dedicated, I recommend taking a drawing class because it will lay a good foundation for future photography endeavors. Drawing is hard, but even if you don't become the next Picasso, the insight gained will probably get you further along than a weekend photography workshop. To draw well, you have to be able to *see* in the proper sense of the word—it cannot be fudged. Those who teach drawing understand the issues involved in making a two-dimensional image from a three-dimensional scene better than anyone who hasn't picked up a pencil ever could. It is no coincidence that many people we now recognize as great photographers spent years studying painting and drawing before they picked up a camera.

A minimalist approach to composition is, in many ways, different than a traditional one, but the best minimalist photographers usually start off by mastering the traditional approach to composition and working with it, often for years, before they start to pare it down and arrive at the essence of the potential image. Traditional composition includes removing clutter and ensuring that the image is not messy. Aesthetic minimalism can be seen as an extreme extension of this process.

The best minimalist photographers usually start off by mastering the traditional approach to composition and working with it, often for years.

An interesting analogy can be found in music. Musicians, particularly in jazz, blues, and rock, tend to play fewer notes as they get older. In their youth, they want to show their prowess and their grasp of technique, but as they age the urge to express ideas takes over. They strip away the inessential, the purely decorative, to force the listener to focus on what's left, the essence. Photography is no different.

At this stage you may be thinking that first going the traditional route and then the minimalist route is a waste of time. Why not just cut out the traditional and go straight to photographing, say, two seagulls and a horizon? Although some photographers have a good enough eye to do this, very few can carve out a career using this approach. The essence of something has to be arrived at by stripping away the inessential, and is not something that can be arrived at instantly or by sheer luck.

Different surfaces present different challenges.

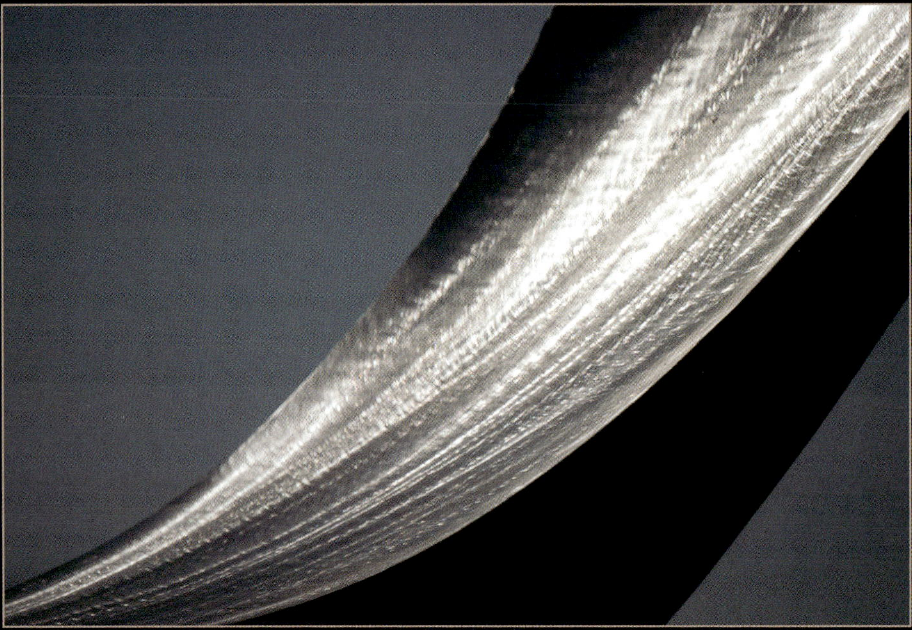

A composition of four areas, three of which are uniform; this helps to emphasize the fourth area, where the sun strikes a steel surface

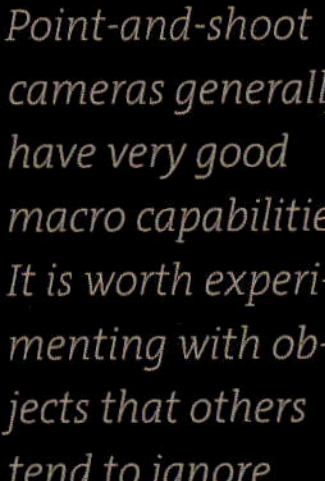

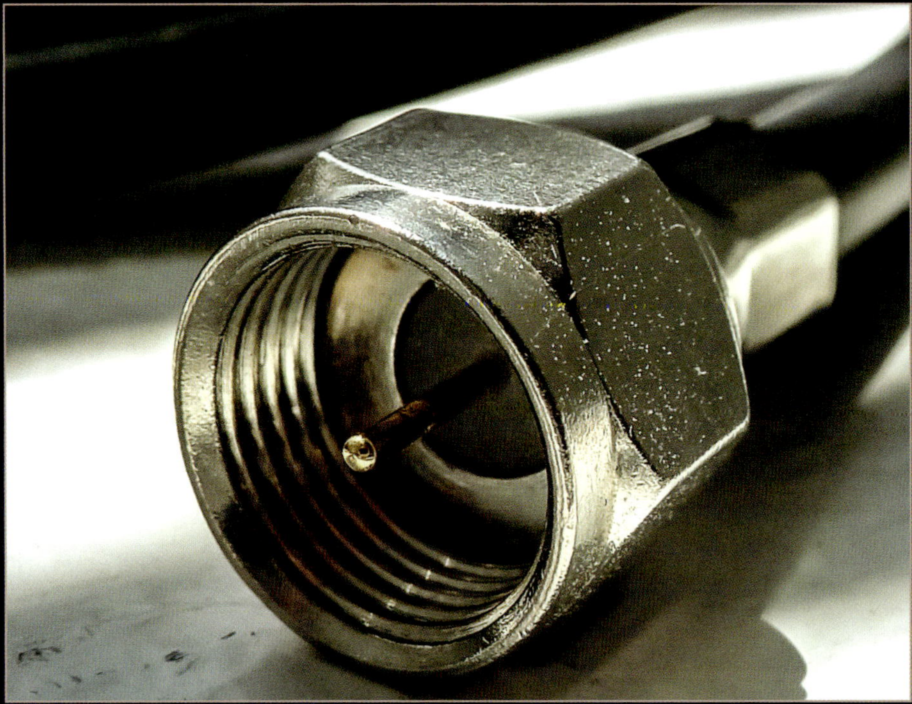

Point-and-shoot cameras generally have very good macro capabilities. It is worth experimenting with objects that others tend to ignore.

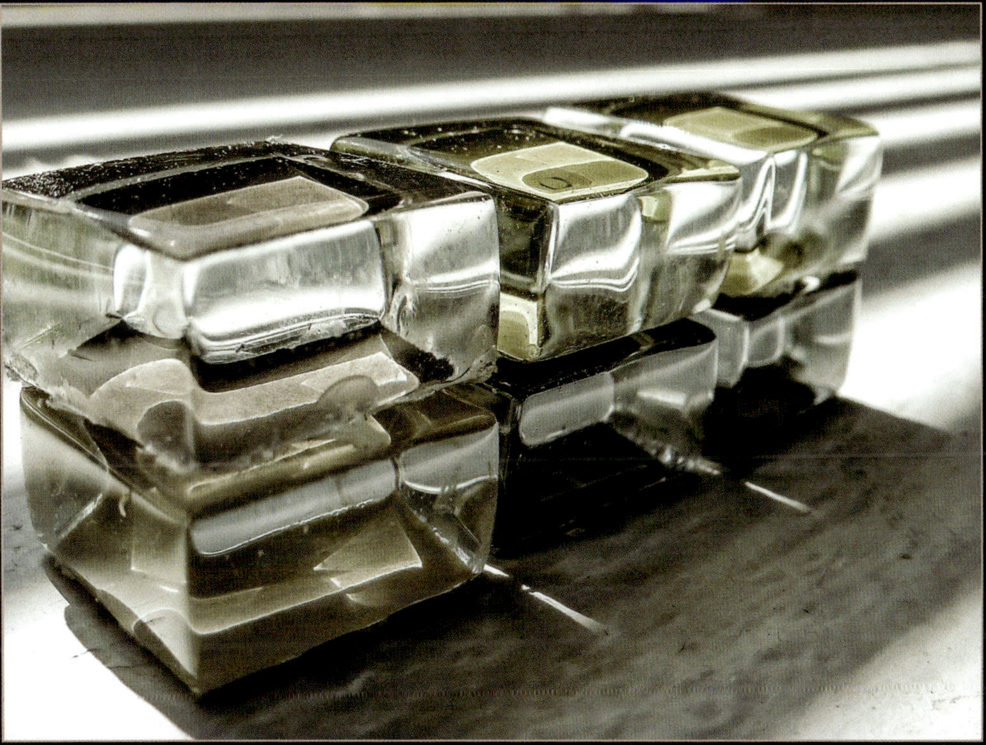

Glass mosaic tiles reflect and refract light in interesting ways

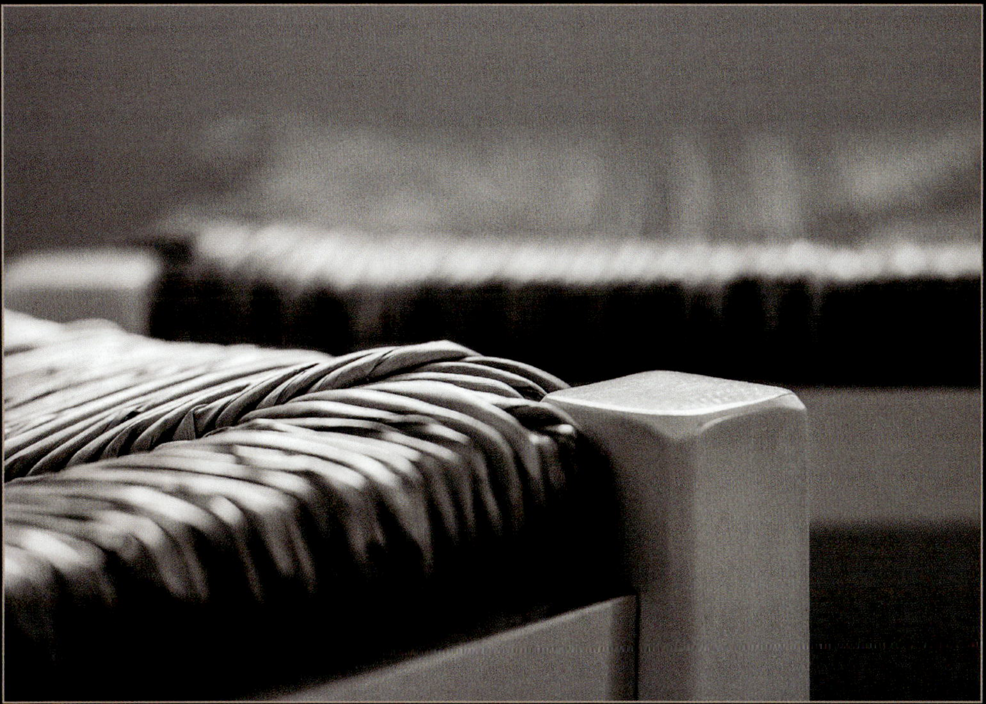

Two stools. Taking time to get the framing right always pays dividends.

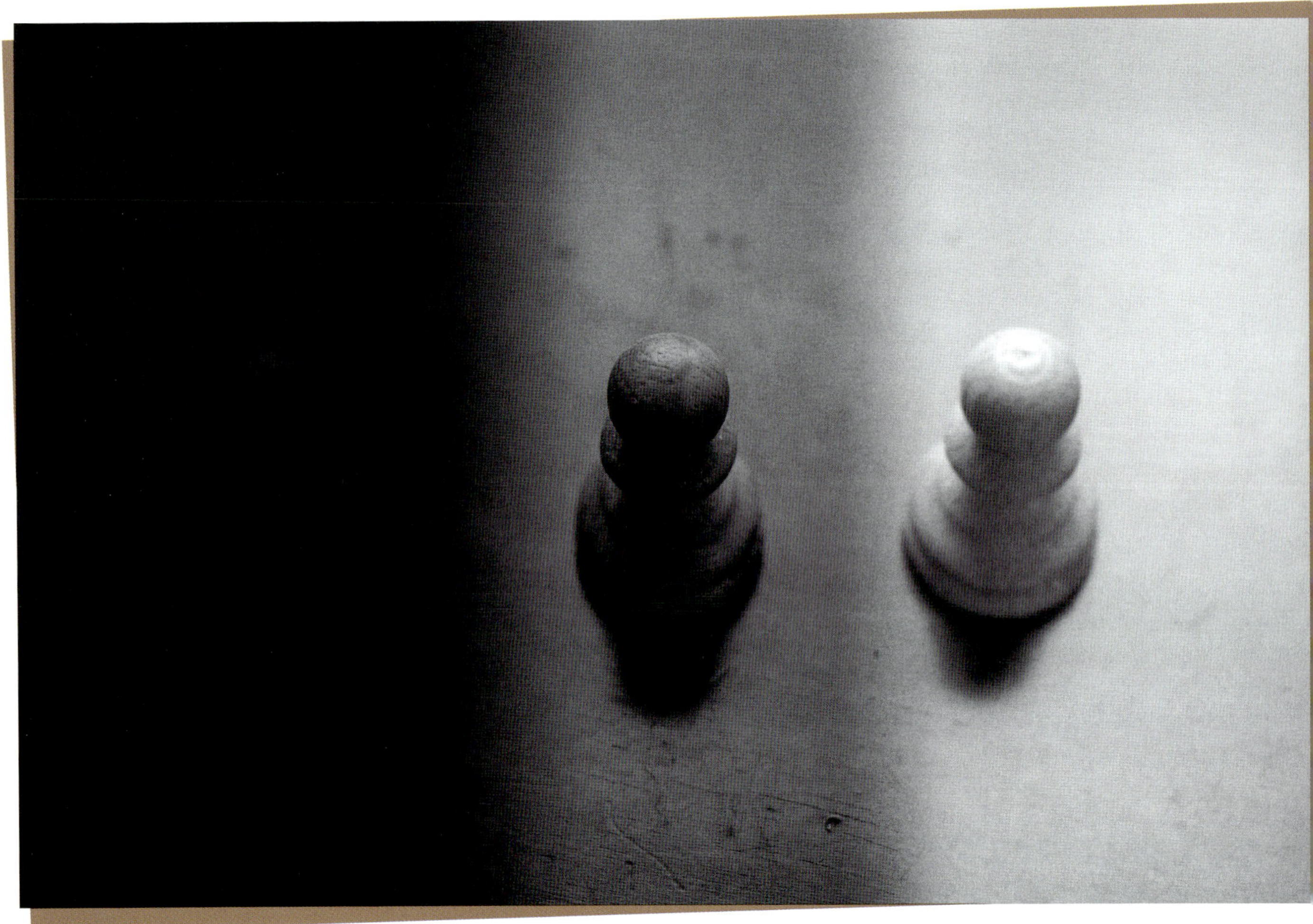

Chapter 3
The Basics

This section consists of two parts. The first part examines the question of what photography is in terms of art, technology, and as a social tool. The second section examines the many aspects of working with light. Light is the fundamental medium the photographer works with, therefore understanding exposure is critical.

What Is Photography?

According to Wikipedia, at the time of this writing, photography is defined as follows:

The art, science, and practice of creating durable images by recording light or other electromagnetic radiation, either chemically by means of a light-sensitive material such as photographic film, or electronically by means of an image sensor. Typically, a lens is used to focus the light reflected or emitted from objects into a real image on the light-sensitive surface inside a camera during a timed exposure. The result in an electronic image sensor is an electrical charge at each pixel, which is electronically processed and stored in a digital image file for subsequent display or processing. The result in a photographic emulsion is an invisible latent image, which is later chemically developed into a visible image, either negative or positive depending on the purpose of the photographic material and the method of processing. A negative image on film is traditionally used to photographically create a positive image on a paper base, known as a print, either by using an enlarger or by contact printing.

To put it another way, photography is the capturing and focusing of light from the three-dimensional real world onto a two-dimensional surface. The camera lens focuses the light onto a digital sensor or film. The technology may change over time, but the fundamentals will not. There is no substantial difference between film and digital, for example. Good film photographers transition to digital photography easily because the basics of exposure and composition are fundamentally the same in both mediums.

A simplified definition: Photography is the capturing and focusing of light from the three-dimensional real world onto a two-dimensional surface.

That is the bare bones, science-based definition, but it doesn't even begin to answer the question, what is photography? A more useful answer can be realized by looking at photography and its role in society. This is covered in much more depth in later chapters, but here is the two-minute version. Up until a couple hundred years ago, the only way to make a visual record of the world was to draw or paint it. Obviously, these skills are beyond the ability of most people and are very time consuming; therefore, with rare exceptions, only carefully selected and usually contrived moments were recorded. This is why portrait painting was so dominant up until the 19th century, after which time the camera replaced the brush and pencil and portrait paintings waned.

It was some time before technology was such that the camera could be used for candid work, the taking of a photograph on the spur of the moment of subjects that were unaware they were being photographed. This was the point at which photography became more than a cheaper and more convenient form of painting

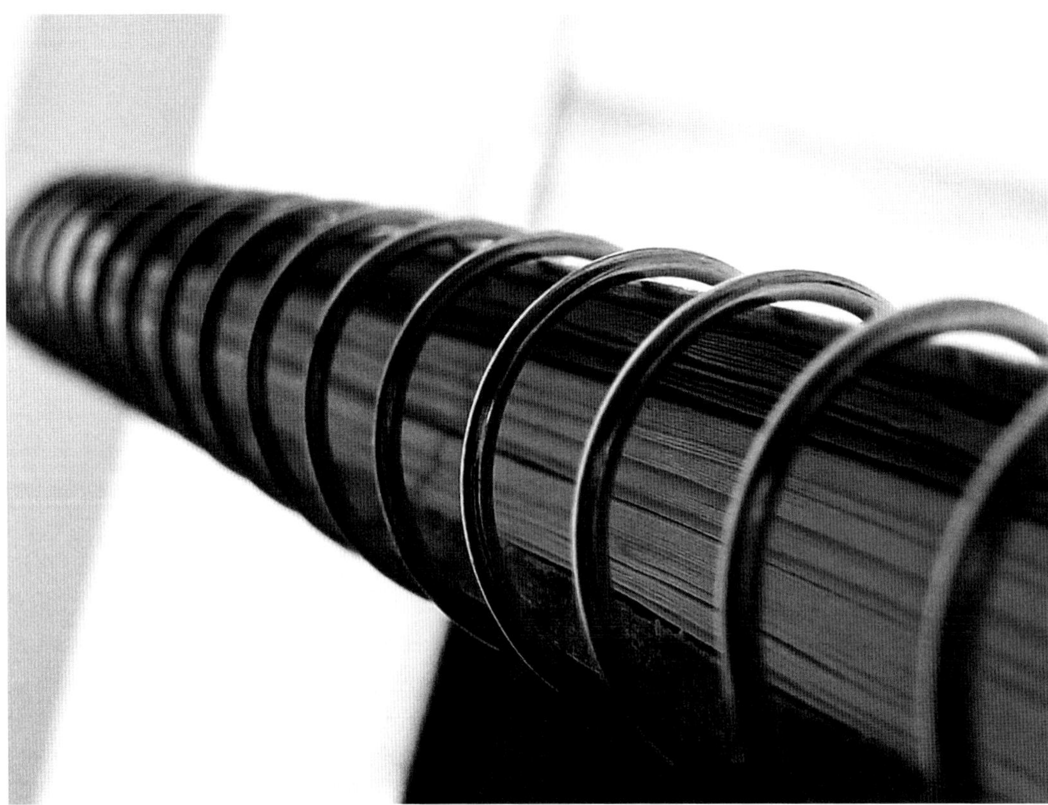

This is an example of an image that just wouldn't have happened prior to digital photography. I was writing some notes for this book and I became curious as to how the spiral binder would look in a photograph. All I had to do was turn on my compact camera and fire off a few shots. The image stabilization meant that I didn't have to set up lighting or spend time setting up a tripod, and the macro setting meant that I could get in as close as I needed to.

or drawing. For the first time, the camera could be used to record something approaching reality, and not just a version especially contrived for the photographer, such as a portrait sitting.

Most of the recent developments in photography, from those first candid images until the present day, have been ones of convenience. A perfectly good compact camera can now be purchased for around a hundred dollars, and the darkroom has been replaced by the computer, which is a device most of us already own. With digital, so called "film" is now virtually free. The upshot is that millions of people are recording every conceivable part of reality, and also publishing their efforts for the world to see on social networking websites such as Facebook. Photography is no longer a separate thing that looks in on society from the outside, but rather is an integral part of society.

The relationship between the photographer and photography as a whole is one of the most important parts of the question of what photography is, but it is a chapter you will have to write yourself. Even if you never write an article about your own relationship to photography—a manifesto describing what photography is to *you*—any time spent considering this relationship will bear fruit. It is also good to realize that we are a part of something much bigger than ourselves. This awareness can ease the sense of isolation that can come from a photographer being a somewhat detached observer as opposed to a full-on participant in events.

To my mind, it is impossible to define photography without addressing the issue of whether or not it is a legitimate art form. My view on the subject can be summed up very simply by the following statement: *Photography is an art form every bit the equal to other visual arts, such as painting and sculpture.* Many disagree with this statement and seek to pigeonhole photography as nothing more than a technical skill. As far as I am concerned, this is an old argument that was laid to rest in the early part of the 20th century. Chapter 8, which is about the history of photography, covers this in some depth.

Exposure Explained

Exposure refers to the amount of light that is allowed to hit the recording medium, usually either a digital sensor or film. What is the correct amount of light that should be allowed to hit the sensor or film? As much or as little as the photographer wants. There are ways to mathematically calculate this, a fact that automatic settings on cameras take full advantage of. A photographer who doesn't bypass these settings and experiment, however, is giving up a huge amount of creative control. If a layperson looks at a photograph, two things will determine whether they think the photograph is a snapshot or the work of a professional: composition and exposure, with the latter being more influential. This explains how important it is to understand exposure.

Understanding exposure in applied terms is pretty straightforward. Three separate things control exposure, and they are set either by the camera, the photographer, or a combination of the two. The three controls are *aperture,* which determines how much light hits the recording medium, *shutter speed,* which determines how long the light hits the recording medium, and *ISO,* which refers to the sensitivity of the recording medium to light. The most important thing to grasp at this point is that any one of these can be used to balance out one or both of the others. For example, if you were to increase the aperture, decreasing either the shutter speed or the ISO by a set amount will cancel out the change in exposure.

So far so good, but it raises the question, why change anything? Why allow more light in by increasing the aperture, only to then reduce it to the exact same amount by increasing the shutter speed? The answer is that changes to these three settings do more than simply increase or decrease the amount of light that is allowed to hit the sensor; or in the case of ISO, it changes the sensitivity of the sensor. It is these other changes, and managing and understanding them, that turns someone with a camera into a *photographer*.

Aperture

The aperture is basically a hole, the area of which determines how much light hits the sensor over a given period of time. Increasing or decreasing the size of this hole does more than just determine the amount of light, though. A photograph is a two-dimensional interpretation of a three-dimensional reality, and much of the resulting effect is directly related to aperture size. For an image to appear sharp from near to far, a small aperture must be used. Conversely, the larger the aperture the smaller the range of depth that will render sharply. *Depth of field* is the term used when discussing this aspect.

It doesn't take much to realize the potential of using aperture size as a creative tool. A large aperture is often used to isolate a subject from its background or to add some creative bokeh. A smaller aperture is often used in landscape photography, where sharpness right through the depth of the image is required.

> *The word* bokeh *means* blur *and is used in photography to describe the aesthetic qualities of any areas of a photograph that are not in sharp focus. There is much discussion about what constitutes good or bad bokeh. When the out-of-focus area is attractive—not* what *is out of focus, but the* way *it is out of focus—it is said to have good bokeh.*

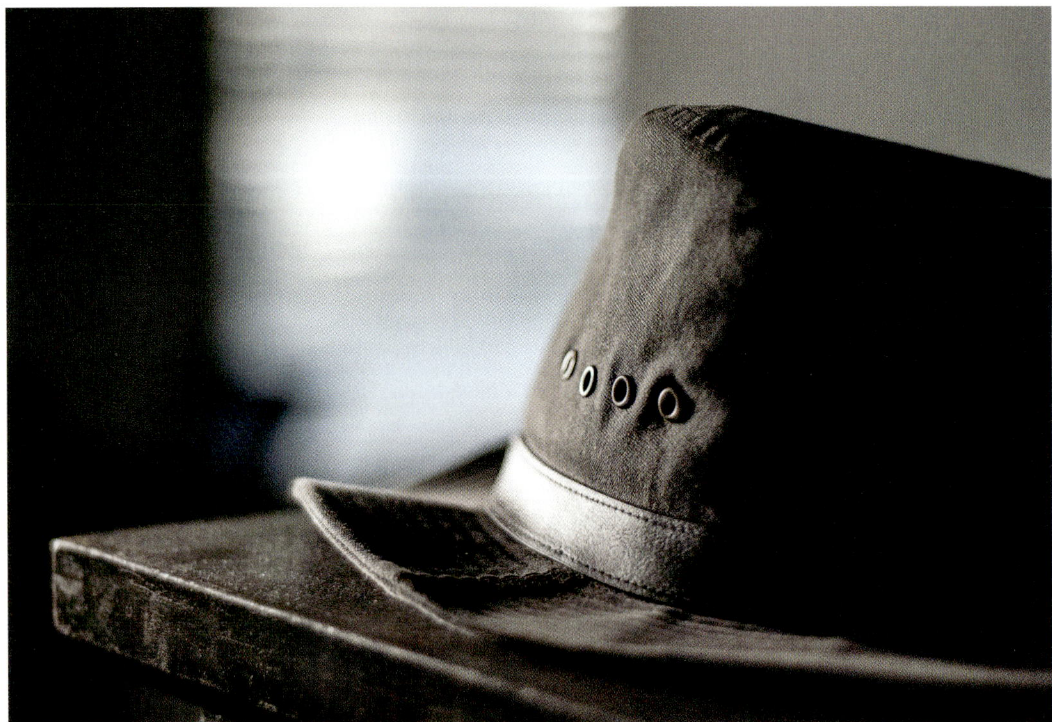

A large aperture setting (f/1.8) gives a very small depth of field

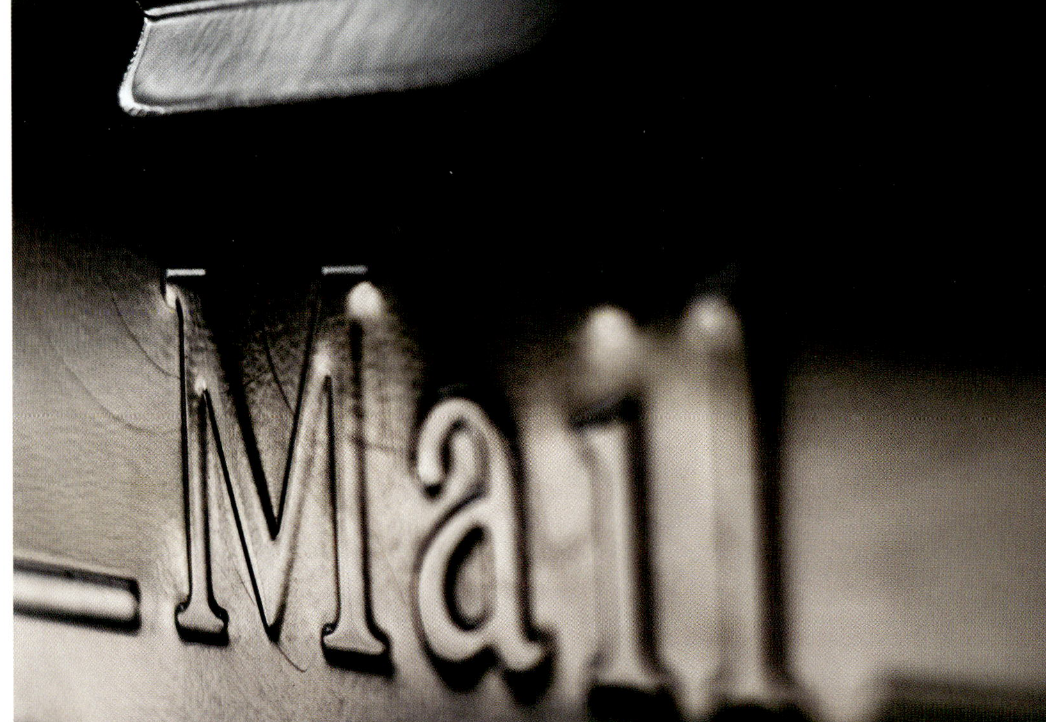

This is another example of using a large aperture to limit depth of field. This type of shot is only possible with a sensor that is larger than those available on a typical point-and-shoot camera.

It is important to mention at this point that depth of field is not only a function of aperture size, but also of sensor size. An identical aperture size will have a very different effect on a full-frame sensor on a DSLR than on the much smaller sensor of a compact camera. The smaller the sensor, the greater the depth of field. This is why for macro work a compact camera can be preferable to a DSLR.

Aperture is measured in a scale called f-stops. A full f-stop is exactly twice the area of the one below it and half the area of the one above it. This is important to understand, especially in relation to shutter speed.

Shutter Speed

A shutter speed of 1/500 second will let in half as much light as a shutter speed of 1/250 second, and twice as much as a setting of 1/1000 second. Therefore, if the aperture is increased by a full f-stop—that is, twice the size—doubling the shutter speed will lead to no net change in the actual amount of light allowed into the camera.

Let's take this out of the realm of the abstract and apply it. If you want to use a smaller aperture to increase the depth of field, you can do so by making the shutter speed slower to compensate.

Just as there are situations in which the aperture setting is the priority, there are others in which shutter speed is the important consideration, because there is a minimum shutter speed at which a camera can be held steady. This varies according to the camera's design, the focal length being used, and the steadiness of the photographer's grip.

ISO

ISO is different than both shutter speed and aperture size because it doesn't influence the amount of light entering the camera, but rather it affects the *amount of light required to form the image*. It is also the only measurement of the three that is not standardized among camera manufacturers. Whereas an aperture of, say, f/8 is a constant, and a shutter speed of 1/500 second is also an absolute value, ISO readings vary. The doubling principle still applies, though, and this is what is important. ISO 200 on a given camera will allow the sensor to absorb light twice as fast as ISO 100 and half as fast as ISO 400.

Increasing the ISO does come with a cost; the higher the ISO, the lower the quality of the image, which is due to some pixels not being rendered accurately. Raising the ISO may be enough to force the shutter speed to be high enough to avoid camera shake, but the resulting image will not be as clean. That said, some photographers like the added low-fidelity effect that so-called *noise* adds to their images.

Cameras with smaller sensors, such as point-and-shoots, are much more prone to noise than those with larger sensors, such as DSLRs. The whole noise issue is continually being lessened by improvements in software, both in the camera and on the computer. This, along with the now-ubiquitous image stabilization technology, means that low-light and nighttime photography without a tripod are now available to just about anyone who possesses a camera.

How Does the Camera Know How Much Light to Let In?

The amount of light entering the camera and the sensitivity of the medium—whether it be film or an electronic sensor—combine to give what is commonly called *exposure*. The aperture size and shutter speed control how much light is allowed to enter the camera, while the ISO setting controls the sensitivity of the sensor. The question, though, is how much light is actually needed for the correct exposure? Almost all cameras nowadays have some means of measuring light and

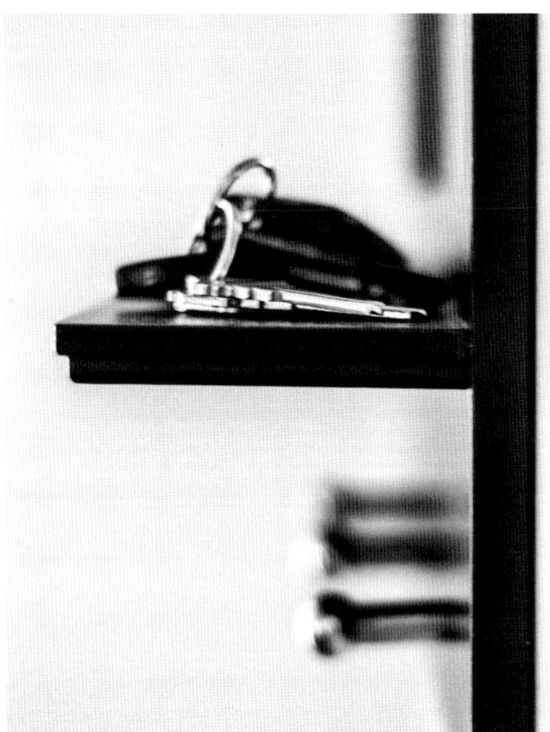

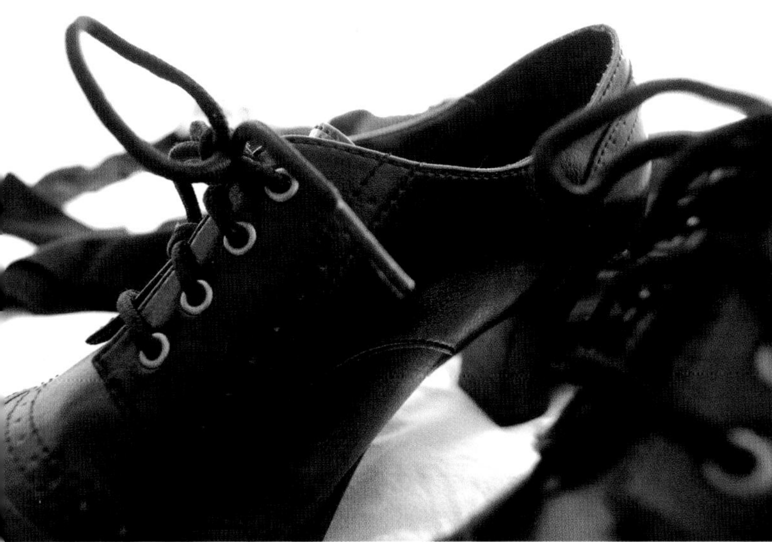

Overexposing the image or "blowing" the highlights can really help to focus attention

suggesting three settings that will allow this amount of light in.

The photographer can then do one of three things with the camera's suggested choices:

1. Accept the camera's choice of settings
2. Change more than one of the settings, but keep the exposure the same; for example, double the shutter speed and make the aperture a full stop larger
3. Change the exposure, which will result in the image being lighter or darker than if either of the first two methods were used

The Importance of Tone in Relation to Exposure

The camera's internal light meter, or an external handheld light meter, measures the light reflecting off a surface, representing a tone within the range the camera is able to record. Two things determine tone: luminance and available light. A pale color will convert to a lighter gray than a dark color—this is due to luminance. The same surface will show different tones under different lighting conditions. For example, the tone will be much darker if a surface is in shadow rather than in bright sunlight.

If this concept is a little abstract, think of an artist making an accurate pencil drawing and producing a grayscale version of the scene. When considering metering and tone, forget about color. Whether the initial color of a subject is red, green, yellow, or blue does not matter; you want to think of it in grayscale, as in a pencil drawing.

Light Metering Methods

Most cameras are capable of measuring the amount of available light in several different ways: *averaged, spot, center weighted,* and the manufacturer's *matrix/evaluative* settings. If averaged or spot metering is selected by the photographer, a single value for the entire image area is being calculated and returned. Matrix/evaluative metering is not so cut and dried, and it is hard to make a definitive statement because methods tend to be proprietary and manufacturers are loathe to share details. Some manufacturers do, however, state that they expose different parts of the image differently using electronic techniques. Darker parts of the image are boosted while very bright parts are underexposed.

Averaged Metering

Averaged metering is when the camera takes measurements across the whole scene and simply comes up with a value based on the medium (average) tone in the scene.

Spot Metering

Spot metering is when a measurement is taken from a single, very small part of the image. The idea is that this part of the image will expose perfectly at the expense of the rest of the image. A couple of examples of when this type of metering may be used are on a face, where exact skin tone is required, or on a candle flame, to not overexpose the flame, which averaged metering would do. Averaging would see mainly black and would therefore interpret a tone as close to black as middle gray, and try to lighten the entire scene accordingly. Spot metering is great for drama, and what we often think of as cinematic-type lighting is often the result of spot metering.

In practical terms, spot metering usually involves pointing the camera at the part of the scene that is to be perfectly exposed, half pressing the shutter-release button to lock the exposure, then reframing the shot and fully pressing the shutter-release button.

Center Weighted Metering

Center weighted metering may be thought of as a compromise between spot and averaged. It gives the highest priority to tones in the center of the scene and the least priority to the tones at the edges, but it does take them all into account.

Matrix/Evaluative Metering and Others

Camera companies often use their own formulas for a metering system that is likely to get the exposure correct in all situations. This often involves a database inside the camera that contains comparative scenes and the best settings for such scenes. Manufacturers tend to keep the details of these systems to themselves, so it is not possible to come up with a definitive description. If your camera has such a setting, it will be good, but that doesn't mean it's always the best option. I tend to swap between this setting and spot metering.

A Practical Demonstration

If your camera has a live view LCD screen, you can try this:

- If you can, and normally you can, set the screen to monochrome
- Set the metering mode to either center weighted or the camera's default mode
- Find a scene with a wide tonal variation—indoors is best, a room on a sunny day is ideal
- Slowly pan the camera while watching the LCD screen
- Now set the metering mode to spot, and pan the camera over the same scene while watching the LCD screen

This is what should have happened:

- On the first setting, the brightness of the image on the LCD screen changed gradually, if at all

- On the spot setting, the changes should have been much more dramatic, going from very light to very dark and back again, with very little movement of the camera

Exposure Basics from a Minimalist Perspective

Some musicians can play instruments superbly without ever learning to read a single musical note, while others need sheet music in front of them to perform. Parallels to this can be drawn with regard to photographers: some work instinctively, while others require a more formal approach and need to have a good grasp of the theoretical.

Most of us fall somewhere in the middle. I find that an understanding of the theory behind exposure is a tremendous help, but I don't have to keep the mathematical equations that underpin this stuff in my head, or even to know them, in many cases. It is enough to understand the interplay between ISO, shutter speed, and aperture size. Understanding the underlying principles involved is important, but knowing the exact equations and numbers is optional.

Of course, this is all academic if it cannot be used when actually taking a photograph. My understanding of exposure allows me to use several methods, and that suits me. As an example, when I use a DSLR camera, I first set it to spot metering and set the lens to manual focus, and then I proceed as follows:

1. Check that the camera is set to aperture priority
2. Roughly frame and manually focus
3. Note the shutter speed that the camera wants to use
4. Decide how I want the image exposed and note how much this varies from the camera's choice—this gives me a shutter speed to aim for
5. If I want to underexpose, I point the camera at a relatively bright spot; if I want to overexpose, I point it at a darker spot, and then I adjust until the shutter speed I want appears in the viewfinder display
6. Halfway press the shutter-release button
7. Reframe and adjust focus
8. Fully depress the shutter-release button

This probably looks like a complicated way to take a photograph. Believe me when I say that it isn't. After a few attempts, it will become second nature, and it is much more instinctive than twiddling with dials. It will also provide an instinctive understanding of exposure.

The main points about exposure are as follows:

- Exposure determines how light or dark the photograph will be
- The camera determines an exposure, but this can be changed by the photographer
- The photographer can determine how the camera chooses an exposure value
- The exposure is always a single value regardless of what type of metering is used, unless the manufacturer's own proprietary method is used

The main points about exposure are as follows:

- *Exposure determines how light or dark the photograph will be*
- *The camera determines an exposure, but this can be changed by the photographer*
- *The photographer can determine how the camera chooses an exposure value*
- *The exposure is always a single value regardless of what type of metering is used, unless the manufacturer's own proprietary method is used*

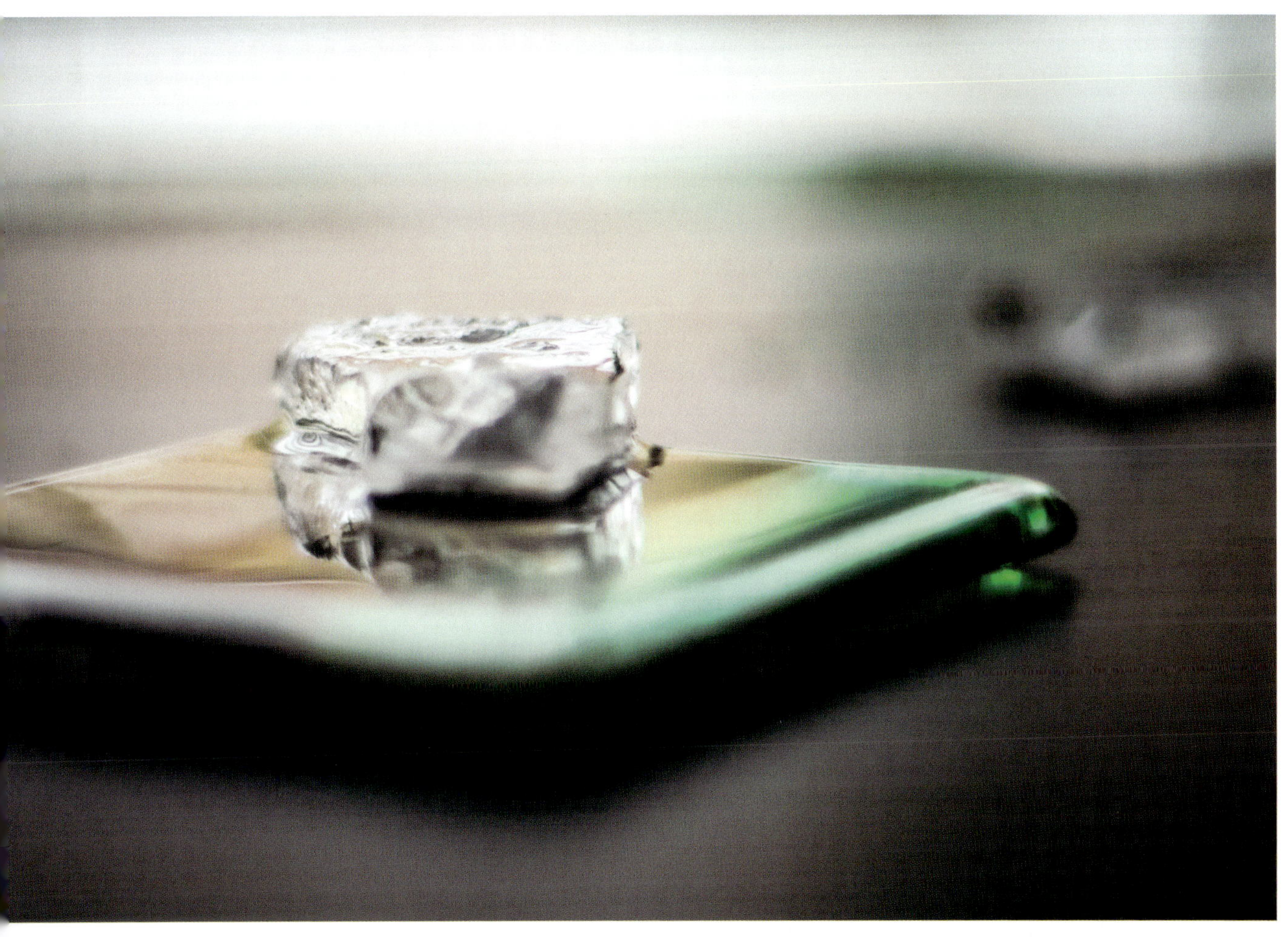

Ice melting on a glass coaster

Gallery 3: Railroad Tracks

Photographers tend to use railroad tracks as a device to draw the eye through the depth of the image. Railroad tracks can, however, make for interesting compositions when used in different ways.

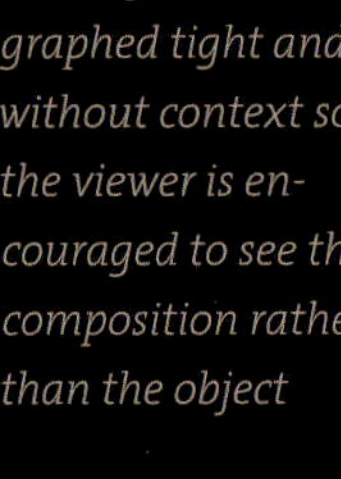

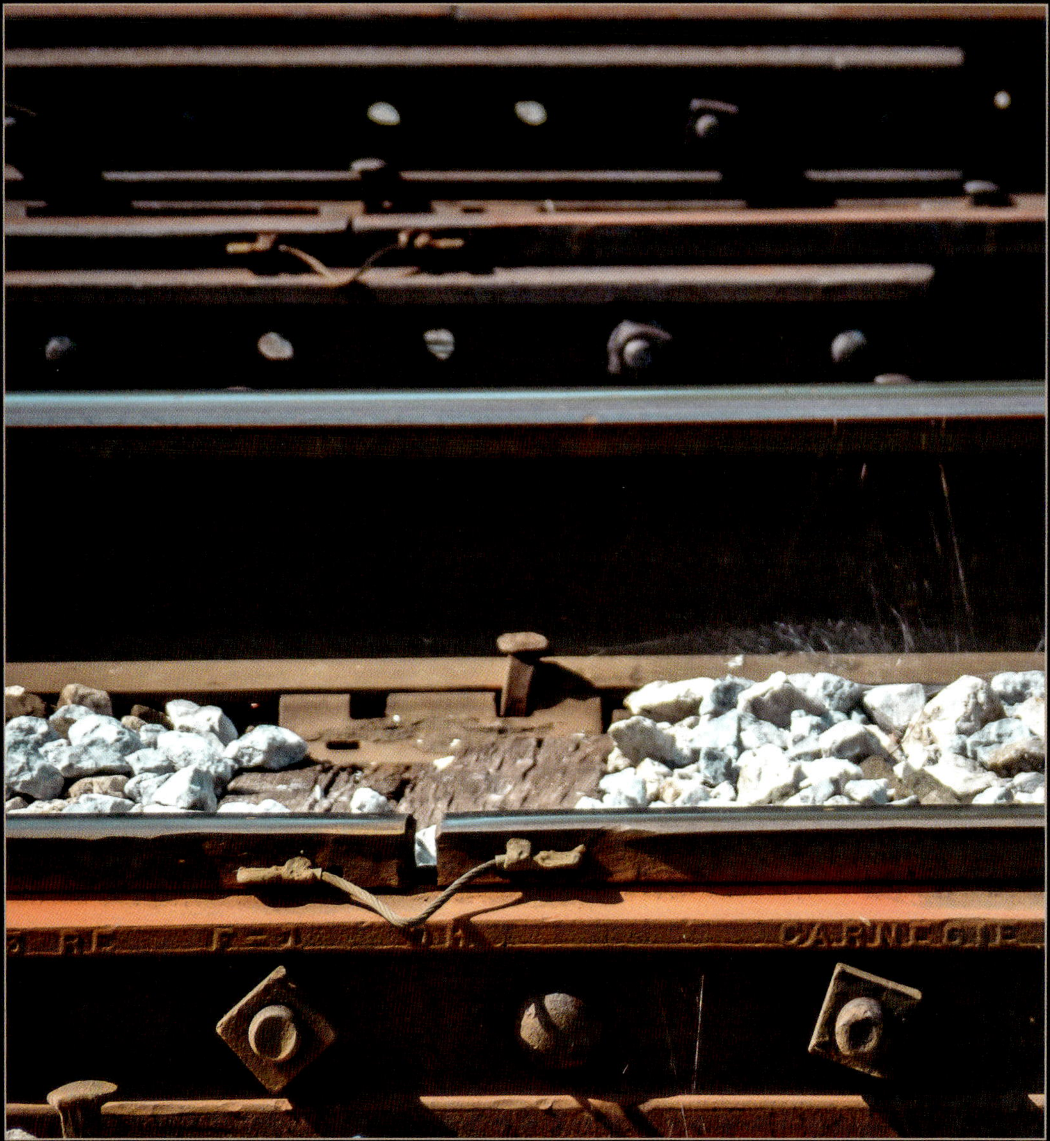

Tracks photographed tight and without context so the viewer is encouraged to see the composition rather than the object

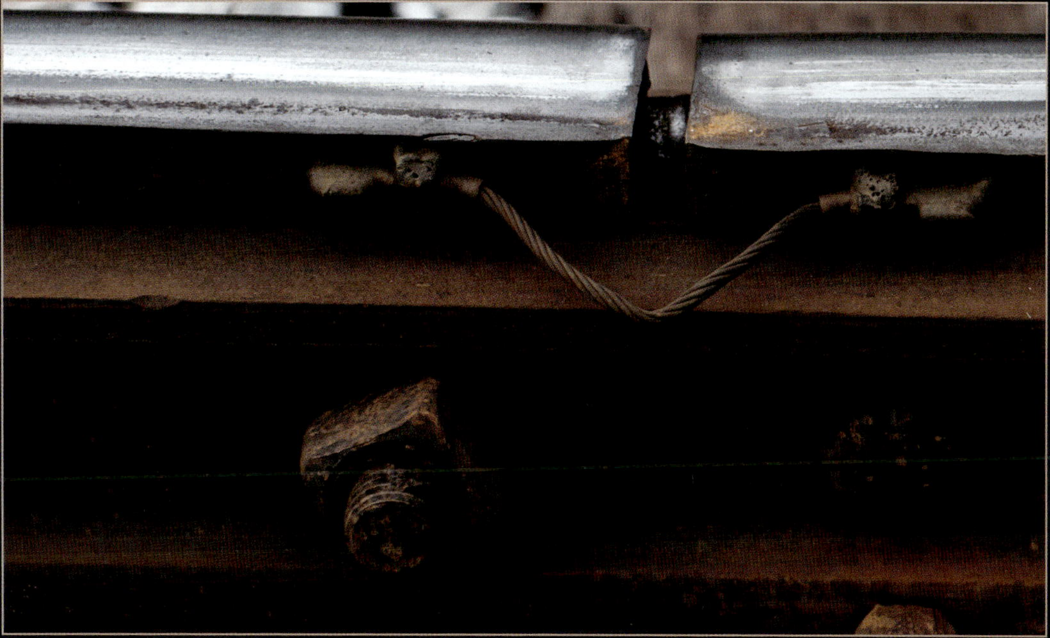

Lots of interesting details

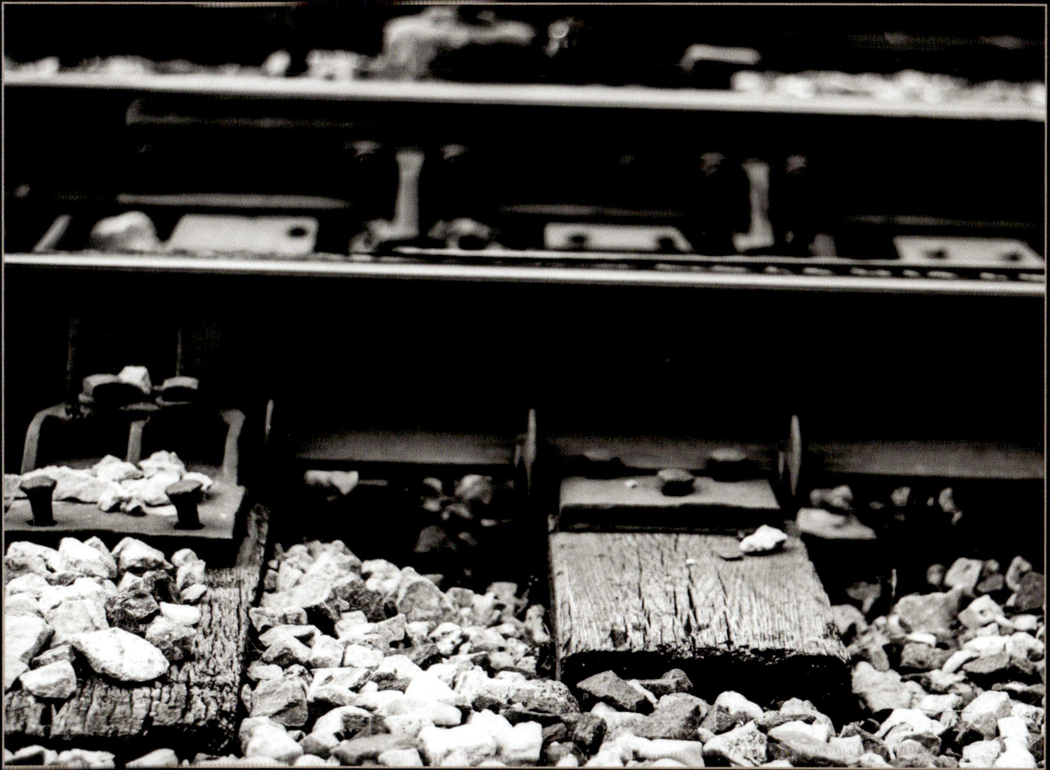

Black-and-white helps to emphasize the age of these tracks

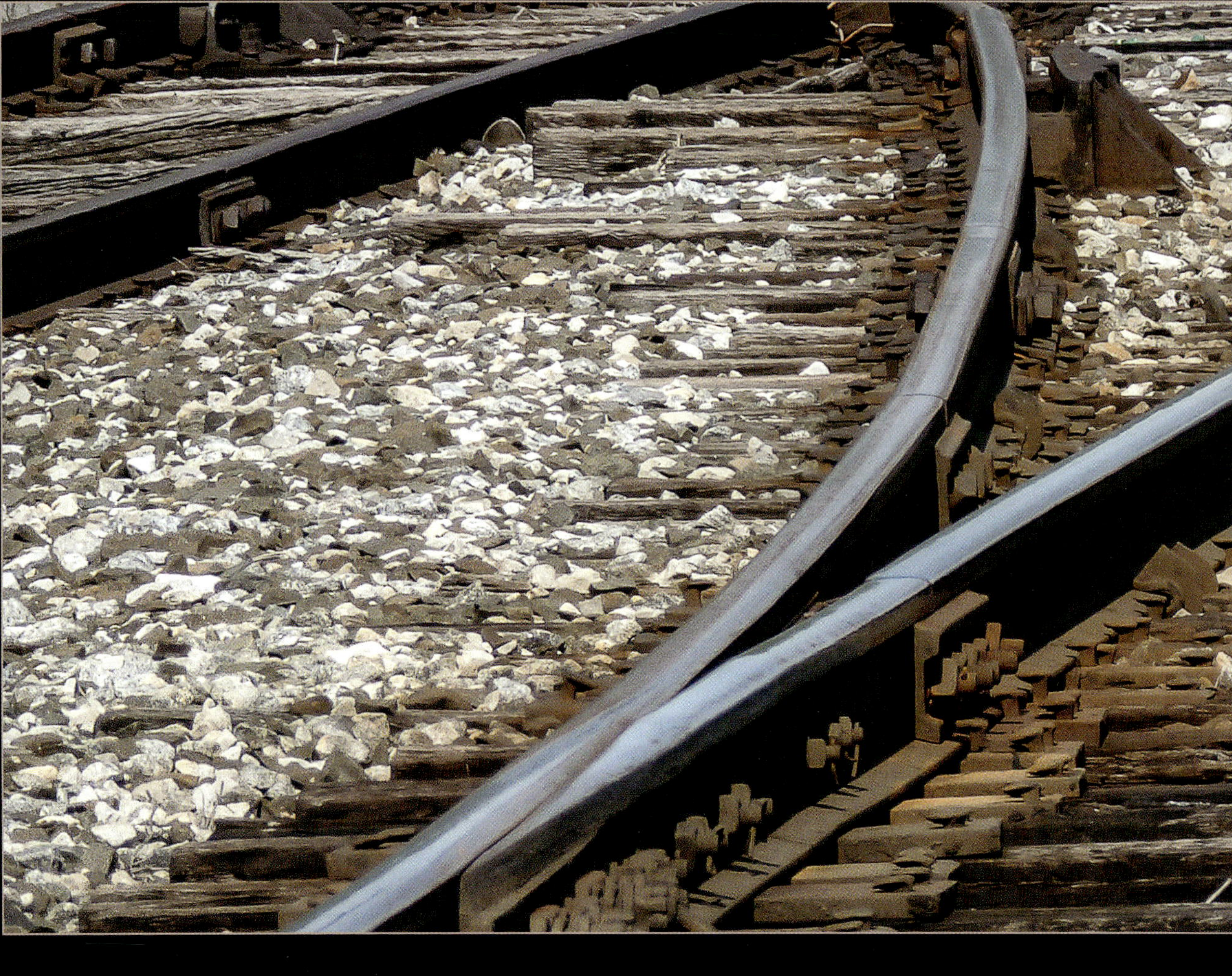

Railway lines used to form triangles, again with the intention of emphasizing the composition and not the actual object

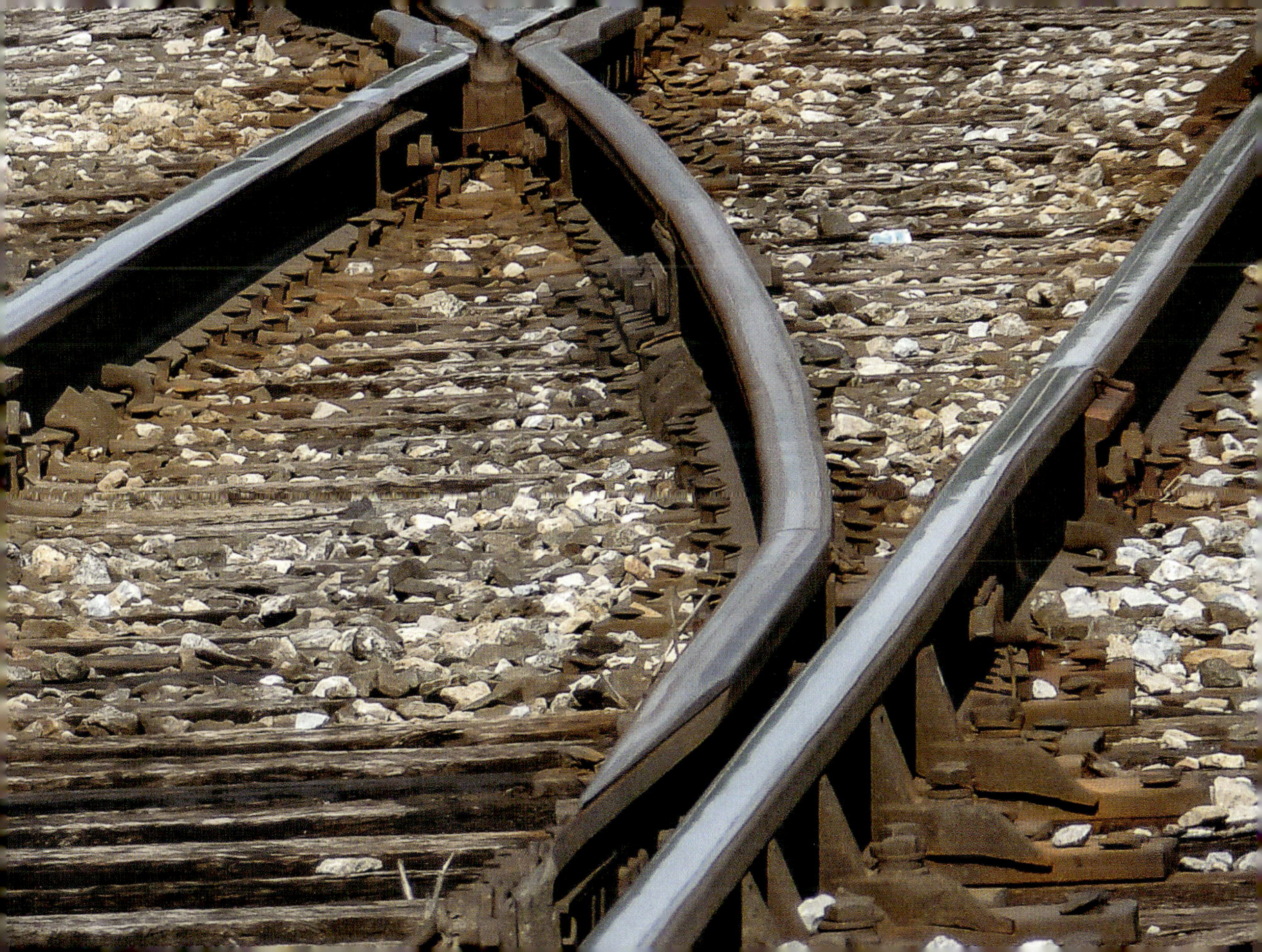

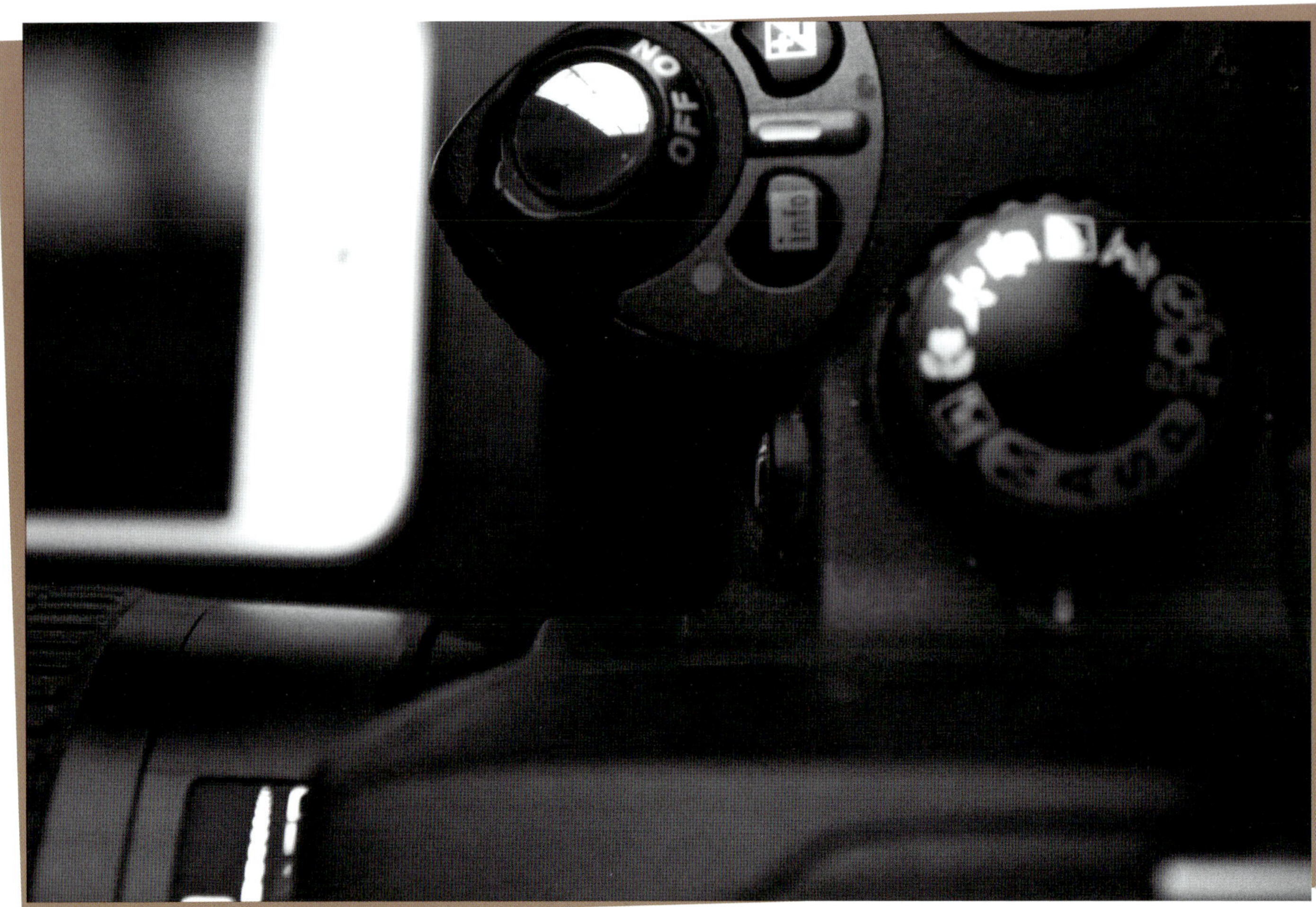
ON
OFF
info

Chapter 4
The Camera

If you want to take photographs, you will need to choose a camera. Until fairly recently, entry-level options were extremely limited. At the beginning of the 1980s, for example, a typical first camera was a fixed-focus film camera with virtually no bells and whistles other than a small built-in flash, an ability to know the film speed without being told, and a cloudy or sunny light setting. Zoom lenses on compact cameras were just beginning to make an appearance, but they were expensive. Zooming in or out was generally done by walking closer or farther away from the subject. For roughly the same price as this basic but serviceable early eighties camera, today's consumer would expect, at the very least, a zoom lens, a macro function, low light functions, various scene modes, and a movie function.

It is essential to carefully research which camera to purchase before parting with any cash. Extreme price differences and an ever-growing choice of camera types combine to make selection tough. As you do your research, carefully consider which type of camera is best suited to your purposes, and also consider the sources of any camera reviews you may read.

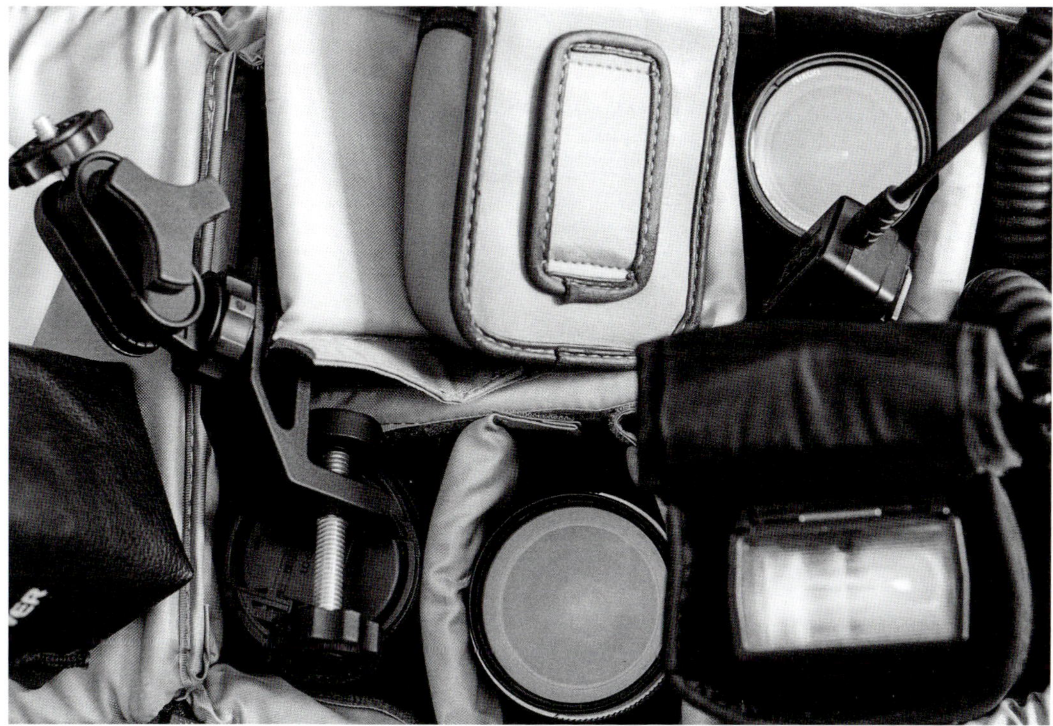

Photography can become very expensive very quickly!

The Photography Equipment Industry

I really hope the following statement doesn't come as a revelation to you:

The photography equipment industry's first priority isn't to make you an *ideally* equipped photographer; it is to make you an *expensively* equipped photographer.

It is important to bear this in mind when deciding which camera and accessories to buy. The industry spends a lot of money on marketing and advertising with a goal of separating you from as many of your dollars as possible. This doesn't make camera manufacturers evil; they are just fulfilling their obligations to their shareholders. It does, however, mean that the onus is on you, the consumer, to do your homework.

One lesson we were taught in history classes was to learn about the historians before we drew conclusions about their versions of events. The same can be said for researching cameras and photography equipment. If you are reading an article about a particular camera, for example, it is a good idea to know something about both the writer and the publication in which it appears. Does the writer have any connections with the manufacturer? Who owns the publication, and does it carry advertising for the brand or model in question? Recently, a lens manufacturer offered prominent photography bloggers the opportunity to keep an expensive lens in return for a favorable online review. This became public knowledge only because some of the bloggers who were approached went public with the details.

I am not saying that a potentially biased writer should be ignored, because a biased source can still provide useful information. It is just a matter of knowing when to take something with a grain of salt, and recognizing the difference between marketing and unbiased reporting. That said, a good author or publication will err on the side of caution and declare any conflicts of interest, even in cases where there is nothing more than a possible perception of a conflict of interest.

Camera Reviews

Not all camera reviews are created equal, and the photography industry worked out a long time ago that we pay more attention to writing we perceive as unbiased than to advertising. It has to be said that although many companies in the industry are ethical, there are others that value sales over strict honesty.

There are the obvious considerations, such as whether a magazine that depends on a manufacturer for advertising will write a negative review of that manufacturer's products. More often, though, the process is a little more subtle. A blatantly promotional review will not fool many people, so the reviewer may throw in one or two very minor quibbles to give the impression of balance.

The Internet presents a bigger challenge. There are literally thousands of people who make money by simply directing viewers to a company's website to purchase goods. Just putting a link to the company on a website doesn't work very well. However, writing what appears to be a review—but is actually a disguised sales pitch—works extremely well.

Another tactic is a fake review posted on a big sales website. Some manufacturers who advertise equipment on Amazon, for example, have been known to solicit positive reviews in return for payment. There are also companies with teams of registered writers that broker requests for articles from companies and other clients. Often these requests explicitly state that the articles are reviews for websites like Amazon, and they usually come with instructions to be positive but not obvious—as in obviously writing the review for cash. A wise consumer will read more than one review and be wary if the product has just a few reviews that are all five star.

The trick is not to disregard all reviews but to be aware that the writer may have an agenda. Even if this is the case, there can still be useful information contained in the review. In most cases, the writer's affiliations and interests will be fairly transparent. It should also be mentioned that these practices are by no means exclusive to the photography industry.

Choose Your Camera (Don't Let it Choose You)

With the vast range of available features and prices, choosing a camera, especially if it is your first camera, can be extremely confusing. At one time, you could decide on a budget and then purchase the model that was priced accordingly. These days, however, there are so many variables that not only is it hard to make a choice, you also risk breaking the bank for what may or may not turn out to be an interest worth pursuing.

The task of choosing a first camera can be simplified. If you think photography is something you may be interested in but are not sure whether it will be a marriage-threatening part of your life or just an occasional weekend pursuit, then purchase a budget compact camera. Something with the basic features will do just fine: around a 5x zoom, image stabilization, some flexibility with settings such as ISO, and an option to shoot and preview on-screen in black-and-white. Features that I would not care about one way or the other are face recognition, GPS, and whether the camera can upload images and movies straight to the Internet. A camera that fulfills the basic criteria can be purchased new for less than $150 without ongoing, additional costs.

There are several advantages to the low-budget approach in addition to reducing monetary risk. Compact cameras are pocket sized and therefore are more convenient than DSLRs. This means you are more likely to keep the camera with you. Just about everyone has a small camera that they use, whether it's a smart phone or a compact camera, so the pressure to perform is minimal. Using a DSLR comes with a little more social pressure. If you use a big, serious-looking camera, others' expectations will tend to be higher because they will assume you have a certain level of expertise. Now, you may have the skin of a rhino and this may not bother you, but self-confidence, especially early on, can be fragile.

A compact camera is a great learning tool, and will adapt to most situations surprisingly well. Of course, framing and composition are more or less the same regardless of camera type, and expertise in these skills can be gained only with practice. Due to the convenience of a compact camera, you will take more pictures than you would with a DSLR. At this stage it is a numbers game. Photographers improve by taking lots and lots of photographs of lots and lots of ordinary things, not by taking a dozen shots once a month of a stunning vista or a beautiful model. Trying to make the everyday visually interesting is the best way for photographers to hone their skills, and a compact camera is the right tool for this particular task.

It is also perfectly possible to get very good results from the onboard camera on a cell phone, and this may be enough, but even a basic compact camera will give you more control over your photography. Features such as exposure compensation and a 5x optical zoom lens will provide more control than is available on even the most up-to-date cell phones. Of course this could change in the future, and cell phones are likely to become as fully featured as the more sophisticated compacts that are currently available.

Trying to make the everyday visually interesting is the best way for photographers to hone their skills, and a compact camera can be a great tool for this particular task.

Many fine photographers are now using cell phone cameras for everything from fine art photography to award-winning photojournalism. To the best of my knowledge, though, these photographers have all mastered the more traditional types of cameras before deciding that a cell phone camera was for them.

A compact camera does have limitations, which may or may not be an issue for you, including the ultimate quality of the image, the lack of flexibility in exposure settings, the lack of ultrawide angle or extreme telephoto capability, and depth of field limitations. These issues can be overcome in a camera with a bigger sensor and the ability to swap lenses. Currently a DSLR, a mirrorless interchangeable lens camera (MILC), or a rangefinder camera would be the way to go in order to solve these issues, but this may not be the case in the not-too-distant future. Smaller cameras are now coming onto the market with interchangeable lenses and larger sensors, albeit not quite as large as in a 35mm DSLR. The one scenario when a DSLR camera is still irreplaceable is when extra lighting is required, such as studio or model shoots. If your type of photography involves using anything other than available light, you will need a level of control and options that are not available on compact cameras.

After you are completely confident with a compact camera and its limitations have started to become an issue, the time is right to start looking at more sophisticated options. The advantage of this approach is that you will now be purchasing a more expensive camera to solve specific problems. You will know exactly what kind of camera features you need, and this will propel your photography forward.

Types of Cameras

Until recently, deciding what type of camera to purchase was relatively easy. If you were a professional photographer or a serious hobbyist, then a DSLR was the way to go. For everyone else, a point-and-shoot camera was the answer. There were other types, such as bridge cameras, which, as the name implies, was an intermediate step between a DSLR and a compact, but the choices were limited.

All this has now changed. Improvements in technology have led to an explosion of camera types, all capable of taking reasonably good photographs. Photographers can now factor in things such as portability, convenience, and—it has to be said—style when choosing a camera. The two most established types are still DSLRs and compacts, but now there are other options. Serious photographers are looking beyond DSLRs, and hobbyists are looking toward solutions other than compacts. In fact, some people think the advent of decent-quality smart phone cameras could all but squeeze compact cameras out of existence. I do not agree with this view because I think there will always be a place for a small dedicated device as opposed to one in which a camera is just one of many functions.

DSLRs

DSLRs use a prism and a mirror, allowing the photographer to view the scene through the lens. This means that what appears in the viewfinder will be the same as what is captured. Until recently, DSLRs were the only type of camera, other than medium- and large-format cameras, that came with interchangeable lenses. This ability means that DSLRs can be used to capture just about any type of image in just about any situation.

In addition to the flexibility offered by an interchangeable lens system and accurate framing, DSLRs have many other strengths when compared with other types of cameras. They have much larger sensors than compacts, which allow for a much higher-quality image. Sensor size is a greater factor than lens quality for sharpness and accuracy in an image. In fact, an average lens on a DSLR will give technically

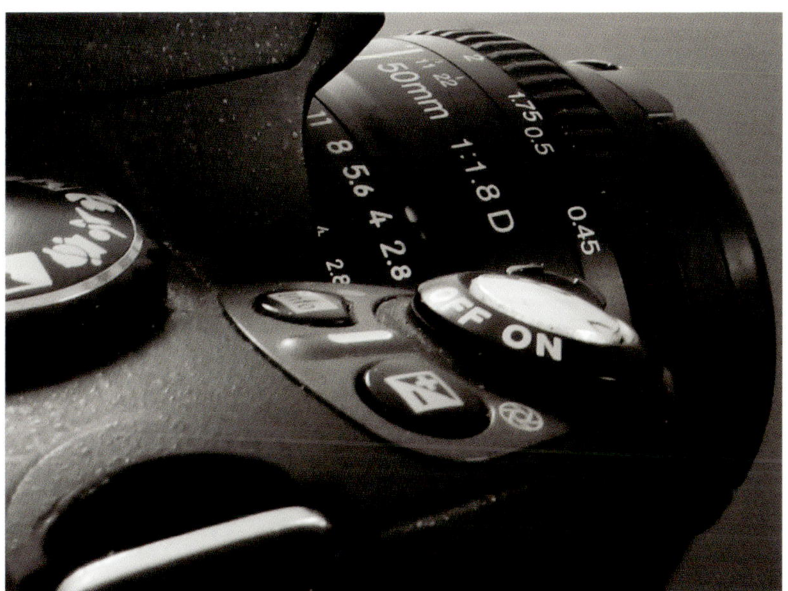

Nikon D40X. A crop sensor DSLR with my favorite lens, a 50mm f/1.8

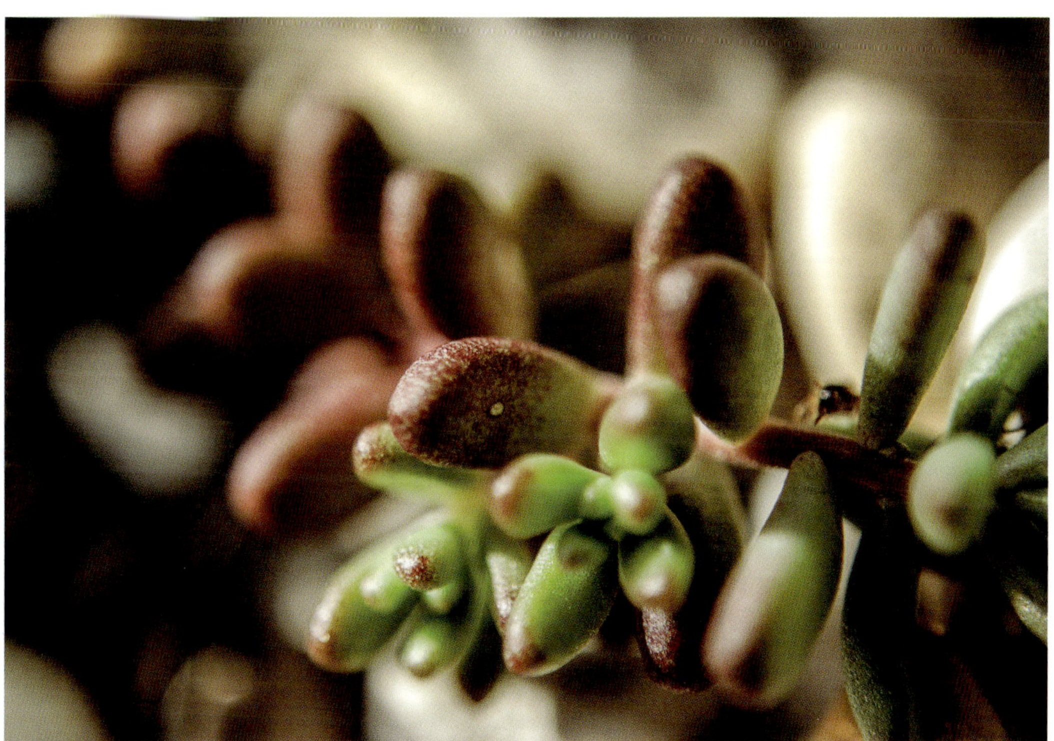

In macro photography, you can use the DSLR's limited depth of field for impact. If a larger depth of field is required, it may be worth switching to a compact camera.

better results than the best-quality lens on a compact camera, with its much smaller sensor. The large sensor also allows for a much narrower depth of field, allowing for greater separation of the foreground and the background. This is especially important in portrait photography.

DSLRs are large, and even the smallest of them are cumbersome compared to most compact cameras. There is no DSLR that will fit in a shirt pocket. There is a saying, however, that the best camera is the one you have with you, and many people choose to go with a smaller, more convenient camera. A recent development that could challenge the DSLR as the mainstay of serious photographers is the growing trend to use larger sensors in compact-sized cameras. Some of these even have interchangeable lenses.

DSLRs are relatively large because they need to house the mirror and prism arrangement that enables accurate viewing and framing through the lens. Cameras are now coming onto the market where the prism, mirror, and optical viewfinder have been replaced with all-digital solutions. Digital or electronic viewfinders have been around for a while, but there was a long time lag between the view changing and the camera displaying the change, making serious photography with these cameras more or less impossible. This major problem has recently been resolved.

Point-and-Shoots

Generally, the term *point-and-shoot* is used to describe a compact camera that is small, doesn't have interchangeable lenses, and is simple to use. The term is a little misleading because the majority of compacts produce better images when the user is confident enough to override some of the camera's settings.

There is wide variation in just how much the photographer can control. Simpler models offer few options, whereas more advanced models allow the user to set ISO, shutter speed, aperture, metering, and just about everything else.

The major pluses of point-and-shoots are small size and ease of use. Just about all have at least one fully automatic setting that leaves nothing to be set by the photographer. Many of these cameras are small enough to fit into a shirt pocket, so they can be taken just about anywhere. People are more likely to relax around a photographer when the camera is not an obvious part of an event, which provides a great advantage when taking candid shots. If you own both a compact and a DSLR camera, take them to different social gatherings and see how differently people react to you. If you have a compact camera, you are part of the crowd, someone who happens to have a camera, but with a DSLR you become seen as an interloper who is there for the photographs and not for the people. It may not always be this cut and dry, but it certainly is an eye-opener and makes for an interesting social experiment.

Another thing that factors into the convenience argument is not having to change lenses. It is now possible to purchase a so-called superzoom point-and-shoot that can cover the focal lengths of several DSLR lenses. Cameras capable of 20x optical zoom have been on the market for some time. In DSLR terms, these lenses give optical zoom ranges of around 24mm to 480mm (the exact figures depend on the smaller value), which is impressive.

Sensor size is the limiting factor with compacts. There is a ceiling on the quality of images that can be obtained using a very small sensor. That said, improvements are continually being made, and the possible quality of images today is much higher than even a few years ago.

The quality—or to be more precise, *fidelity*—of a photograph may not be a major issue. There is a growing trend toward the more stark aesthetics and less subtle images produced by small compact sensors. Of course, this is a matter of taste and the type of photography required. Information can always be removed

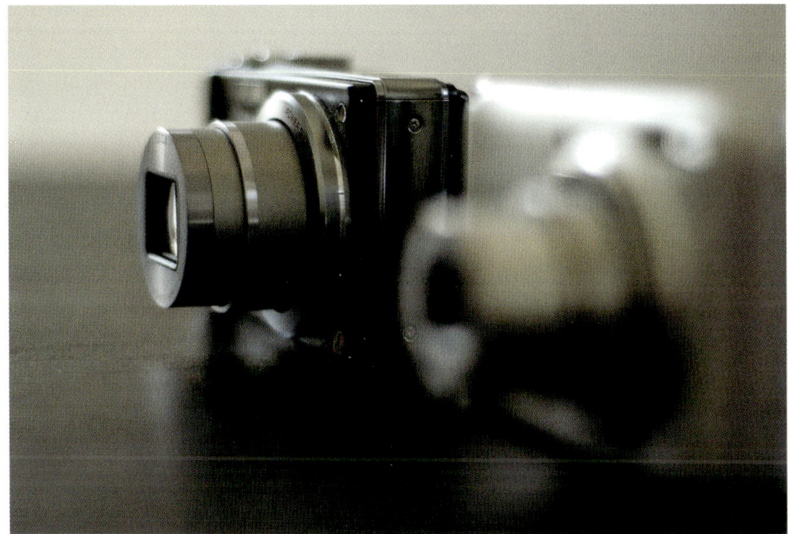

Point-and-shoot cameras

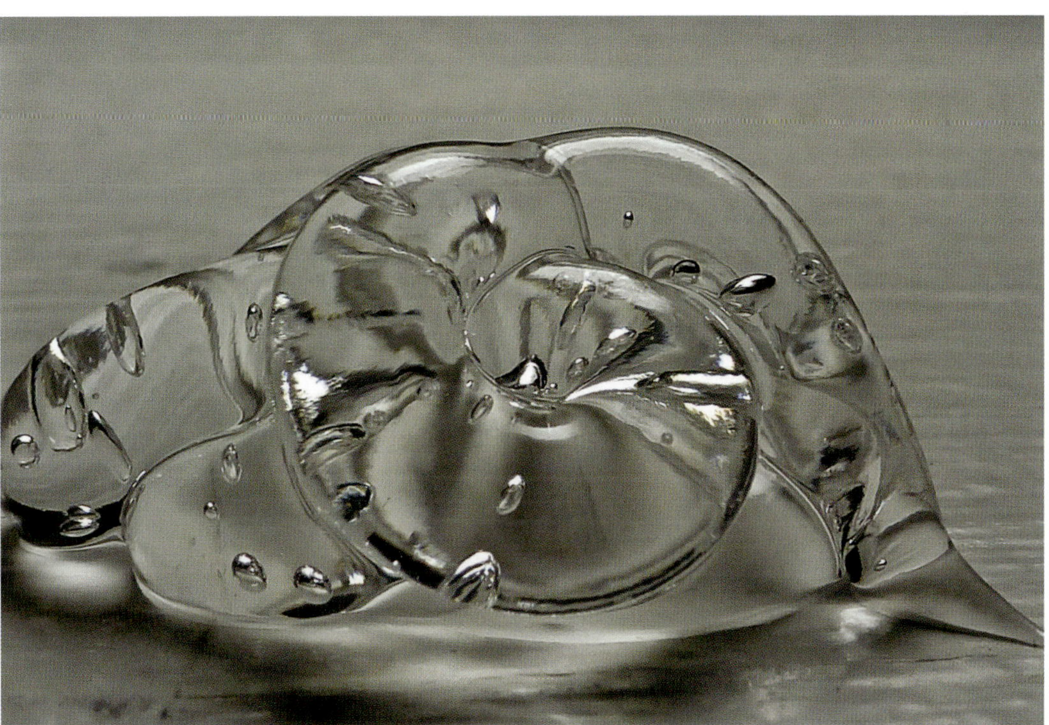

Curiosity is a great driving force in photography. This image was the result of wondering what hair gel would look like just squeezed onto a surface. If technical perfection is not an issue, a basic point-and-shoot is ideal for spur-of-the-moment photography.

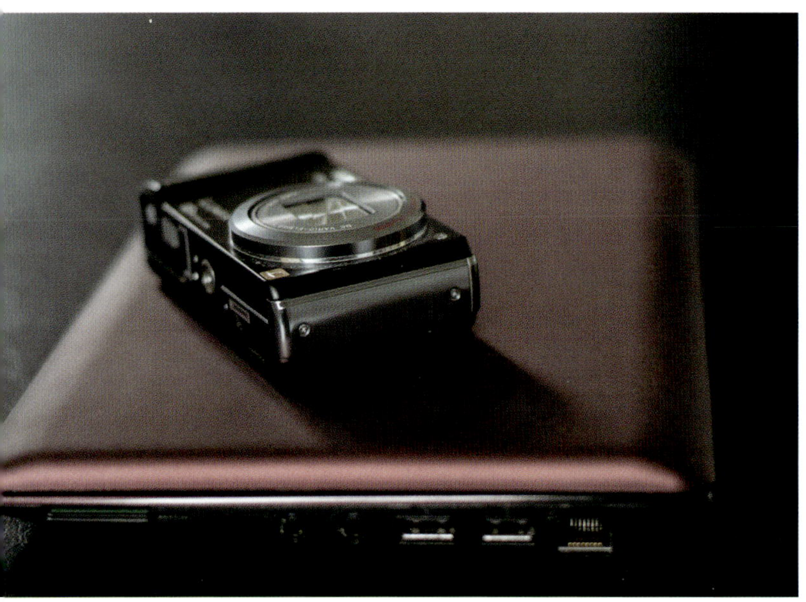

Photography has never been so portable. A camera and a netbook are everything required for taking and editing photographs. Find the nearest coffee shop with a wireless Internet connection, and the images can be published as well.

from an image, but it cannot be put back in; therefore, the larger the sensor, the greater the options.

Micro Four-Thirds System

If there is a holy grail in the camera-manufacturing world, it is a camera that has the quality of output and flexibility of a DSLR with the convenience and size of a compact. The most serious attempt at bridging the divide comes in the form of the micro four-thirds (MFT) system. Olympus and Panasonic created this standard and announced it to the world in 2008.

The MFT does not have a mirror box or pentaprism like DSLRs or their predecessor, the four-thirds system, which allows the camera to be compact in design. The downside of not having the mirror assembly is that an optical viewfinder is not an option. All of these cameras have a live view screen, and some come with an electronic viewfinder or a separate (not through-the-lens, or TTL) optical viewfinder. In the case of electronic solutions, the time lag between an event and when it appeared on the viewer used to be a major problem. It is fair to say that this has recently become much less of a problem.

Lenses on MFTs are interchangeable and, providing an appropriate adapter exists, just about any lens can be used. The sensor size gives a crop factor of around two, which means that a 200mm lens (designed for a 35mm camera) will have the same effect on an MFT as a 400mm lens on a 35mm camera. In comparison to a DSLR, this is good news when you're looking for greater reach but not so good when you're coming down into wide-angle territory.

The MFT sensor is a quarter of the area of a standard 35mm DSLR sensor and just more than half the area of a crop sensor DSLR. It is, however, five to nine times larger than the sensor in a compact camera. Bigger sensors are better; unlike pixel counts, which don't give a lot of useful information on their own, sensor size tells us a lot. A full 35mm sensor is better than a crop sensor, and a crop sensor is better than a compact sensor. Whether the quality boost of a larger sensor is important to you as a photographer, only you can really know. If you try to glean information from Internet forums or groups, all you are likely to end up with is a headache.

Larger sensors do two things much better than small ones: with them, image noise is greatly reduced, and they are much better at handling subtle contrast differences. The sensor size isn't a big issue to me because, as a normal part of my minimalist workflow, I tend to simplify contrast and often use noise reduction software to soften detail.

I know this will seem like sacrilege to many people, but I do see MFT cameras, or at least a descendant of the format, taking the place of DSLRs as the camera that the vast majority of photographers will either own or want to own. Over time, the technology will continue to improve and the recording quality of small sensors will keep getting better. If you have trouble believing that, just look at how much better sensors are today than the same-sized sensors were a decade ago. This applies to all sizes, but especially to those at the lower end of the range. The electronic viewfinder lag issue has been solved, and the autofocus is now more than good enough on most recent models. Currently, MFT cameras are priced about the same as lower-end DSLRs. For most people this would make an MFT a more likely replacement for a DSLR than a compact camera.

Other Mirrorless Interchangeable Lens Cameras

The micro four-thirds system is arguably the most established format that bridges the divide between high-end point-and-shoot and DSLR cameras, yet there are other mirrorless interchangeable lens cameras in production. Unfortunately the popularity of these cameras has led to an increase in the number of acronyms that a prospective buyer has to know. The most commonly used terms are:

- CSC – Compact System Camera
- MSC – Mirrorless System Camera
- DSLM – Digital Single Lens Mirrorless
- DILS – Digital Interchangeable Lens System
- EVIL – Electronic Viewfinder with Interchangeable Lens
- MILC – Mirrorless Interchangeable Lens

The term EVIL does not apply to cameras with an optical viewfinder, but apart from that all these terms are interchangeable. For the sake of this discussion, I will refer to all of these as Mirrorless Interchangeable Lens Cameras (MILCs).

As with the MFT system cameras, the purpose of the MILCs is a camera that accepts interchangeable lenses, and is smaller than a DSLR but capable of comparable image quality to a DSLR. Whereas one of the defining characteristics of an MFT system camera is the sensor size, this is not the case with the rest of the MILC group. Sensor sizes go from the small point-and-shoot 1/2.3" up to the crop sensors of the so-called entry level DSLRs. I do not recommend purchasing a model with a sensor size at the lower end of the range, though, as any benefit from the ability to change lenses would be rendered irrelevant by a small sensor's shortcomings.

It is important for the potential buyer of these types of cameras to consider lens compatibility and the number of available lenses on the market for any given model of camera. Whereas the owner of a DSLR camera manufactured by one of the big names in the industry may now have hundreds of lenses to choose from, often from multiple manufacturers, this is not the case with the MILCs. Adapters provide a partial solution to this problem, allowing for a greater range of lenses to be used with a given camera, but the autofocus function is usually lost.

Rangefinder Cameras

Modern rangefinder cameras often get classified with MILCs but this does not meet with universal approval for a number of reasons. Other MILCs are all-new designs, and unlike the rangefinders, did not evolve from film cameras. The rangefinder history dates back to the 1920s and the modern digital models represent an evolution of these earlier versions rather than something completely new.

The rangefinder also performs differently to others in the MILC category in a number of respects. Unlike DSLRs and other MILCs, rangefinders have separate viewing and taking lenses. Because the viewfinder and the lens are in slightly different positions, the image seen through the viewfinder is not framed the same as the image seen through the lens. This effect is known as *parallax error*. Over long distances the effect of this variance is minimal, but the closer the subject is to the camera the more pronounced the deviation, making macrophotography all but impossible.

Telephoto zoom lenses do not work well with rangefinders, as the viewfinder has to be engineered differently for each focal distance. Wide-angle and ultrawide-angle lenses on a rangefinder or an MILC present less of a problem than with DSLRs. Because they lack a mirror, the rear part of any lens assembly can be positioned closer to the sensor or film surface. Consequently, wide-angle lenses for rangefinders and MILCs tend to be much cheaper and more compact than their DSLR equivalents.

Toy Cameras

Just as many audiophiles prefer the imperfect sound of vinyl recordings to those made on CDs, many photographers prefer the imperfect images captured on old, cheap film cameras to the predictable digital cameras we now take for granted.

Most of the cameras that fall into this category were originally intended to be a budget alternative to a normal camera, novelty items intended as gifts, or cameras for children.

These film cameras are cheap, yet fully functional. They do, however, come with numerous faults due to imprecise manufacturing. They tend to leak light and they have cheap plastic lenses that cause optical aberrations. It is precisely these flaws that are the basis for their appeal, and many professional photographers have produced superb work with them.

The technically imperfect look produced by these cameras has become so popular that a whole mini-industry has sprung up to aid photographers who want to achieve the same look digitally. Lenses are now available that can selectively blur parts of a shot, software that imitates the look of various toy cameras is ubiquitous, and the number of online articles proposing do-it-yourself solutions, such as petroleum jelly on a cheap ultraviolet filter, is increasing all the time.

One of the names most often associated with the toy camera industry is Lomo. This is due, so the story goes, to a couple of Viennese marketing students, Matthias Fiegl and Wolfgang Stranzinger, who found an old Lomo LC-A toy camera and used it during their travels. Of course, they had no idea how the photographs would turn out until the film was developed. Apparently they were really sold on the color and saturation and they proceeded to heavily market their new discovery.

This took place in 1991, which predated digital cameras in the marketplace by a good few years, so the fact that these cameras use film is perhaps not as significant as some people think. It just so happened that film was the medium still in general use at the time.

Some of the better-known names in the toy camera world, along with Lomo, are Holga and Diana. The Holga was originally a mass-marketed Chinese 120 film camera, the Lomo was originally a mass-marketed Russian 35mm film camera, and the Diana was originally a child's 120 camera.

The retro and toy look goes beyond specific cameras and software tools. Lenses that can be used on digital cameras are now manufactured to purposely emulate the flaws and quirks of cheap cameras.

One type of lens that now has a dedicated following has optics that can be tilted in relationship to the sensor surface. Until recently, lenses that had the ability to do this, called tilt-shift lenses, were used primarily for photographing architecture because they could compensate for converging parallels. To understand this, just point a camera up at a tall building from the sidewalk. Lines that are in fact parallel will appear to come together as they increase in

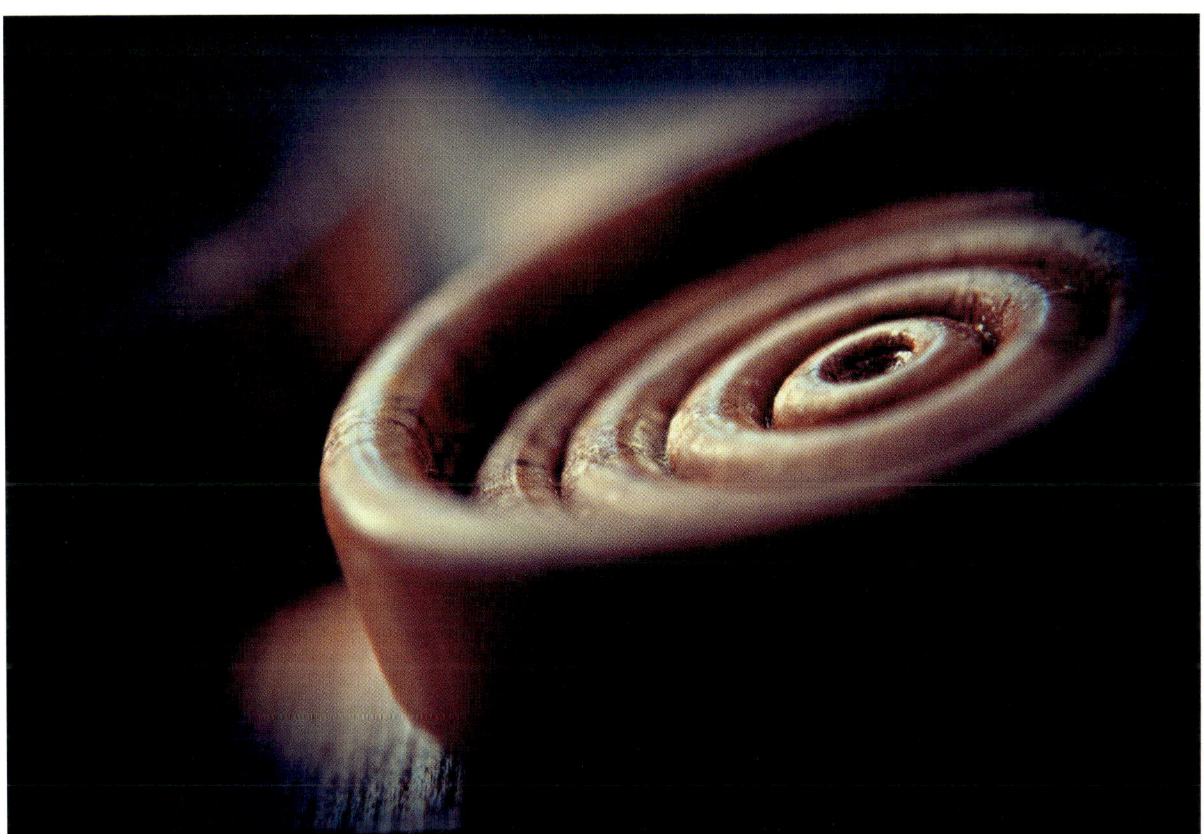

This image was taken with a DSLR, and then the Lomo effect was added with editing software

height. A tilt-shift lens compensates for this and keeps parallel lines parallel, so to speak. These lenses are incredibly expensive because the optics must be absolutely top notch to get a high-quality image in the traditional sense.

One cheaper lens that works on this principle goes by the slightly odd name of Lensbaby. There are now several different lenses on the market under this manufacturer's name, made for most of the popular DSLRs and some other cameras, but they all operate on the tilted lens principle. The interesting thing is that what cost a small fortune to correct in the original tilt-shift lenses used by architects, such as unwanted distortion, chromatic aberration, and a host of other optical nasties, actually became desired features of the Lensbaby. The flaws are as important as the tilt-shift effect.

It is interesting to think for a moment about the fundamental change that has taken place in photography; for example, a selling point of a lens can be its flaws—its lack of fidelity. Even though these lenses are cheap when compared to the tilt-shift ones, they still start at around $80 at the time of this writing, which is not far short of the cost of a so-called nifty fifty, a fast (f/1.8) 50mm prime lens for either a Canon or Nikon DSLR. Many photographers tend to be tinkerers by nature, and it may be due to this fact that there are a lot of do-it-yourself versions of tilt lenses out there. Fortunately, many photographers also enjoy posting their projects on the Internet, and a quick search will yield many interesting examples of images taken with these types of lenses.

Cell Phone Cameras

Cell phone cameras represent one of the biggest shifts in society's relationship to photography during the past 100 years. For the first time ever, a large proportion of the population has a camera with them at all times, whether or not they are interested in photography. This, coupled with the rise of social media on the Internet, has made photography a part of people's everyday experience, not something that happens only at special times such as birthdays and vacations. I'll cover this topic in greater depth in chapter 9.

The early cell phone cameras were pretty much a novelty and of limited value for ordinary photography, let alone for something more serious. That has now changed, and while cell phone (or smart phone) cameras cannot rival a DSLR in terms of quality, they could rival compact cameras at some point down the road.

One device in particular has done more to change things than any other in this department, and that is the Apple iPhone, first released in 2007. The iPhone has been extremely influential due to its large user base and Apple's decision to allow third-party application (app) development.

One app, Instagram, became hugely popular by doing two things well. It tapped into the retro aesthetic, and the company got the social networking part of the equation right. Just in case anyone thinks this is a quirky fad of little interest to anyone not obsessed with the history and development of photography, here are a couple of names and numbers. In 2012, Facebook (a name doesn't get much bigger than that) acquired Instagram for $1 billion—that is billion with a *b*. To put that in perspective, in 2005 Yahoo! paid only $35 million for Flickr, which is arguably the best-known social photo sharing service out there.

Instagram's user base is currently estimated at somewhere north of 100 million users. There were 5 billion Instagram photographs uploaded as of October 2012. Instagram is the biggest company working this particular retro/social-sharing niche, but there are several others, the most notable of which is Hipstamatic.

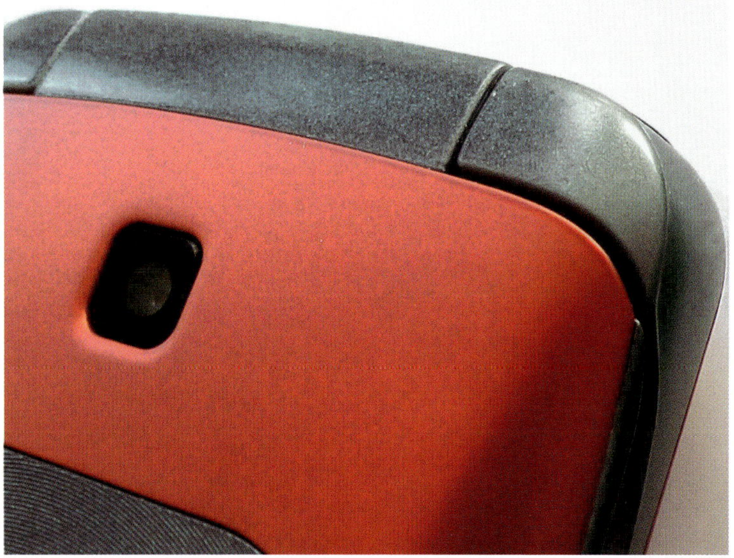

Even the most basic cell phones now come equipped with a camera

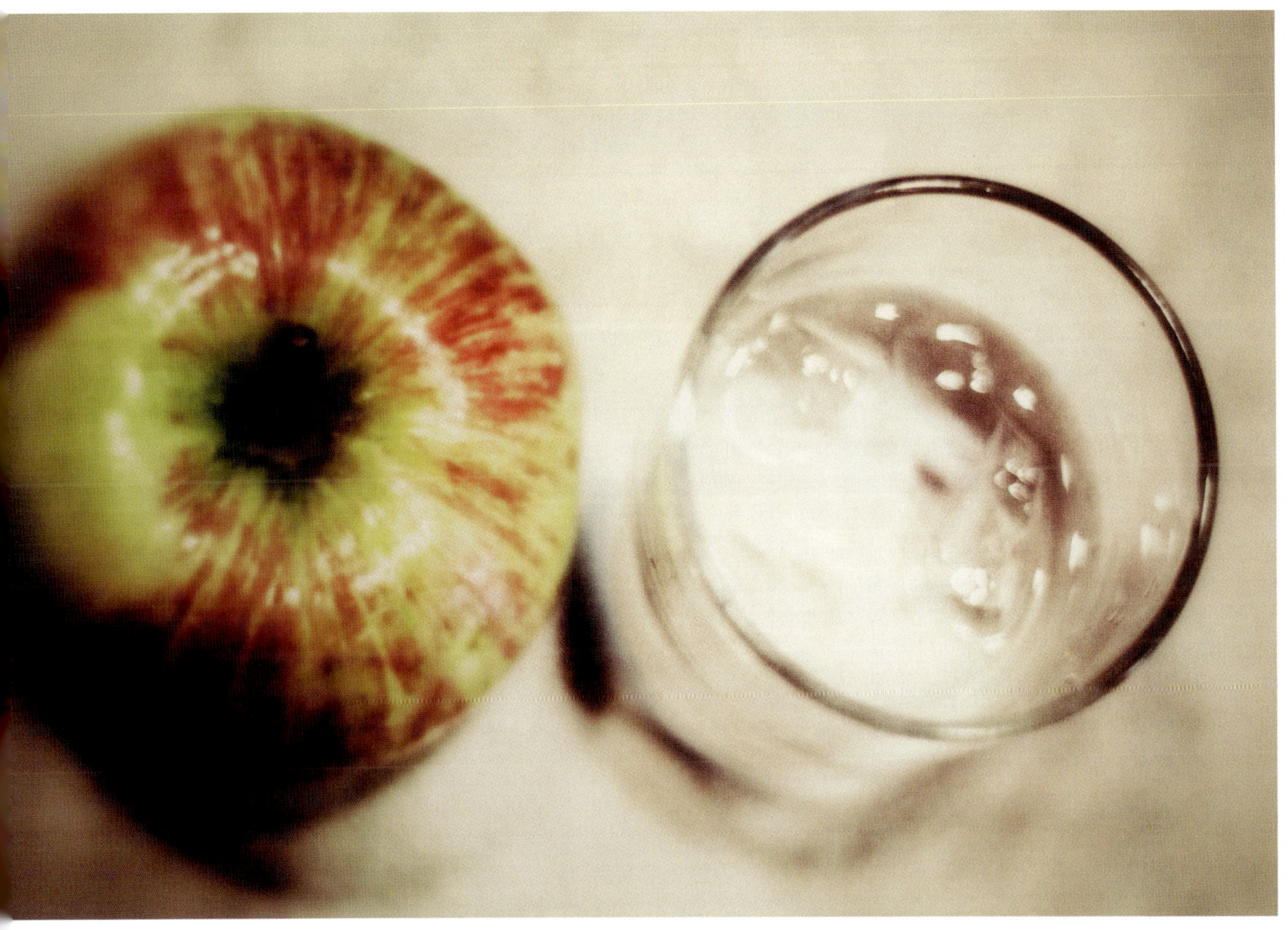

An apple and a glass of iced water

Gallery 4: Building Blocks

Repetition is a common theme in minimalism, and building materials used in construction provide an endless source to draw upon.

The reflections define a crooked line that pulls the viewer's eye through this photograph

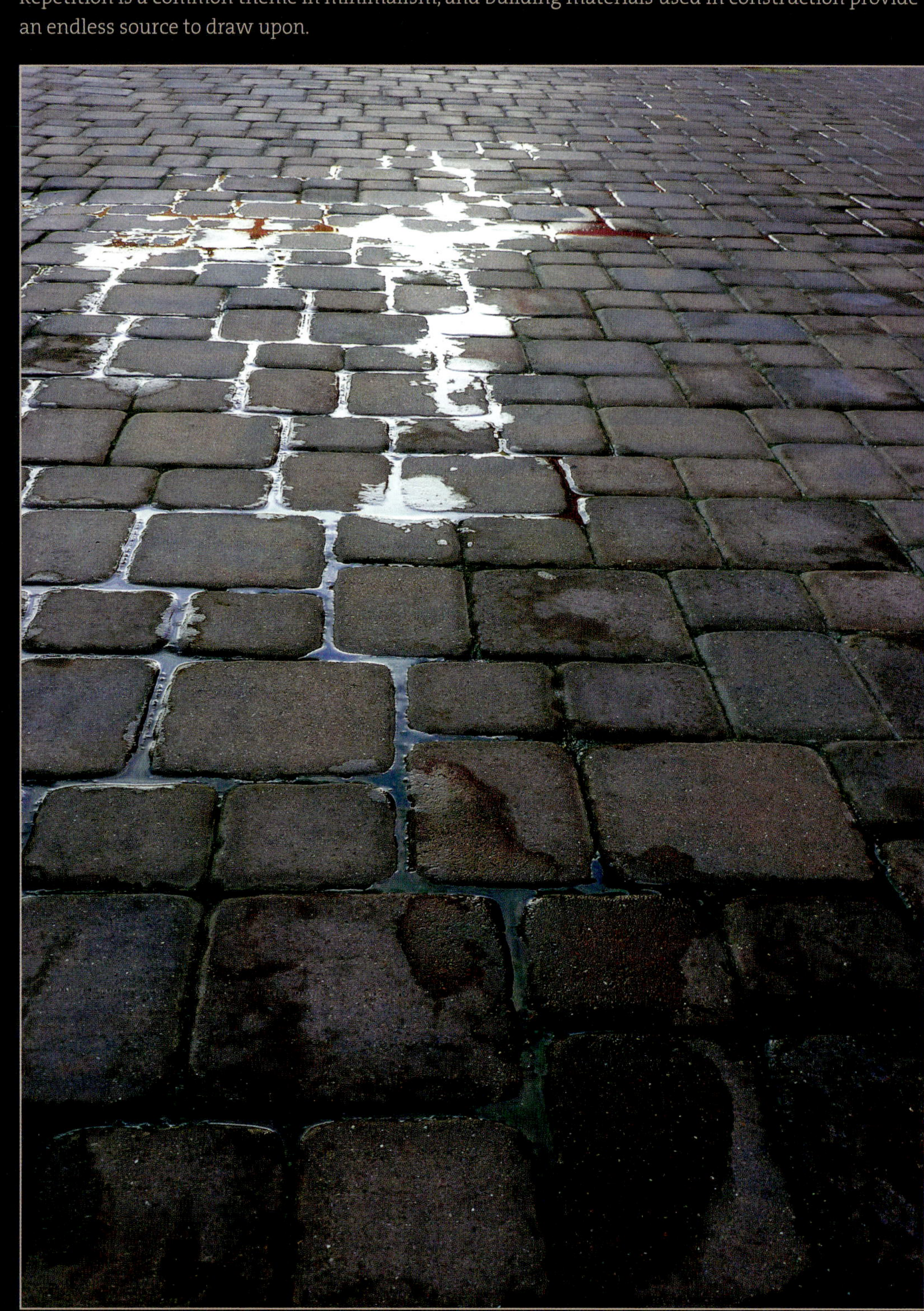

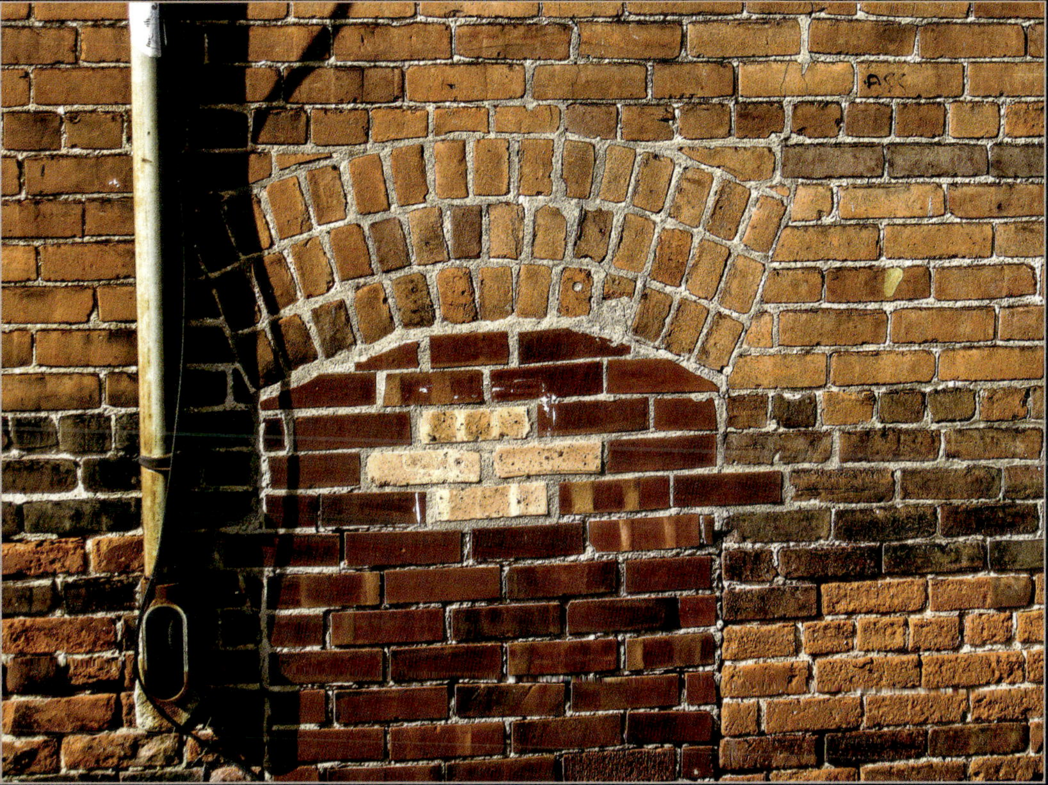

Every old brick wall tells a story

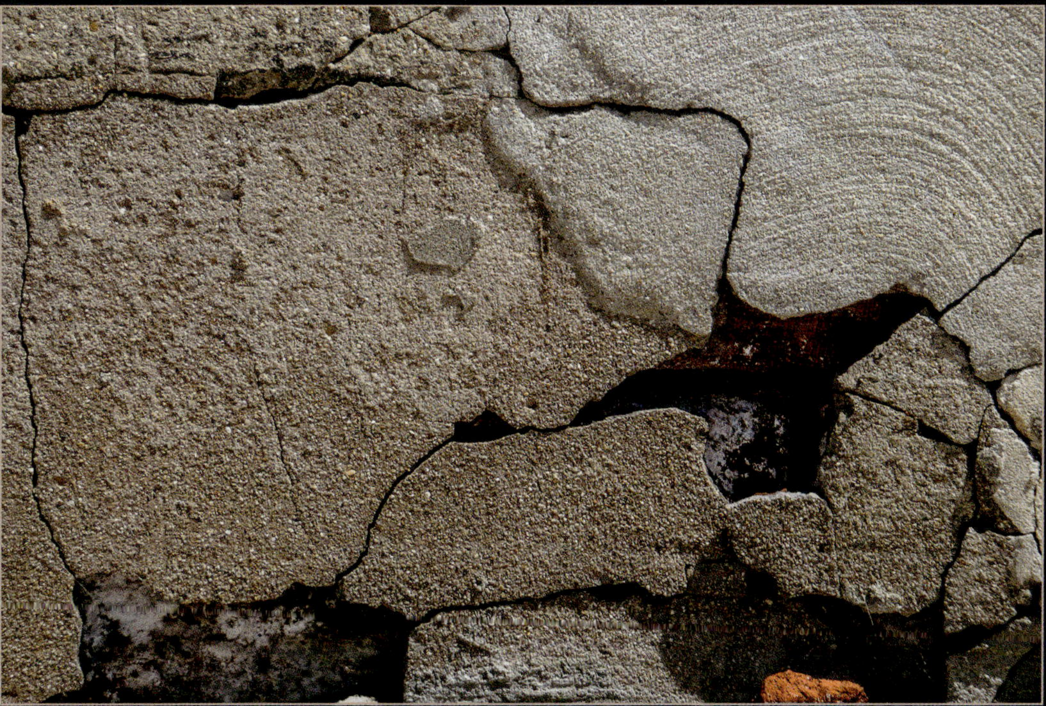

Old walls in disrepair provide good opportunities for practicing composition

reet pavers

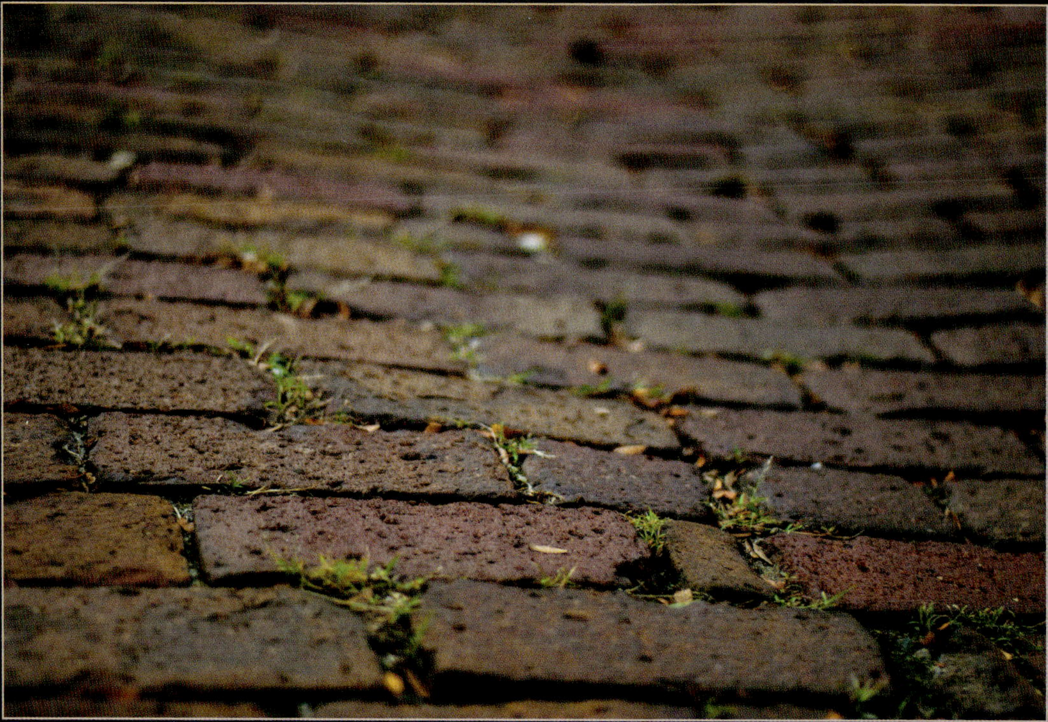

and brick wall

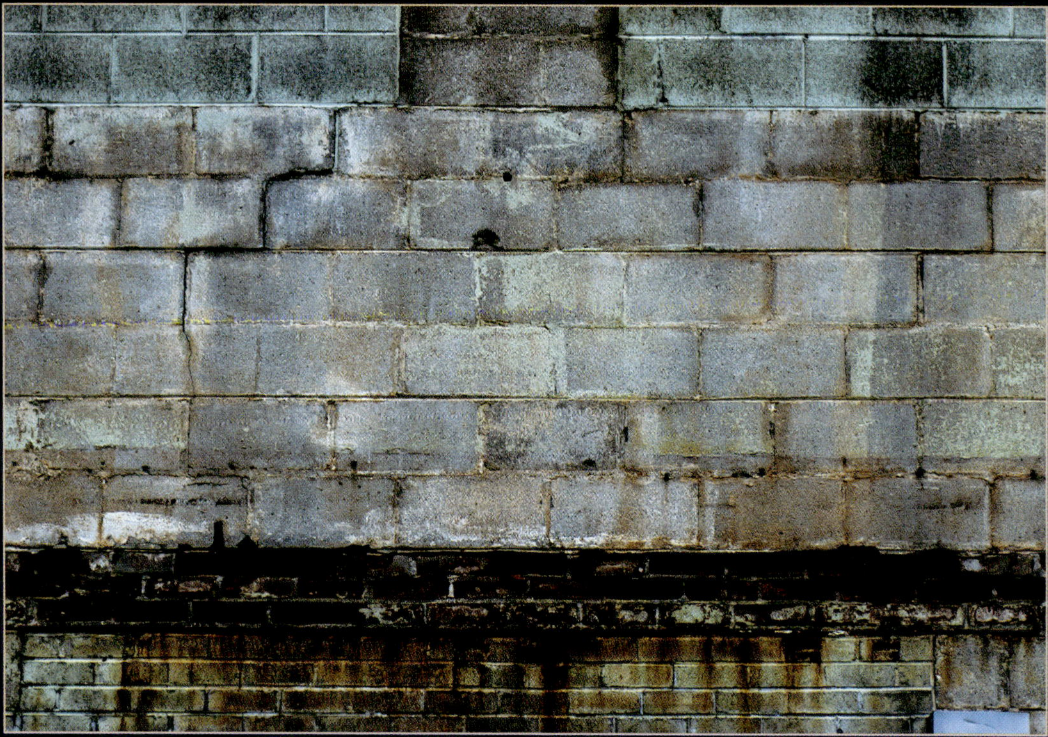

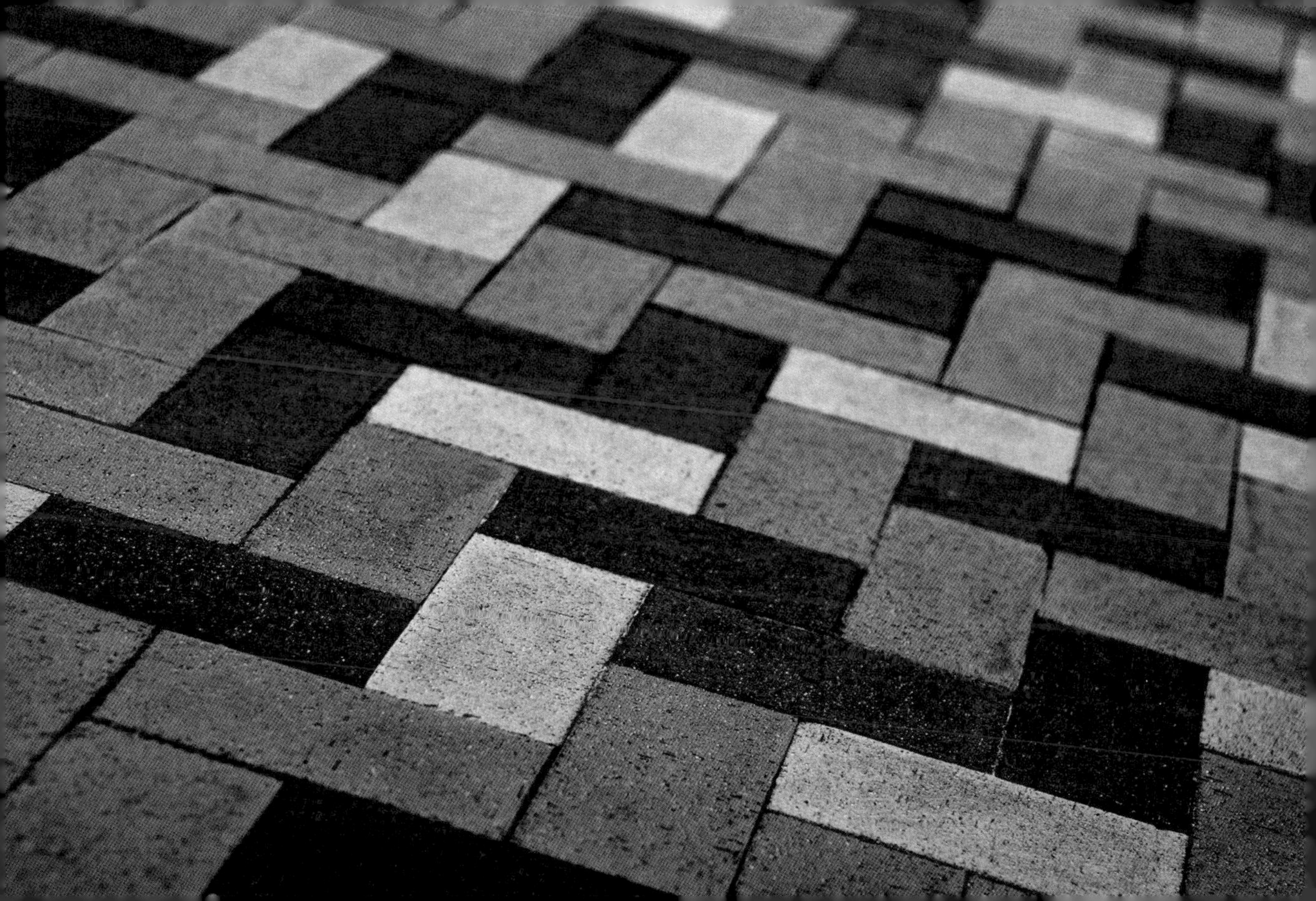

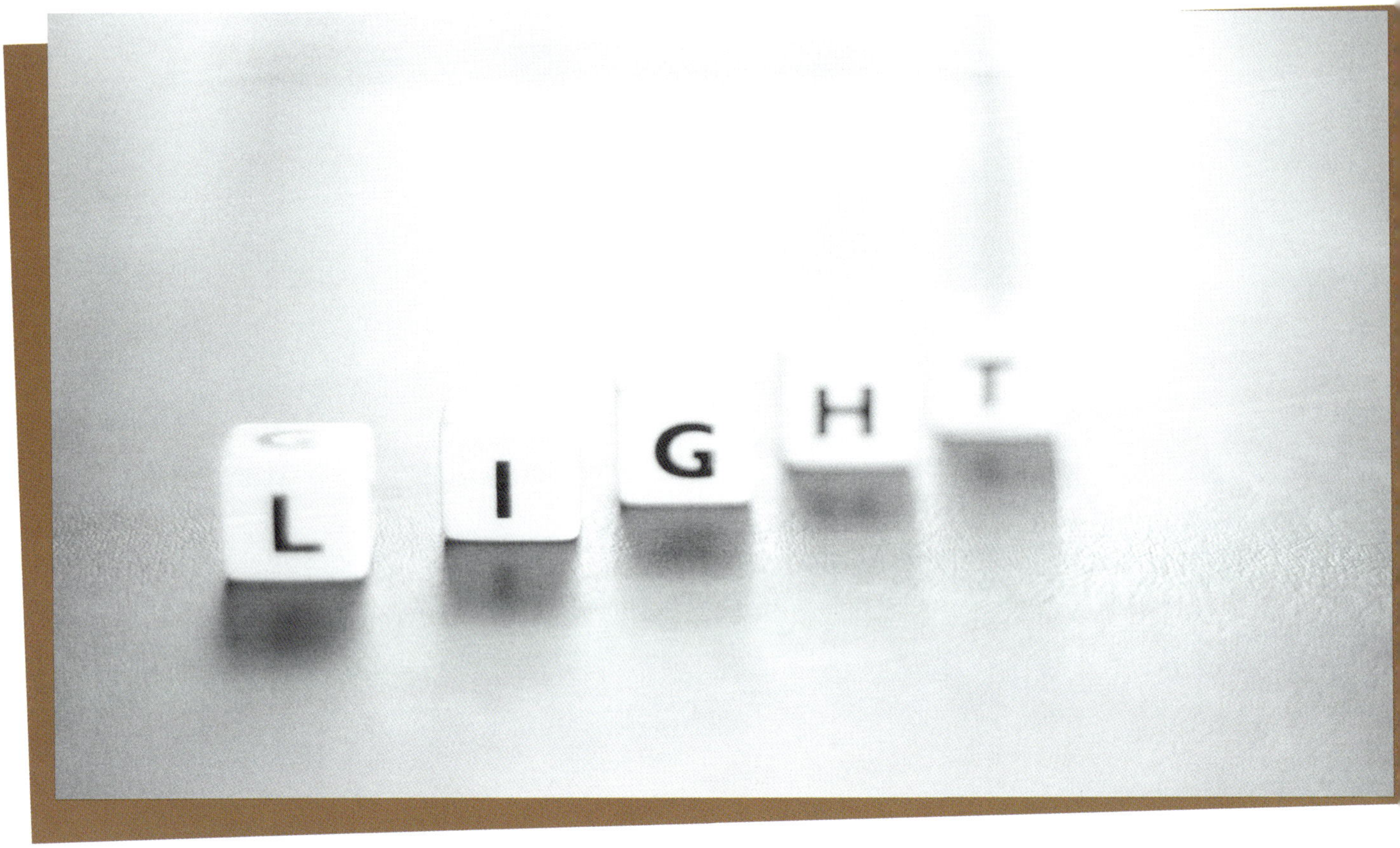

LIGHT

Chapter 5
Light

Without light there would be no photography. In this chapter, I will cover some of the following aspects in regard to light that are most important to you as a photographer:

- Soft versus hard light: Understanding the difference between soft light and harsh light is an essential skill for photographers, so there is something of a conventional wisdom in photography that soft lighting is desirable, and harsh lighting should be avoided. These types of light have very different properties, but both have their place in photography.
- Equipment: Lighting equipment designed for photographers is very expensive; however, much cheaper alternatives can be created or obtained.
- Color temperature: Mixing different types of lighting, otherwise referred to as color temperature, can cause problems.

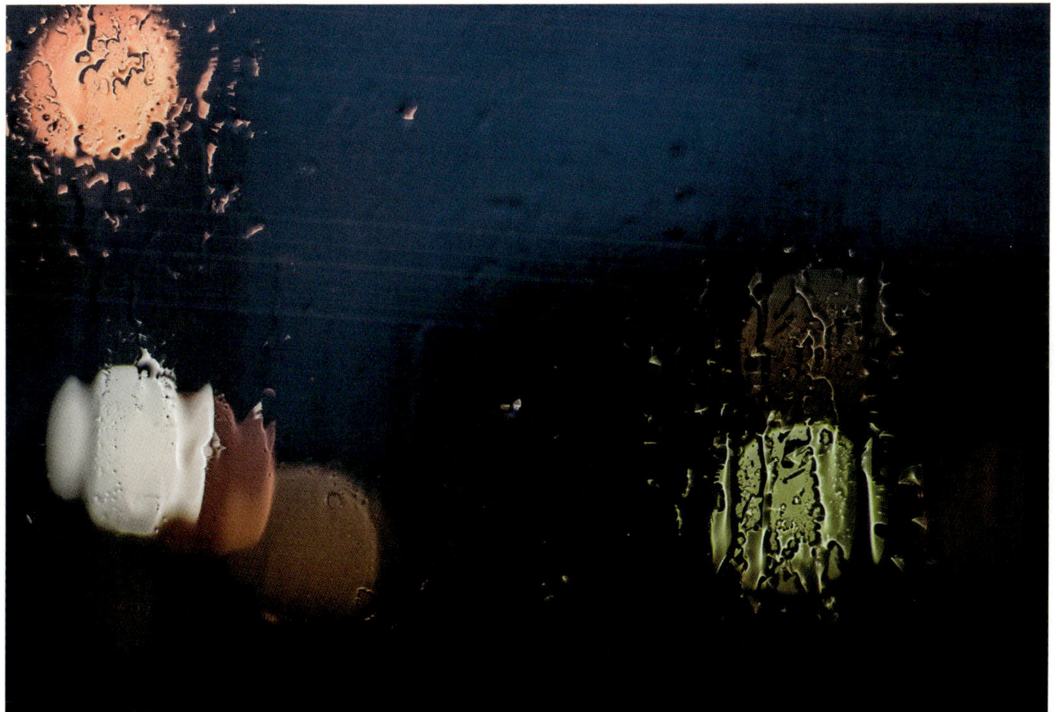

Here a wide aperture is used to blur everything beyond the window and create bokeh from car lights and streetlights. There is a large element of luck involved with this type of abstract photography because the exact positioning or color of the circles cannot be predicted.

Harsh Light, Soft Light, and Shadows

The harshness or softness of the light depends on the size of the light source in relationship to the object being photographed.

Some people have an instinctive grasp of lighting and how all of the different elements of this vast subject come together, but most of us need a little help. Here are two statements to get the ball rolling:

1. The closer the light source is to the subject, the softer the shadows
2. The bigger the light source, the softer the shadows

I recommend testing these statements before going on, and to do so, I suggest doing a few exercises that may seem like simplistic and possibly even insulting suggestions to aid understanding, but please try the exercises and experiment with them. Try to get interesting photographs because this will make the whole exercise more enjoyable. Understanding something in the abstract is of limited use. It is when the lesson is applied that real learning takes place.

First, find a desk lamp and an object, such as a toy or a ball. Make sure the desk lamp is the only light source, and draw the blinds or curtains. Place the object close to the lamplight and take a photo of the object and the shadow it casts. Move the light farther away and take another photo from the same position. This will force an understanding of the previous two statements about light sources.

Second, get a piece of parchment paper or a piece of semitransparent plastic, place it between the desk lamp and your object, and take a picture of the object. Now move the paper different distances from the light and take more pictures. You should see the shadow getting softer and its edges getting more blurred as you move the paper—which acts as a diffuser—farther away from the light and closer to the object.

The take-home message here is that the softness of the light (which we see by looking at shadows) depends on the size of the light source in relationship to the object being photographed. Moving the light source closer or placing a diffuser in front of the light increases its size, making for softer light. Moving the light source farther away makes it harsher.

Let's apply this to photography in the real world. The sun is a large object, but it is a long way away. This distance means that the sun is a small light source. This is why photographing in direct sunlight—other than in the early morning and late evening—produces harsh shadows and extreme contrasts that are way beyond what most camera sensors can capture. Shortly I will return to why this is different when the sun is low in the sky.

Now, let's consider clouds. You may have already worked out that clouds serve exactly the same function as the parchment paper or plastic diffuser that we used in the desk lamp experiments. The cloud cover works like a huge diffuser, in effect increasing the size of the light source many times, thereby giving a much softer light. The most even natural light is found on a foggy day, where we are essentially working inside a cloud. I love shooting in fog because it adds a sense of mystery to a photo, and it is nature's way of removing background clutter. The reason that light is softer at dawn and dusk is that it has to travel through much more of the earth's atmosphere than it does at midday, and thus the atmosphere can be thought of as a very diluted cloud.

Let's see how this applies to lighting provided by a photographer. The standard-issue flash on a point-and-shoot camera is all but unusable because it is tiny and not diffused. It is also all but unusable for several other reasons, including close proximity to the lens and a lack of power, but those are subjects for another time. The best advice I can give regarding the use of on-camera point-and-shoot flashes is this: don't.

The bigger strobe units on DSLRs are a bit better because the area that the light comes from

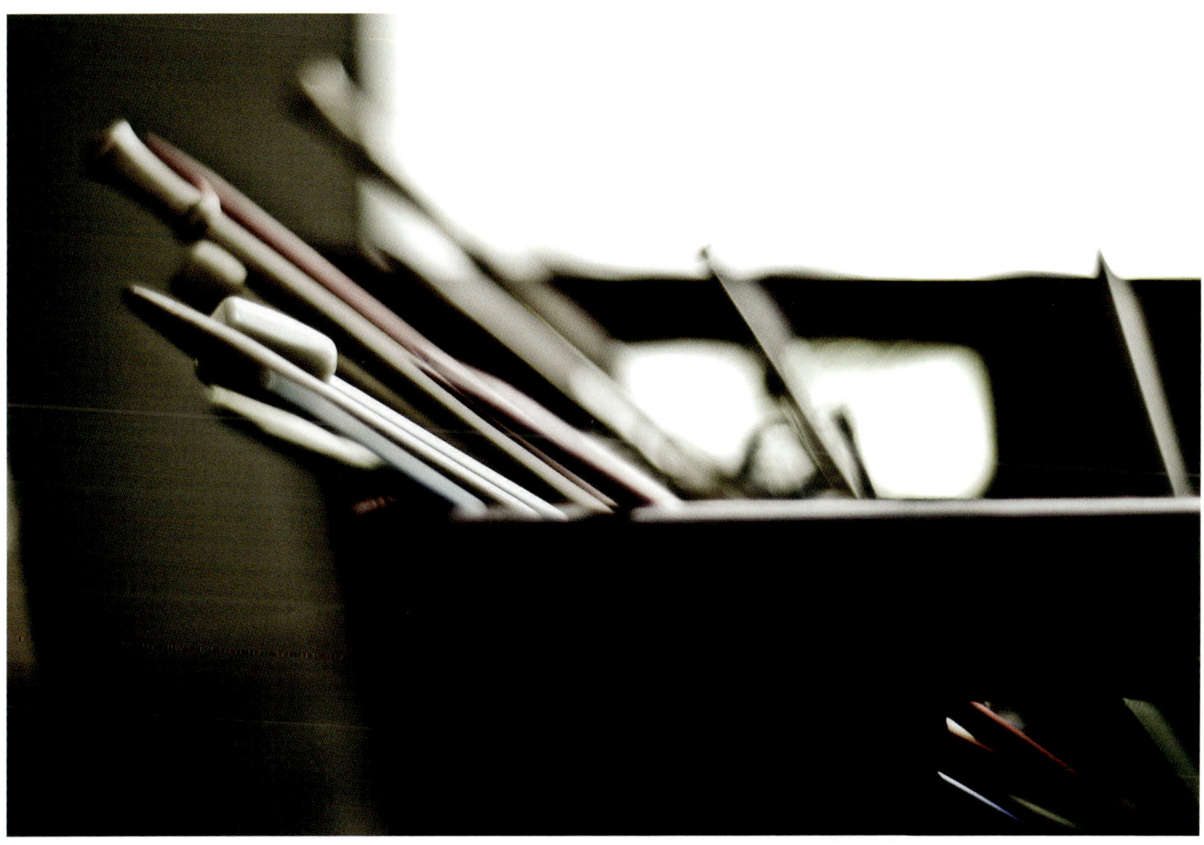

A window provides light for this shot. The combination of indirect light and a high aperture setting gives this image its softness.

is larger, yet it is still too small to give soft light. The strobe lights are more powerful than the built-in compact camera flash units and, even on the camera hot shoe, are farther away from the lens. The flash can be used off-camera by means of either remote control or cable, which is the best option by far. Unless a hard light is desired, a strobe light usually needs some help. You can fit a diffuser over the top of the flash or bounce the light off of a white ceiling or wall. Either of these methods works well. Bounce flash changes the quality of light, though, because the relatively small surface of the light is greatly increased.

A good photograph does not depend on soft light. Some of the most striking photographs come from the use of harsh direct sunlight and the corresponding hard, well-defined shadows. Many photographers treat shadows as something that should be minimized at all costs. It is much more productive to treat shadows as something to be embraced, something that can add tremendous impact to an image. We are wired to exist in a three-dimensional world, so our brains treat shadows as very much a secondary, unimportant thing. The best visual artists and photographers understand this and can elevate shadows to be at least as striking as the objects that cast them.

For a practical demonstration, find a room with venetian-type blinds and direct sunlight. Set the meter on your camera to spot metering and expose for a shadow cast by the blind. Now take a picture. It may not be the best photograph ever, but it will be striking, and you may just be surprised by people's reaction to it. We

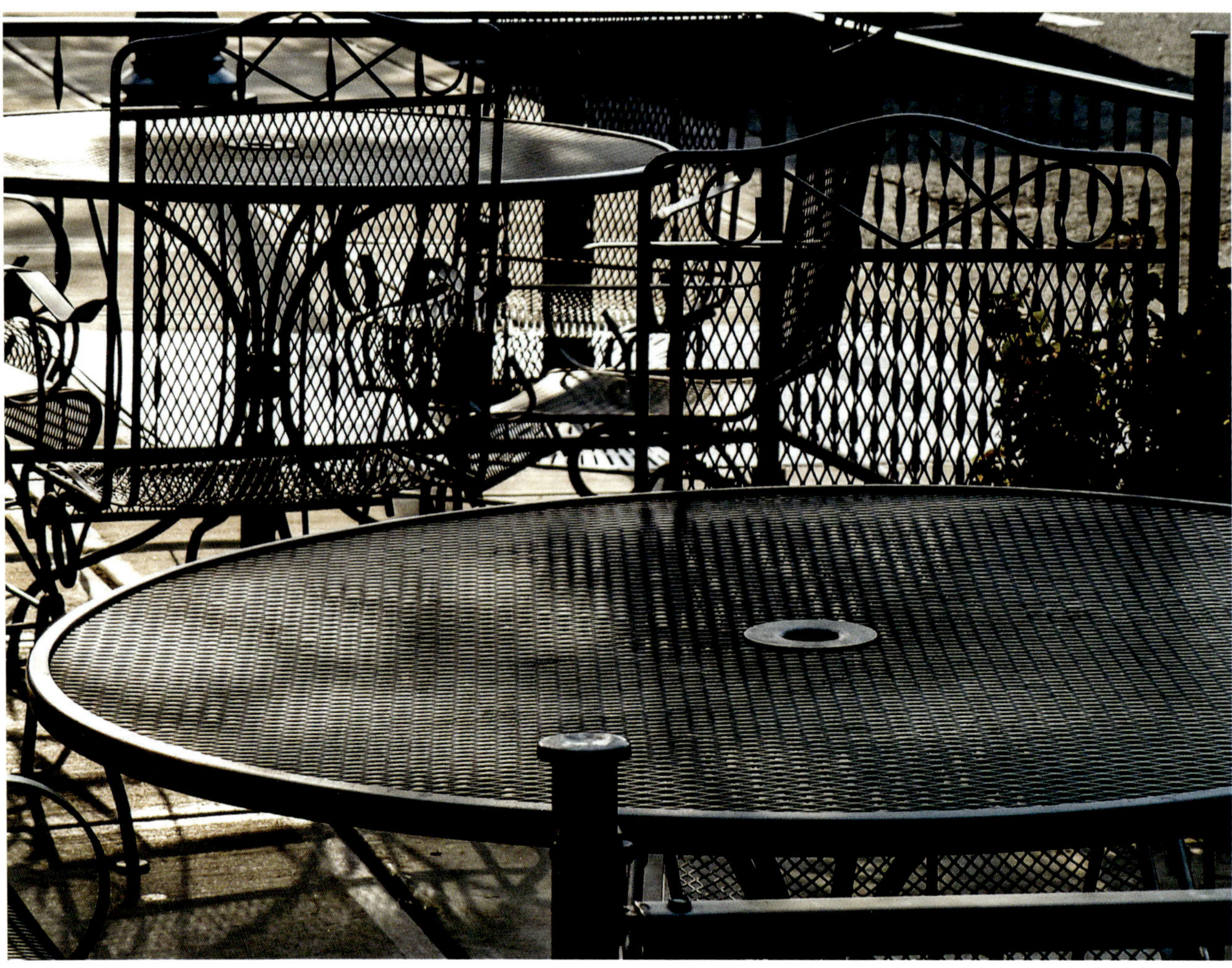

Soft morning light. This image was taken around 8:00 a.m. After this time the light gets harsh very quickly.

are wired, as a species, to be more responsive to contrast than any other visual element.

I am not arguing against using the soft, warm light of dawn, but rather that you at least experiment with other types of light. It is important to know the more traditional theory of lighting because it will enable you to take a magazine-quality portrait or a perfect product shot. The ideal is both to know this and to be prepared to discover something new. The best results often come when our experimentation can be incorporated into more traditional methods. This synthesis produces images that are different enough to get someone's attention, but not so different as to appear gimmicky, which has limited appeal.

Some Cheap Studio Equipment Alternatives

Some photographers have their own studio so they can completely control their working environment. Landscape photographers may have to wait a long time for the sun to peek out from behind a cloud or for mist to lift before pressing

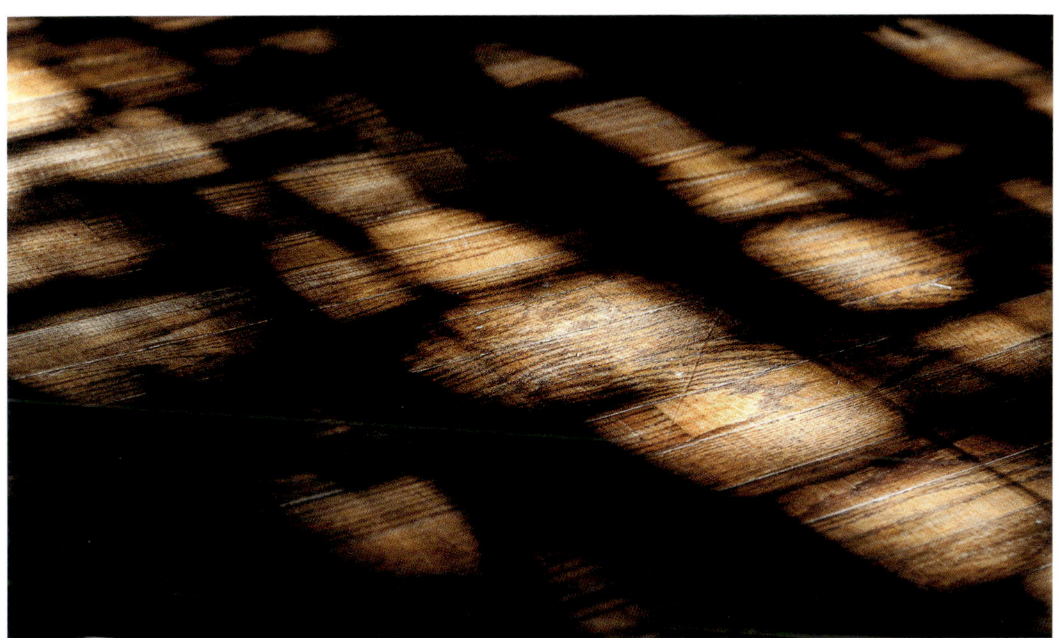

Two photographs of completely different things with a very similar feel because they were photographed in the same room at the same time of day

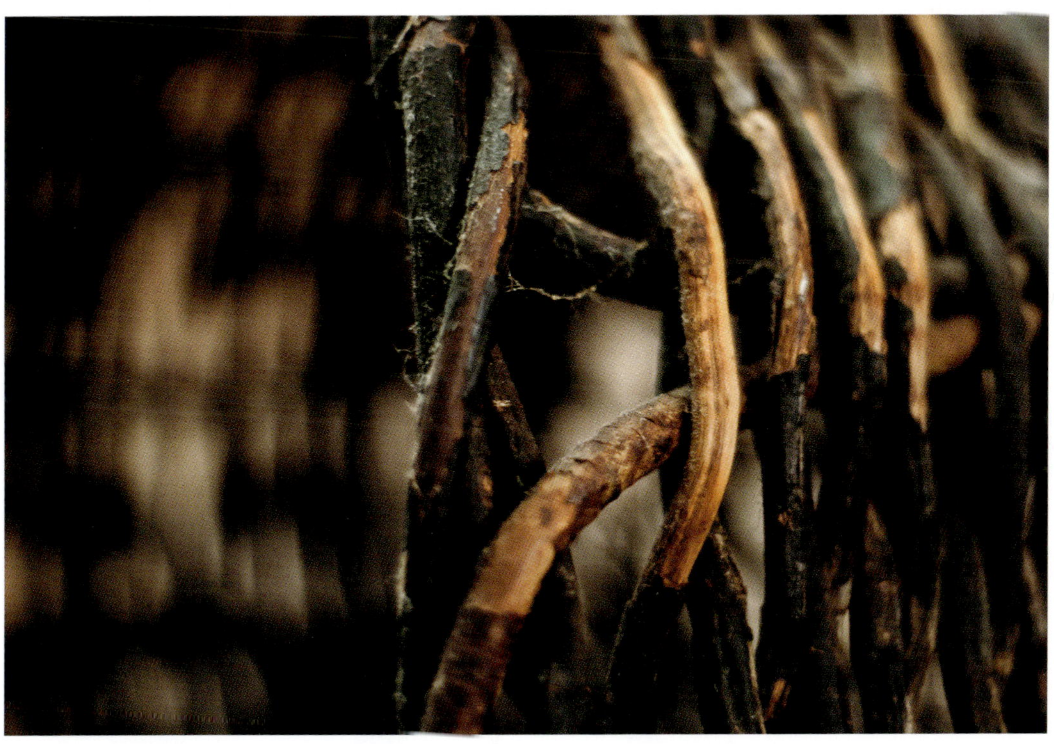

the shutter-release button, but studio photographers have no such problem. If something is not right, they can change it, and the thing they will most likely want to change is the lighting. The basic unit of studio lighting is the strobe, or flash, used either alone or in combination. Strobes work by giving off a short burst of light on a given signal that coincides with the press of the shutter-release button. Studio photographers have many different tools at their disposal to modify the light produced by the strobes, such as soft boxes, reflectors, and other devices.

The problem with this equipment is that it's extremely expensive. Setting up a working studio with even the minimum amount of equipment will run you at least several thousand dollars, and more likely several tens of thousands of dollars. This obviously means that setting up a well-equipped studio is beyond the reach of most people for whom photography is not a major source of income.

Fortunately, there are cheaper do-it-yourself alternatives for most of the equipment that a professional uses. The alternative setup that I will describe next may not look as sleek, elegant, or downright expensive as a professional's equipment, but it will enable you to take extremely good photographs that are perfectly acceptable for publication. The cost is closer to a hundred dollars than tens of thousands, so even if you decide that the studio environment is not for you, you will not have to take a massive financial hit. If, however, you find that you really enjoy working in a controlled environment, just about everything you learn will be transferable to a more traditional studio setup.

The Lights

Construction lights are a great source of cheap lighting. I recommend getting two pairs on stands and a single one that is self-supporting but not on a stand. These will set you back less than $100 and are sufficient for lighting one or two people or most objects. You can find these lights in just about any home maintenance store. There are a few things you should know about this particular type of light, none of which is a problem for me, but your opinion may differ.

Construction lights are a continuous light source, as opposed to the momentary burst of a strobe or camera flash. This is a great advantage because continuous lighting—or solid lighting,

A pair of construction lights

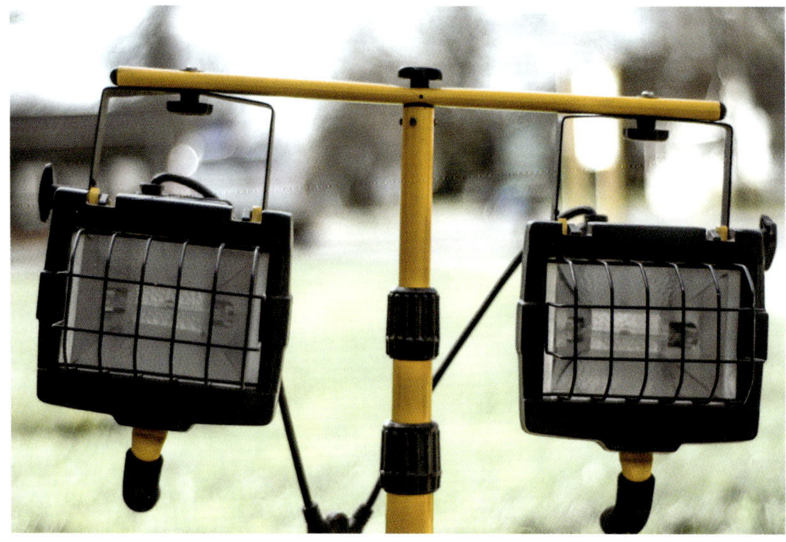

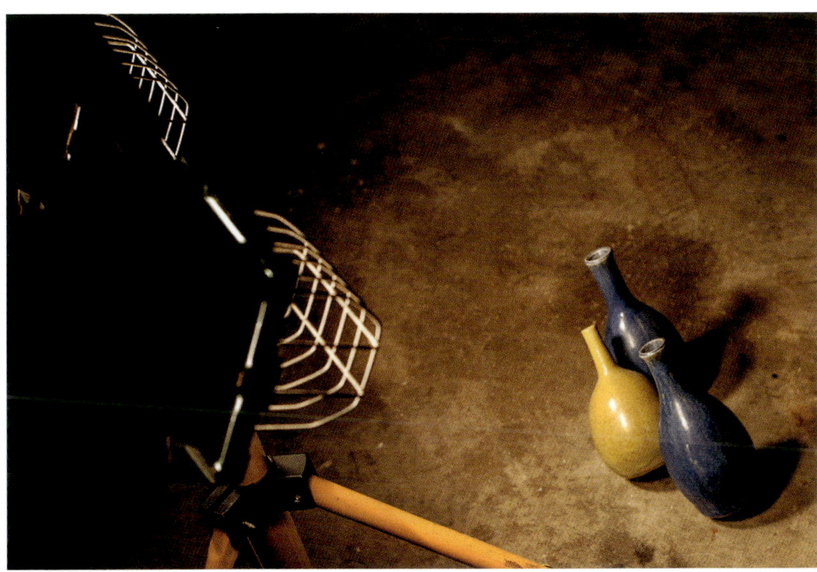

Construction lights illuminating vases

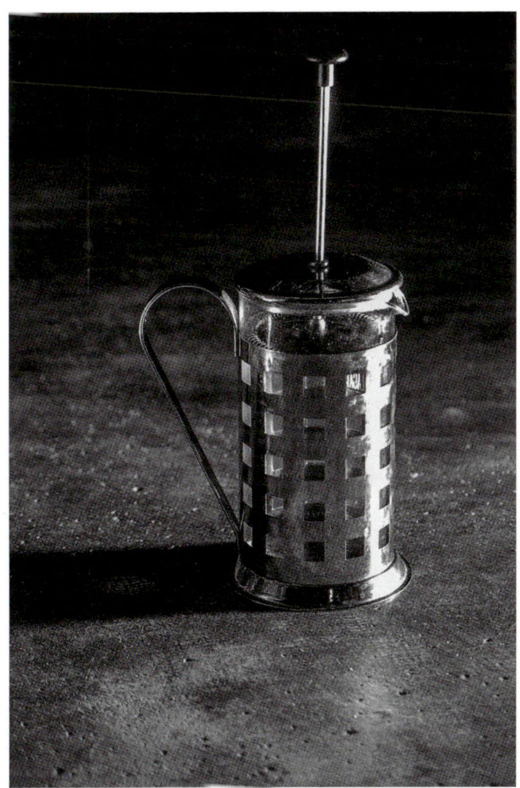

This image was shot using construction lights with no diffuser

as it is more generally referred to—completely takes the guesswork out of the situation. The shadows and other effects can be seen before the shutter-release button is pressed, rather than predicted and then corrected if needed.

Tungsten bulbs continually burn, and can become very hot. I know photographers who have used these lights on cold location shoots as much for their heating qualities as for light. The lights have metal guards on the front, so with reasonable care, there should not be a safety issue. If you are working with models, comfort and unwanted perspiration could be an issue. You would definitely want to be in an air-conditioned room if you use these during a Texas summer.

The next issue is more technical and concerns what is referred to as the *temperature* of the light. This has nothing to do with heat, but rather the way a camera sensor sees different types of lighting. I will go into a little more detail about this later, but the important thing for now is that different types of lighting, such as tungsten and daylight, do not work well together. An image shot with different types of light will look weird, and parts of it will display an unwanted color cast. This means that any room used as a studio has to be blacked out. Daylight coming into the room will spoil the photograph. The exception is when the intended output is monochrome, in which case the lighting sources can be mixed without making any difference. Blacking out the studio is not an issue with strobes because strobes are designed to have the same color temperature as daylight.

A Simple Diffuser

The light from a construction lamp is very harsh. A diffuser is simply a screen that scatters the light and makes it softer. A translucent plastic shower curtain can make for an excellent diffuser and is big enough for using with full-length model shots. Obviously, patterned shower curtains won't work unless you are looking for some interesting special effects. Plastic plumbing pipes can be made into an excellent lightweight frame, and an adhesive hook-and-loop fastener is perfectly adequate for securing the shower curtain to the frame.

A Simple Reflector

A plastic hula hoop supporting a sheet of aluminum-coated bubble wrap (such as the stuff used for ceiling insulation) works well. Simply attach the bubble wrap to the hula hoop with duct tape.

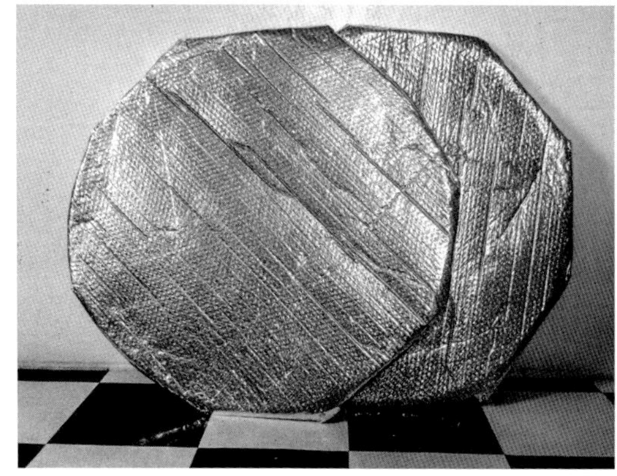

These reflectors are about four feet across and are exceptionally lightweight

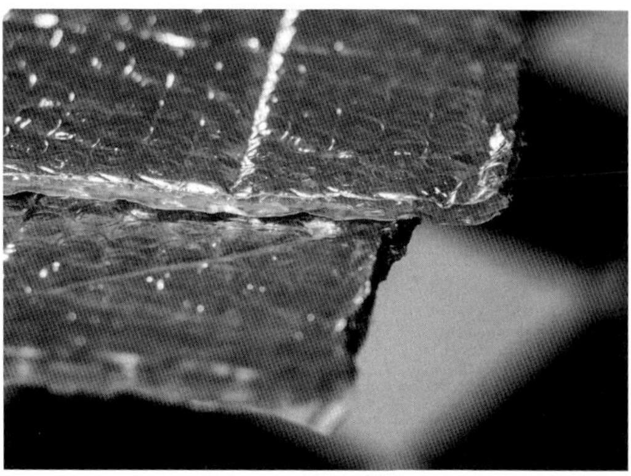

Aluminum-coated bubble wrap

A Cheap Tripod

A tripod is essential for any studio setup. I will go against conventional photography wisdom here, though, and advise against spending a small fortune on one. If you need to steady a camera on a 45-degree slope in gale-force winds, then yes, you are going to have to spend serious money, but in a room where outdoor elements are not an issue, a cheap tripod will do just fine. I'm still using one that I purchased ten years ago for around $20, and it does exactly what it has to do.

Tabletop or Product Photography

Tabletop and product photography is technically demanding, but it can be done well with a compact camera and some cheap equipment that was not originally designed for photography. If you want to photograph something to sell online, then this section is for you. Clean, accurate photographs with minimal shadows and loads of detail work best for selling stuff. In photographic terms, this means diffused light (to soften the shadows), a low ISO (no room for artistic interpretation here), and absolutely no movement from the camera when the shot is taken.

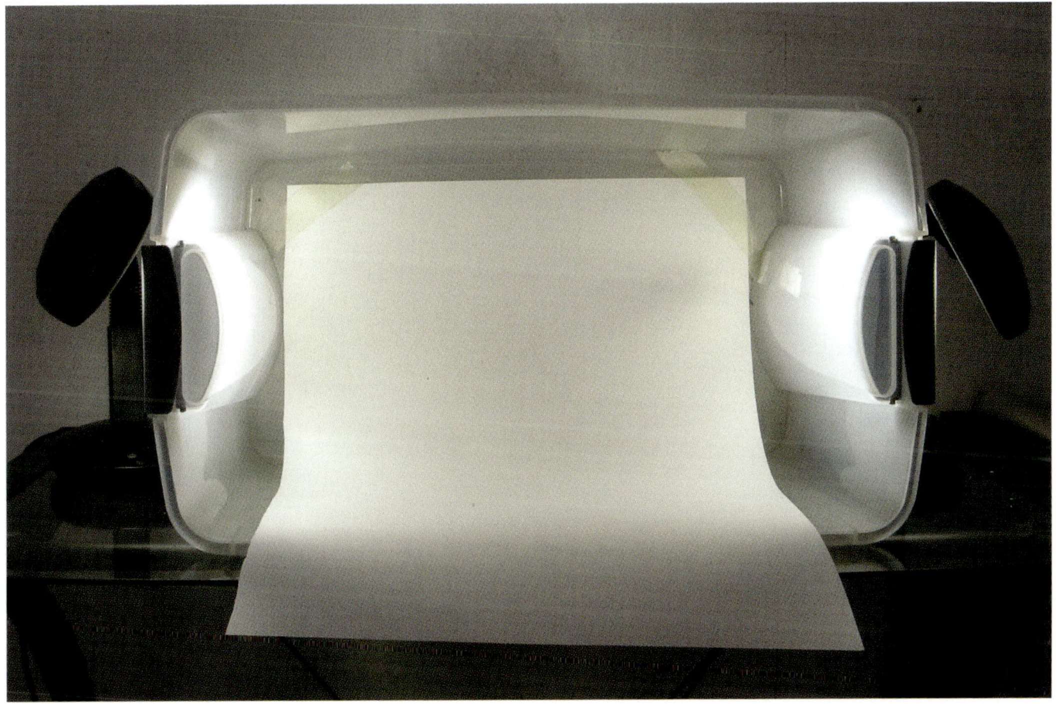

Product photography setup

The equipment required is as follows: two desk lamps with daylight-equivalent bulbs, a white semitransparent storage box, and a sheet of heavy white paper. If you cannot get your hands on a storage box, you can use a cardboard box with the sides cut out and replaced with parchment paper.

1. Place the storage box on one of its long sides with the opening toward you.
2. Cut the white paper to size and stick it to the inside of the box in such a way that there is no crease or seam.
3. Place a lamp on each side so they shine through the sides of the box.
4. Place the object to be photographed on the white paper, ideally behind the line of the lamps.
5. Put the camera on a tripod. Make sure image stabilization is turned off and the timer delay is turned on. Note that it is possible to take the shots handheld with image stabilization on, but the quality will take a bit of a hit.
6. Set the camera's ISO to its native setting. Note that this is not always the lowest setting. Settings lower than native are usually indicated on the display and are used when there is too much light. These artificially low settings tend to produce more noise.
7. Experiment with the zoom, focal length, and distance from the camera to the object to get the best shot. Try to avoid wide-angle shots because the resulting distortion is generally not desirable with this type of photography.
8. If you are shooting a lot of highly reflective objects, it is probably worth investing in a light tent, which has a small hole for the camera lens assembly to poke through, which will stop the camera from being reflected in the object. A basic but perfectly serviceable tent can be purchased for around $30.

A slightly unusual example of mixed lighting. The watering can votive is in natural light, whereas the vase in the backgroung is an image on a laptop computer screen. The camera's white balance is set to daylight, so it renders the votive correctly, but the vase has a blue cast.

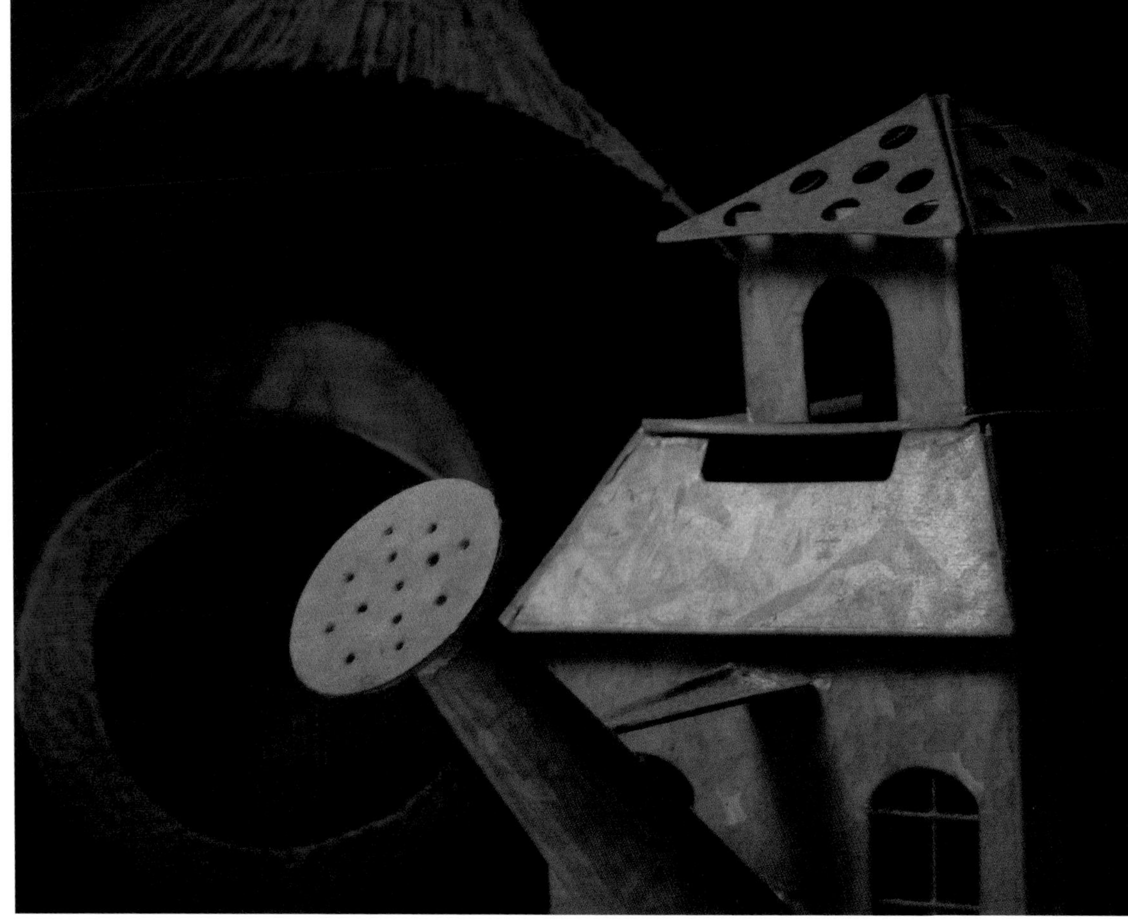

Color Temperature

Color temperature has nothing to do with heat, but rather with different types of light. This can be a little confusing because some light sources are cool to the touch (such as fluorescent tubes) and some are very hot (such as tungsten bulbs), but in this context that is irrelevant.

No camera can compensate for mixed lighting types in the same shot. If more than one type of lighting is used, part of the image will always have an odd color cast to it.

Different types of light that look the same color to us look different to the camera sensor. When you set the white balance on your camera to automatic, you are telling the camera to take care of this issue.

Cameras are now very good at compensating for different lighting types. However, there is one major exception: no camera can compensate for mixed lighting types in the same shot. If more than one type of lighting is used, part of the image will always have an odd color cast to it. If parts of a photograph look strangely blue or orange, then it is a fair bet that mixed lighting is the issue.

Flash or strobe lighting is the same temperature as daylight, so either can be mixed without any problem.

In regard to format type, one big advantage of RAW files over JPEG files is that the white balance settings are not baked into the image and can easily be changed using any RAW image editor. This won't help if the lighting has

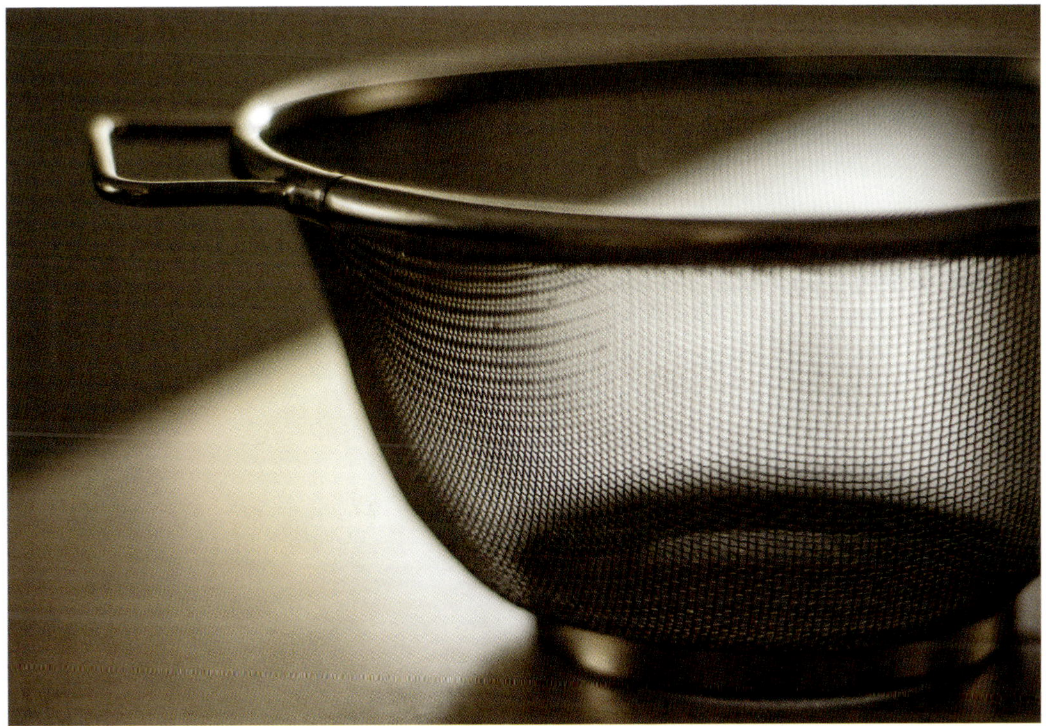

White balance can be used creatively. This image was taken on a sunny day, but the white balance was set to cloudy. This gives the image a warm feel.

been mixed, though; it only works if the white balance wasn't set or was set incorrectly in the camera. JPEGs can be salvaged to some extent, but the end result will likely be inferior to one in which the white balance was set correctly in the camera.

Of course, if you shoot in monochrome, you can mix lighting types to your heart's content, as long as you are not going to want a color version of the image.

Gallery 5: Into the Light

As a youngster, I was taught that the light source should always be behind the camera when taking a photograph. This turned out to be wrong. Excellent photographs can result from pointing the camera toward a light source. A portion of the image is likely to be overexposed, but experienced photographers can actually use this to their advantage. Of course, pointing the camera directly at the sun or a strong direct source should be avoided.

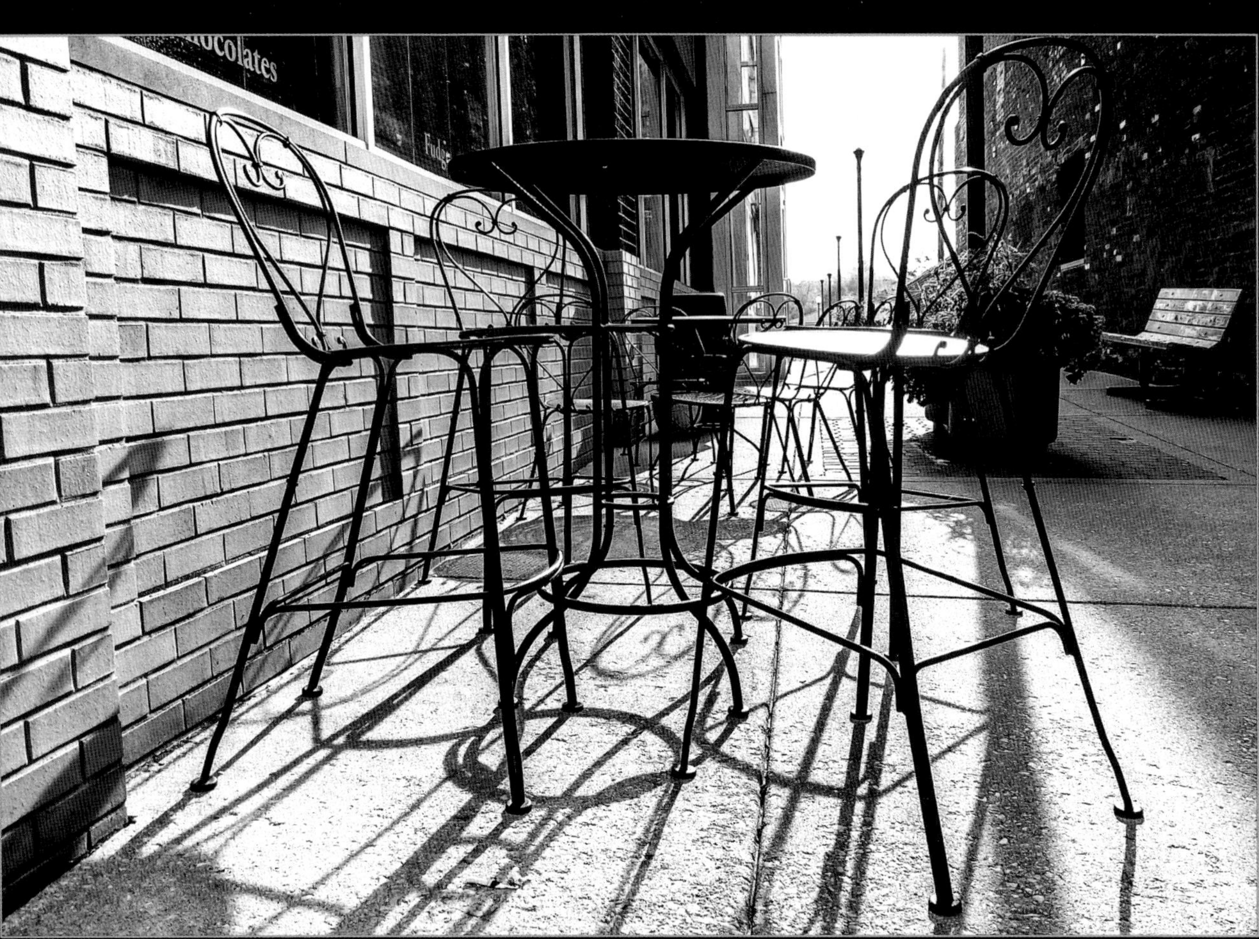

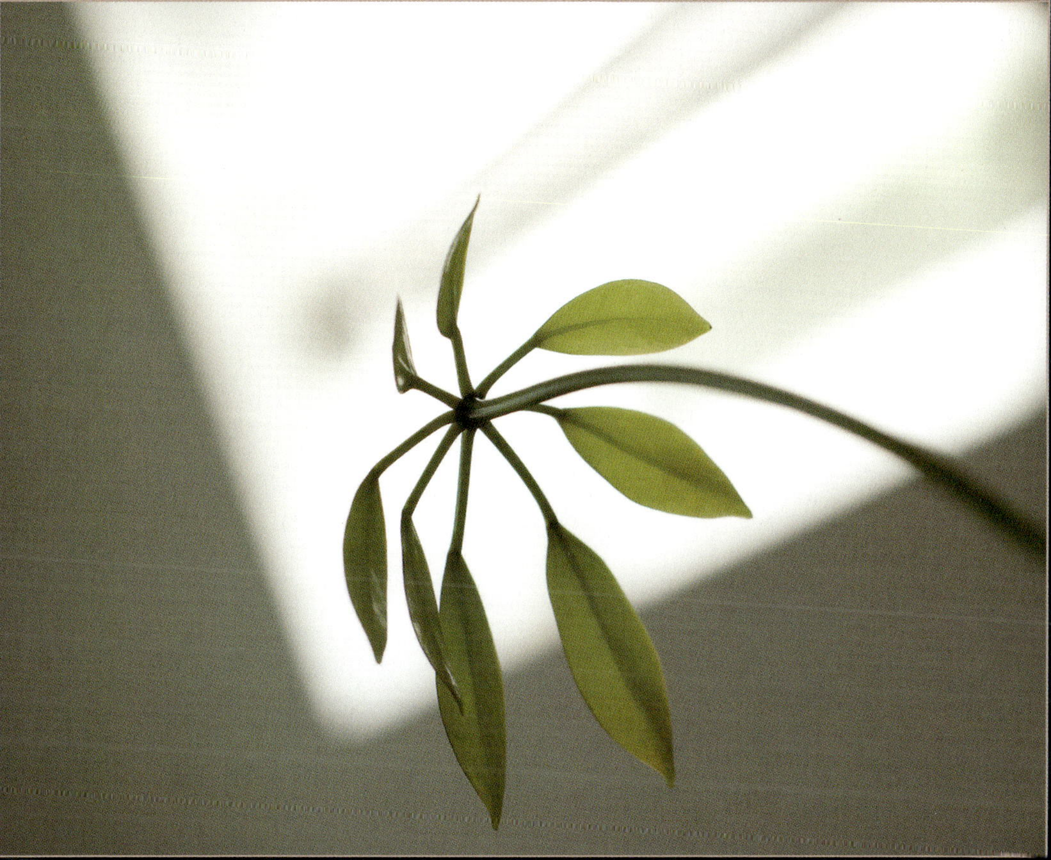

As much thought should be put into the background as the foreground

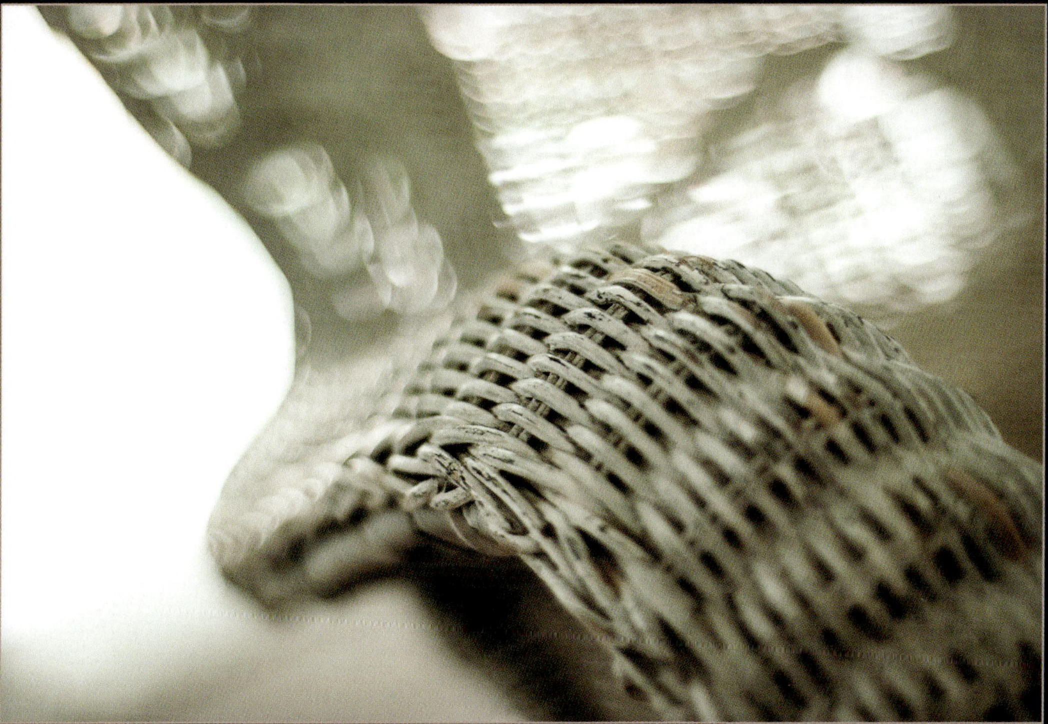

This type of shot is the forte of DSLRs. The small sensor of a point-and-shoot would not be able to replicate the depth of field and the bokeh.

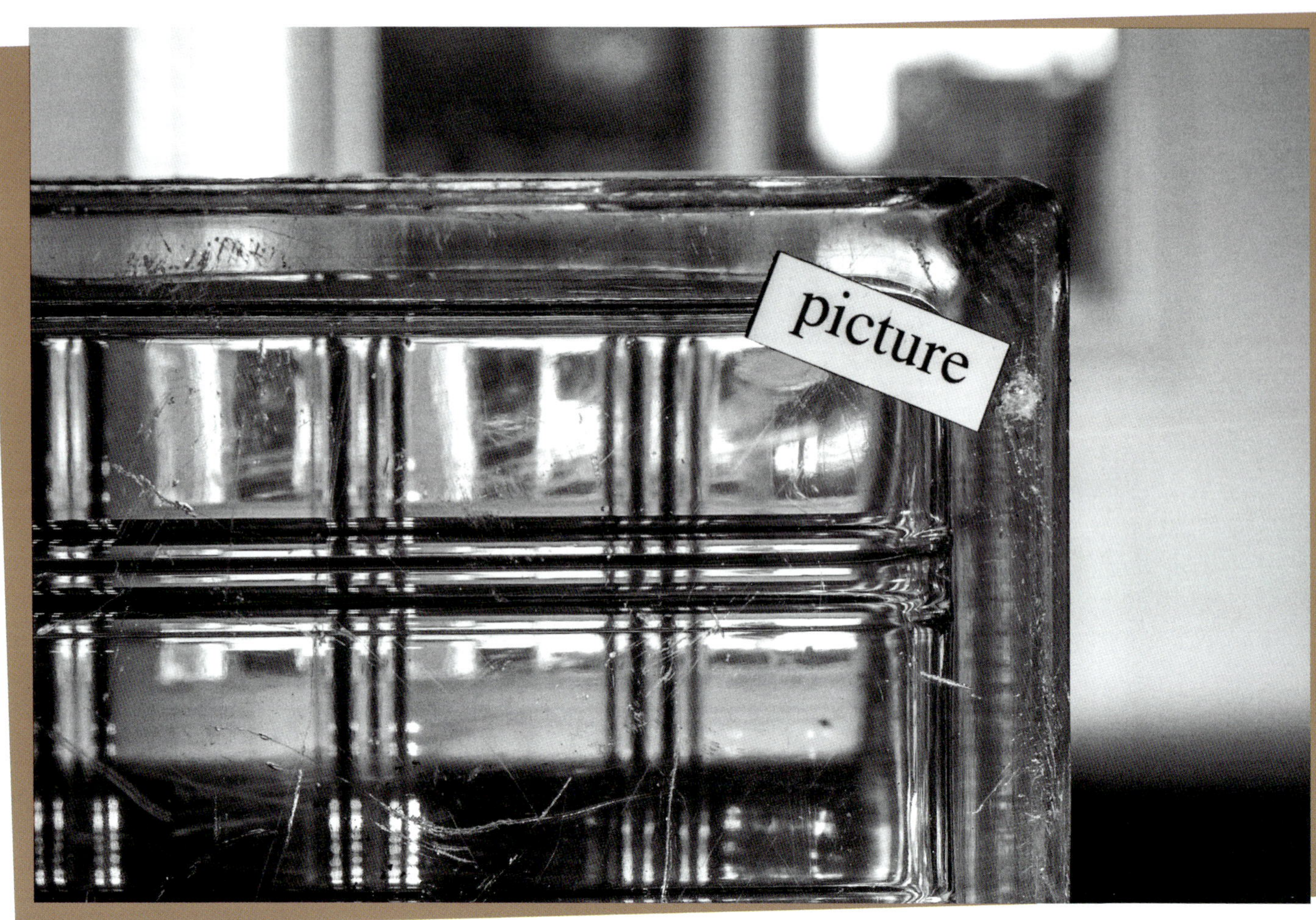
picture

Chapter 6
Composition and Aesthetics

This chapter tackles aesthetics and composition and then goes on to look at the difference between art and design. Rather than just rehashing the standard tutorials on these subjects, I have taken an uncommon approach, and incorporated my own point of view. I believe we learn more from teachers who are not afraid to inject their own thoughts and passions regarding a subject than those who do their best to imitate a textbook on legs.

Composition

Composition is the arrangement of visual elements within the boundaries of an image, or in this case, a photograph. The word *composition* means putting together. This translates easily to painting or drawing because artists start with a blank canvas and are free to place various elements wherever they like.

Composition in photography is a little more complicated because it is not usually possible to rearrange nature, an event, or most other types of scenes for that matter. In most cases, the photographer's task is one of recognition—of seeing what reality presents and determining a pleasing composition. In other words, it is more about recognizing a good composition than forming one from scratch. There are situations, such as in the studio, where photographers have freedom to compose their own version of reality, but for the majority of us, it is a matter of spotting what nature, people, or happenstance presents to us.

We took a brief look at composition in chapter two and now I'd like to flesh out those thoughts. First, though, I want to stress that composition is very much a personal matter. While there are certain rules that are beneficial to know, how those rules are interpreted and at what stage they are applied—if at all— is a matter of individual taste.

I don't think much about rules. I may think about them when something is not working instinctively, such as when I want to take a shot but the best composition will not show itself, or when I'm editing and can't find a good crop. Other times, I might think about rules on the rare occasions when a photograph I have taken surprises me in a good way. I may deconstruct the composition to see exactly why that image works better than others, but it is, at best, a hit-or-miss process. Really good photographs often go beyond the rules of composition. If composition was purely formulaic taking a perfect photo would be nothing more than a technical exercise, I would not have written this chapter, and you would be reading a math book.

Composition should be dictated by the scene that presents itself in the moment and not by a rule learned from a book. Keep this thought in mind when you read the rest of this section and also when you have your camera in front of you. The process of photography is an active one, so it is advantageous to be thinking about capturing the best image rather than wondering how to squeeze what is in front of the lens into a mathematical formula.

Composition should be dictated by the scene that presents itself in the moment and not by a rule learned from a book.

In the following sections, I will discuss some of the rules of composition along with some of the dangers of being hidebound by the rules. Here is a bit of advice that applies to everything you read: read actively. Read a paragraph, then decide whether you agree, disagree, or something in between. The important thing is to know where you stand regarding the point being made. Of course, a second reading or reading a paragraph further may cause you to change your mind, which is fine. When you are reading something with the intention of improving your photography, or just about anything for that matter, become actively involved. Passive reading leads to rehashing the thoughts of others, and will show in your work.

Rule of Thirds

The *rule of thirds* is usually the first rule of composition anyone learns. The best way to envision this rule is to imagine a tic-tac-toe grid over the image in question. If the lines of the grid are close to going over major lines in the image, then the composition is more likely to work. This is why, generally speaking, horizons work best when they are roughly a third from the bottom or a third from the top of the image. If the intersections of the grid lines are in roughly the same spot as the focal point of the image, this will also strengthen the composition.

It is worth emphasizing that the application of the rule of thirds needs to be instinctive. When a photographer tries to force a scene to fit the grid on the viewfinder, it can make the image appear contrived and therefore static and lifeless.

Leading Lines

The one thing that the rule of thirds has going for it is that it can be applied to any image, whether the photo is a pictorial landscape, a modernist closeup of a human body part, or a completely abstract and unidentifiable macro shot. This is not the case with the next compositional device, *leading lines*. A leading line is used to give emphasis to the appearance of depth. Think of a river winding its way through low-lying hills or the center line of a road disappearing into a seemingly infinite desert.

The effect of a line in the image is often enhanced if the line's path is S-shaped. A leading line is a strong visual element intended to draw the viewer's eye to a point of interest, or sometimes out of the photo completely.

There is no doubt that a leading line can add interest to a photograph, but it can also be used as a crutch, producing an acceptable photograph without having to really work at it.

There is another, deeper issue at play here. The prescribed use of a line that draws the eye through the depth of the image is based on the assumption that it is desirable for the two-dimensional image to give the impression of three-dimensional space. This thinking relegates all of the two-dimensional art forms, including painting, as being less than their three-dimensional counterparts. Photography's function, it would seem, is far higher than that of a device for squashing three dimensions into two. Fortunately, as with most things visual, the other two-dimensional arts, such as painting, put this issue to bed more than a hundred years ago.

The Post-Impressionists consciously rejected the idea that depth had to somehow be incorporated into a painting. They deliberately flattened surfaces because they believed this reduction gave the art power and focus. The artist who took this approach the furthest was probably Paul Gauguin, and I recommend studying his work if you would like to gain a clearer sense of composition that goes far beyond what is usually taught to photographers. Although one of his main contributions is the flattening of perspective, his work contains other important lessons. He, along with many Post-Impressionists, believed that the best art combined the real

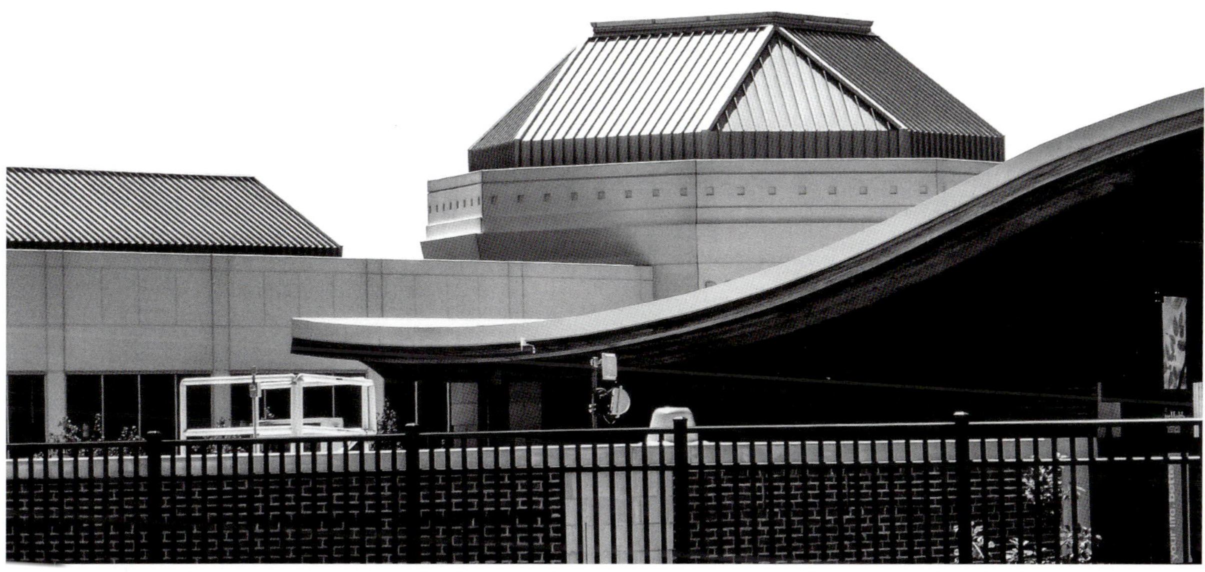

The flattening of depth caused by a telephoto lens achieves, through optical physics, what Gaugin did with his brush and canvas

world with our internal one, and this is the territory that some of the best photographers are now beginning to explore.

Balance

Whereas the rule of thirds and leading lines are easy concepts to grasp, the same cannot always be said for *balance;* arguably the most important single aspect of composition. Unfortunately, many photographers see balance as being synonymous with symmetry. Nothing could be further from the truth. Symmetry in this context is the mirroring of the left and right sides of the photograph. Such symmetry rarely leads to anything interesting, but is obvious, predictable, and sucks the life out of an image. It may have a superficial appeal, but that's about it. Balance, however, is about combining different elements to make the image pleasing, but not in a superficial way.

To give a relatively simple example, imagine just two elements are being balanced. This balance can be achieved by juxtaposing these two elements according to contrast, color, shape, texture, and placement as follows:

- A small shape that contrasts heavily in tone with the background can balance a much larger shape with less contrast.
- A small area of a bright color can be balanced with a larger area of a more muted hue.
- A small complex shape can balance a large simple one.
- A small, highly textured surface can balance a larger, plainer one.
- A smaller object can balance a larger one by being farther away from the center.

Of course, life and subject matter is rarely this simple. Objects or surfaces will display multiple characteristics, and it is these characteristics that determine the best relative positions. Follow this idea to its conclusion, and it is easy to see that in just about every case you will have to approach this problem by instinct and by trial and error. Balance is the most complex element of composition, and the only real way to gain

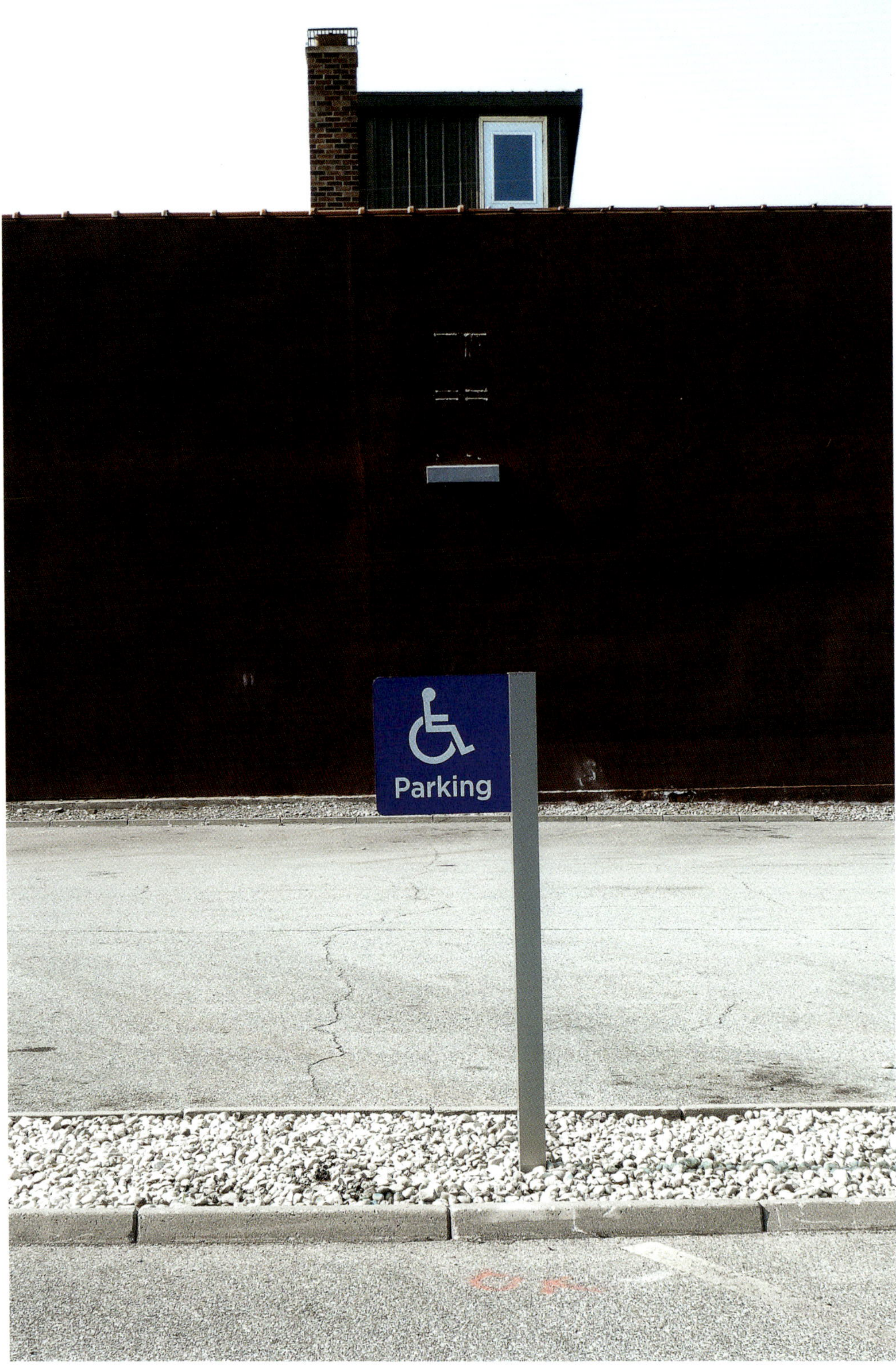
Parking

any control of it is to practice by taking as many photographs as possible, and then learning from the results. Deconstruct the images to see why some work and others fail. If the balance of an image is wrong, it will not work regardless of any other factor. Master the effective application of balance in your images, and you will probably never have to give the formal elements of composition another thought.

Positive and Negative Space

In most photographs, it is fairly easy to work out the areas of positive and negative space. In the traditional sense, the area inside a major object is positive and the area outside is negative. In a photograph of an apple, for example, anything inside the apple shape is positive space, and anything outside is negative space. It is not always that straightforward, though, especially in photography where there is little or no emphasis on depth. With abstract photography, the positive–negative distinction can become meaningless.

The balance that a good use of positive and negative space brings to an image still has an important place in abstract and contemporary photography. Even if there are no objects, as in an image that deals with a texture on a single surface, there will still be areas of differing tone that form their own shapes. Here, light and dark tones can be treated as elements of positive and negative space and balanced against each other, using exactly the same principle as if the image were of a vase or an apple.

It all comes back to balance. Practice with abstract images is never wasted because it forces the photographer to work out exactly which areas of the image have to be balanced with others. Working traditionally, where the positive and negative areas are easily defined, is okay, but to take it to the next level, the photographer needs to be able to work instinctively, without the clues of inside and outside spaces provided by the real world. This may seem like a difficult concept, but it is well worth spending time on.

◀ *A simple composition avoids being boring despite the obvious similarity between the left and right sides of the image. It is the very small differences between the two sides that prevent it from being a static image.*

Scale

Using scale creatively is a great way to get people to stop and look at your image as opposed to looking at the thousands of others out there. The reason for this is simple; as consumers of images, we have become very blasé due to the sheer volume available. For example, on seeing an image of an apple, the brain matches it to its interior model of a generic apple, thinks "boring," and tunes it out. To get a viewer's brain to stay with a photograph, this process of matching up an image with a preexisting template has to be short-circuited. This can be done in a number of ways, including use of unusual angles, dramatic lighting, or placement in an unusual situation, to name just three.

Scale is another way of engaging the viewer and not triggering the "boring" response. Most of us see apples from a distance of 2 to 12 feet, so a good way to hold the viewer is to go into macro mode and get really close. Focus on where the stem joins the apple, or try focusing on a blemish, and work the rest of the image around this. Get in close enough, and nearly any object can be treated compositionally as a landscape. This change in mental approach, from photographing an object to photographing a scene, can really bring an image to life because it shows viewers something familiar in a way they may not have seen before.

I have found that it is the photographs of objects we see or use every day, shot in unexpected ways, that are more satisfying than

Photographs of objects we see or use every day, shot in unexpected ways, may be more satisfying than images of stunning vistas or rare and precious objects, however well those may be executed.

Nature abstracted using macro. The actual area of the closest elements is about an inch wide.

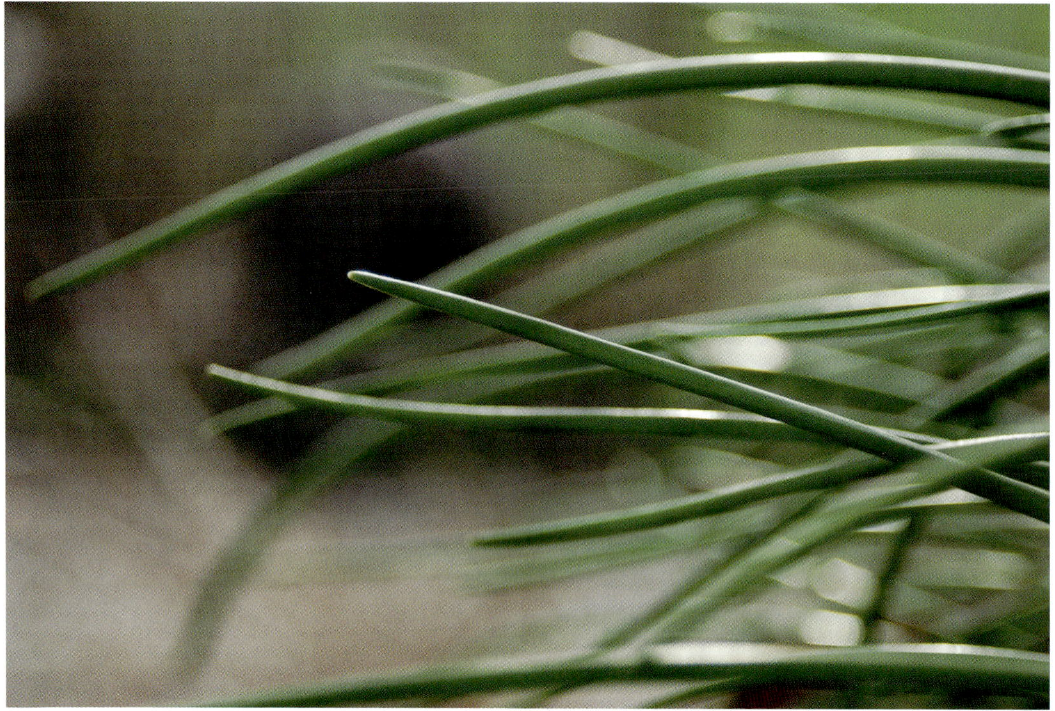

The trick with macro photography is to treat it the same as any other type of photography and not automatically go into shooting a science specimen mode. There are incredible artistic possibilities with macro photography.

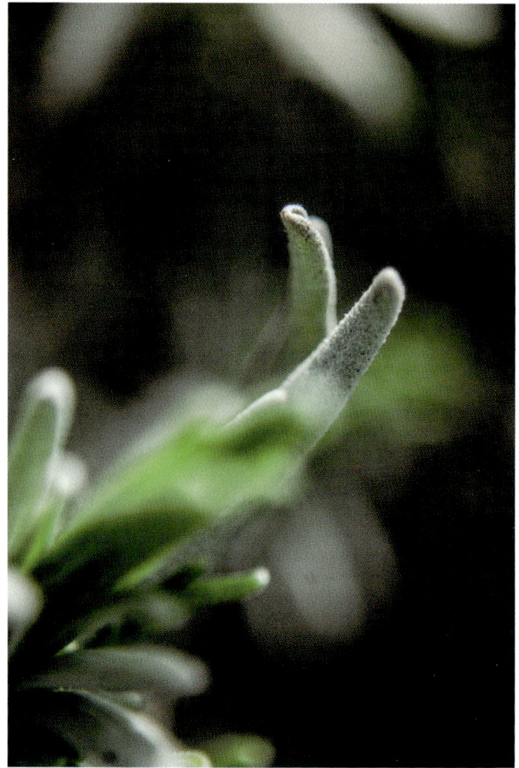

images of stunning vistas or rare and precious objects, however well those may be executed. You may be surprised at just how many viewers respond positively to photographs of things that are normally considered banal.

A combination of creative use of scale and unusual angles can be very effective. If an object is usually seen from above, try photographing it up close and straight on, or even from underneath (a glass-top table is useful for this). There is a caveat to this, though: The line between a striking image and one that just looks wrong is a fine one. As with most things in life, the best way to find this line is to step over it a few times and then pull yourself back.

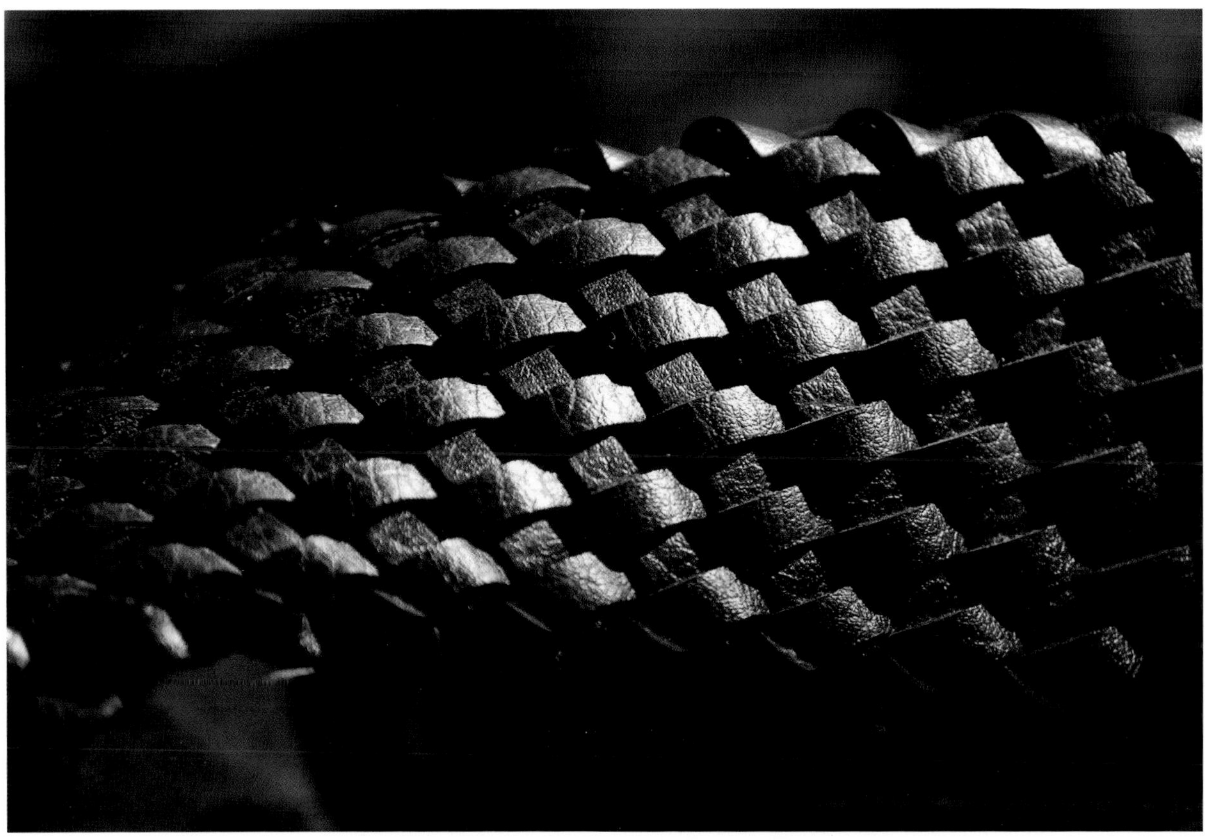

The texture of this belt could be drawn by just using blocks of tone. The lines would appear automatically, as part of the process.

Line, Shape, Tone, and Color

Most discussions about composition start off by discussing line, shape, and tone. This makes sense on the surface, because these elements can be considered the basic building blocks of composition. Elsewhere in this book, I discuss minimalism as a reductive process; we start with lots of elements and then reduce these elements to what is essential (minimalism from nothing to something is not really minimalism, in the true sense of the word). I think the process of learning about composition is also best handled by starting off with the big picture—in this case the concepts addressed in the previous sections of this chapter—and then reducing them to their essence.

You may be familiar with the list of compositional elements—*line, shape, tone, and color*—and you may be familiar enough with it to sense there is an omission. If this is the case, you are correct. *Texture* is usually lumped in as a basic element or building block of composition. It shouldn't be. Texture is a level up from the basic building blocks because it is always composed of those building blocks and therefore cannot be one itself. I am belaboring this point for a reason. The more reductionist you can be in your thinking, the better photographer you will become, regardless of your style or tastes.

The impressionist artist Edouard Manet stated that there are no lines in nature, just areas of color. This is an important and useful concept. If you look at any photograph, you will see that this is indeed the case (obviously tone

Horizontal lines have a calming effect. The muted colors and soft edges add to this effect.

Not clearly defining the subject allows the focus to be on the abstract. Here the vertical lines and the relationship between the two colors is what is important.

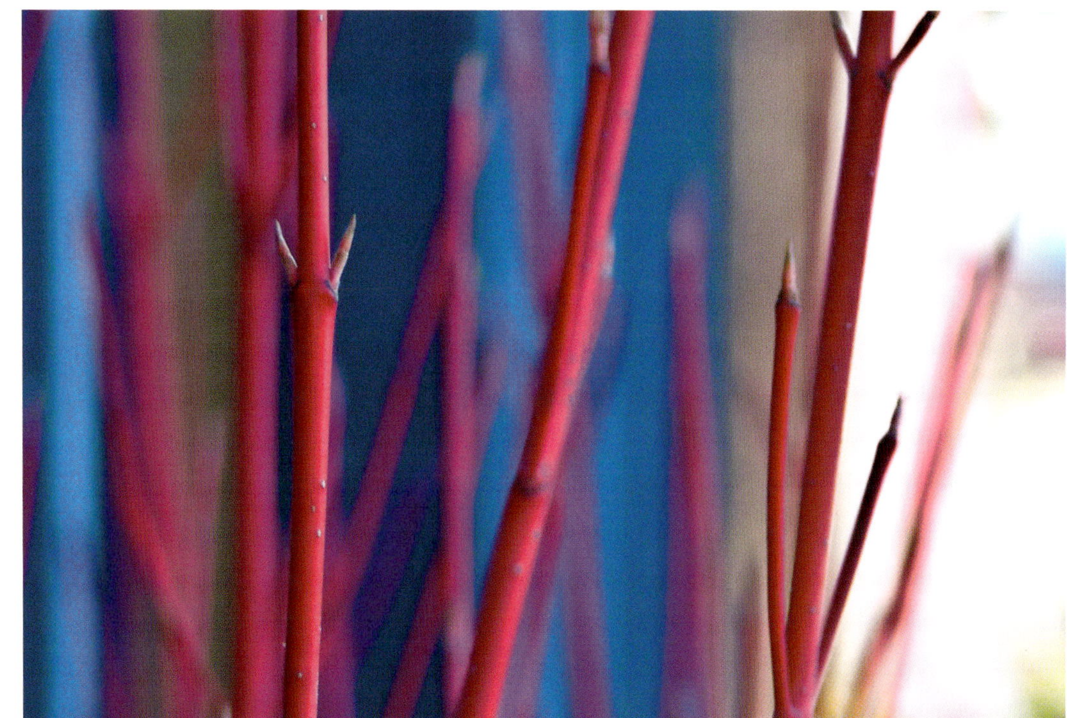

will have to be substituted for color in the case of a monochrome photograph). Many drawing instructors encourage an approach that does not make use of lines in the traditional sense, but rather encourages the building up of compositions by using blocks of tone. The end result of this approach is often much more impressive than making a line drawing and then shading in the areas.

Even if you don't draw, and you don't intend to learn how to draw, it is worth finding a simple solid such as a cube, lighting it from one side, and drawing it—including the shadow—using both methods, first with lines and then with just blocks of tone. This will help you grasp the idea that all we really see are blocks of tone or color, as opposed to a series of lines that are filled in. More important, perhaps, it will give your subconscious something to work with. Learning always has a subconscious component, and this has to be utilized to fully understand any art form.

Despite this, we know there is a part of composition that we instinctively recognize as a line. As you probably realize by now, a line is where two areas butt up against each other. It has no existence of its own. To illustrate this, look at the cube again. It may seem as if the edge is a line with its own existence, but it isn't. Light will never be exactly the same on the two faces that abut to form the edge, and it is the resulting difference in tone or color that gives the illusion of a line.

The one possible exception is a line drawn on a flat surface, but very few photographs contain an element like this. In relation to this, a line that has any thickness at all is in fact an area, albeit a skinny one. This may seem contrived, but with logos, writing on signs, or road markings, it is completely valid. Seeing these elements as either lines or areas can really open up your photography.

More Thoughts on Composition

By now you could be thinking these concepts of composition are far too abstract and esoteric to be of any use when you have the viewfinder to your eye and are composing your shot, or even when you are working in post-production to get the best out of an image. Well, here is the news that is either good or bad, depending on your point of view: that is how the best visual artists and photographers think. Ideally, by the time you press the shutter-release button, the process of composition will be instinctive, but that doesn't happen by magic. Those who are best at composition have considered the subject in far more depth than I've outlined here. Why could this be good or bad news? It is bad news if you expected to pick up a decent camera and automatically take photographs like the ones that appear in galleries; it's good news if you want your work to be better than most people's who pick up a camera and you don't mind putting in a little thinking time.

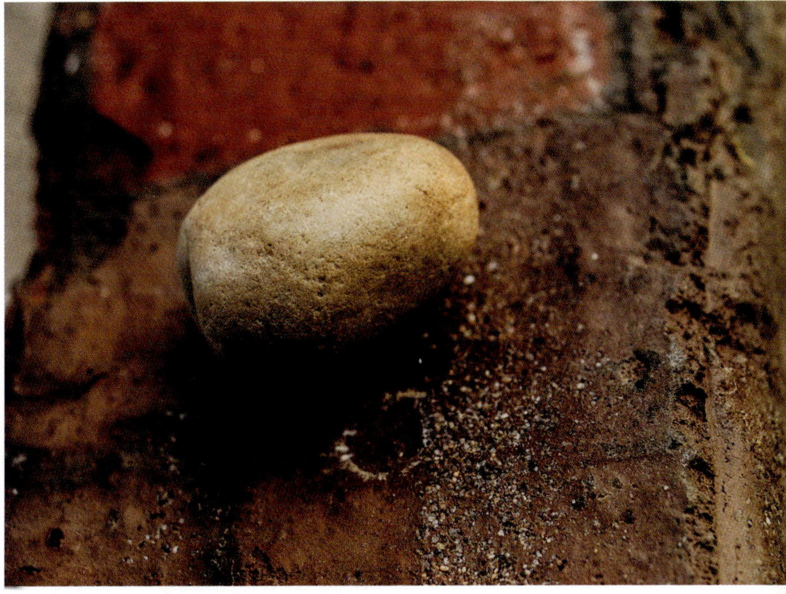

The simple, smooth form of the pebble and the complex textures of the paver provide an interesting contrast

Minimalism and Composition

Minimalism is a great tool for resolving problems with composition. If you cannot resolve composition problems using the rules, then simply take stuff out. If your photographs are not working, point the camera at simpler scenes or, if you are composing your own scenes, put less stuff in. If these are not options, then try moving in closer to the scene. This applies to all photography, but when you are using the lens of minimalism, decluttering becomes a conscious process that will almost certainly improve the image.

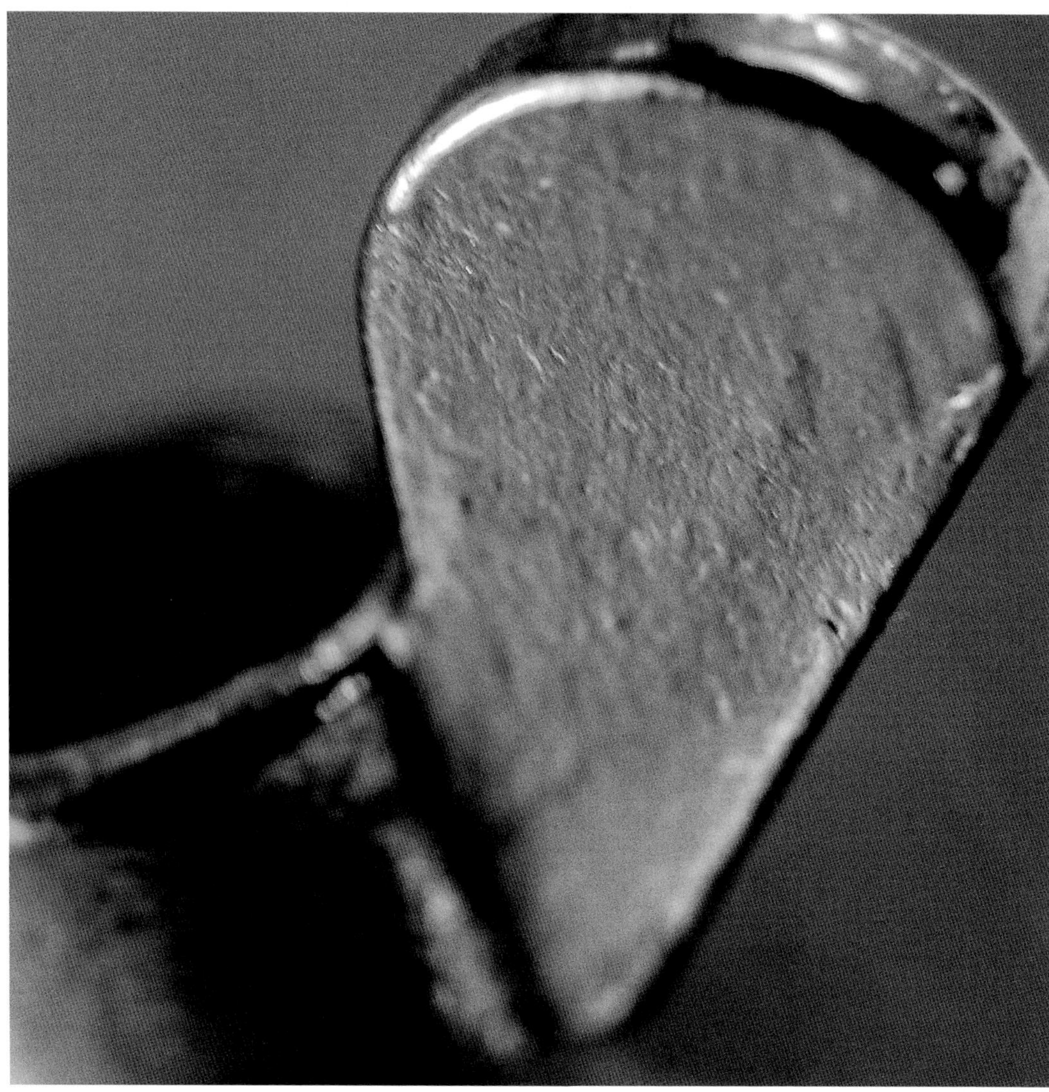

Just because an object is small doesn't mean it shouldn't be cropped

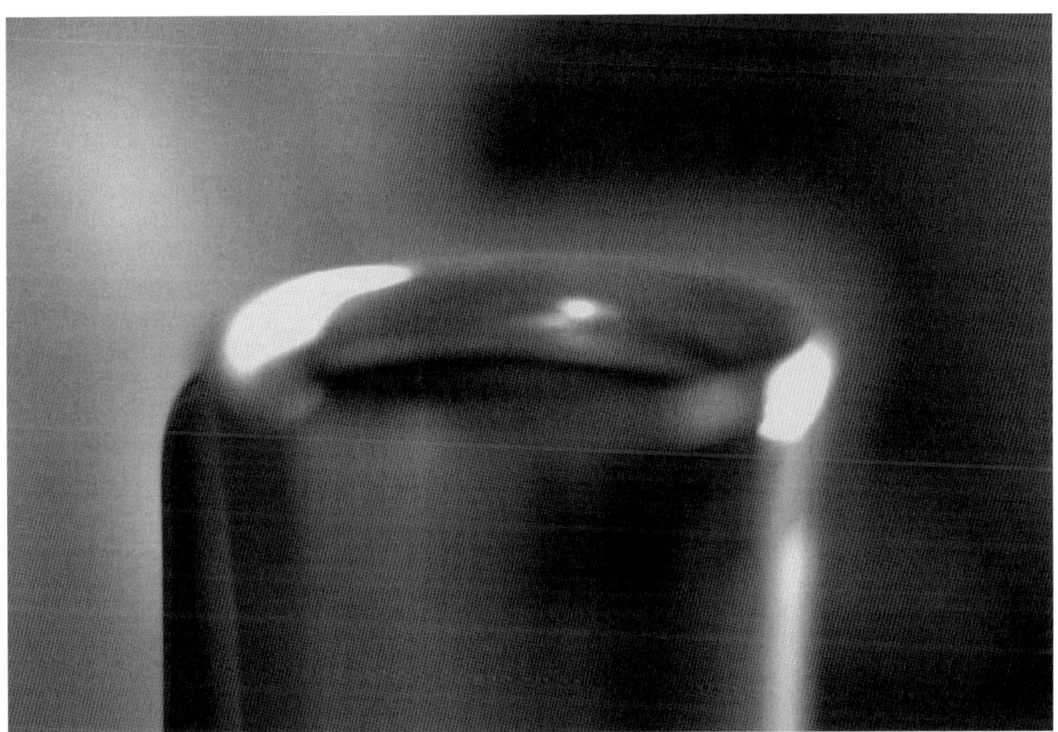

A stainless steel travel mug forms the basis for a tonal exercise

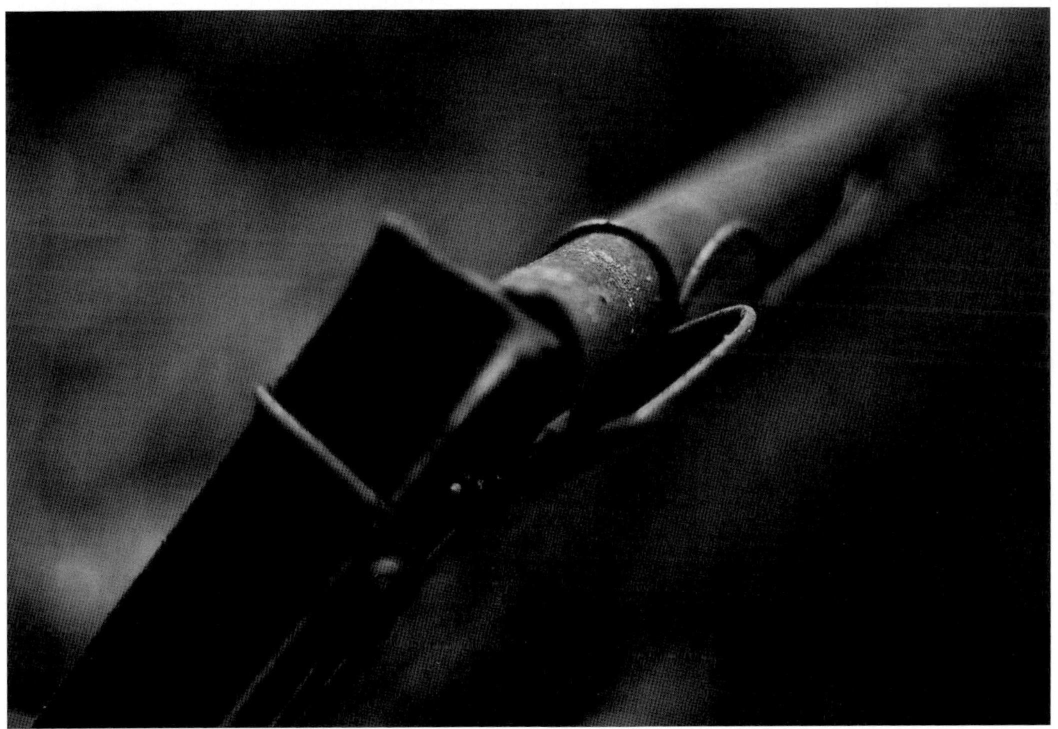

A strong diagonal line heading toward an upper corner usually shoots the viewer's eye straight out of the picture, but in this case the blurring is enough to keep the eye in the picture

Vertical emphasis in the foreground contrasts with horizontal emphasis in the background

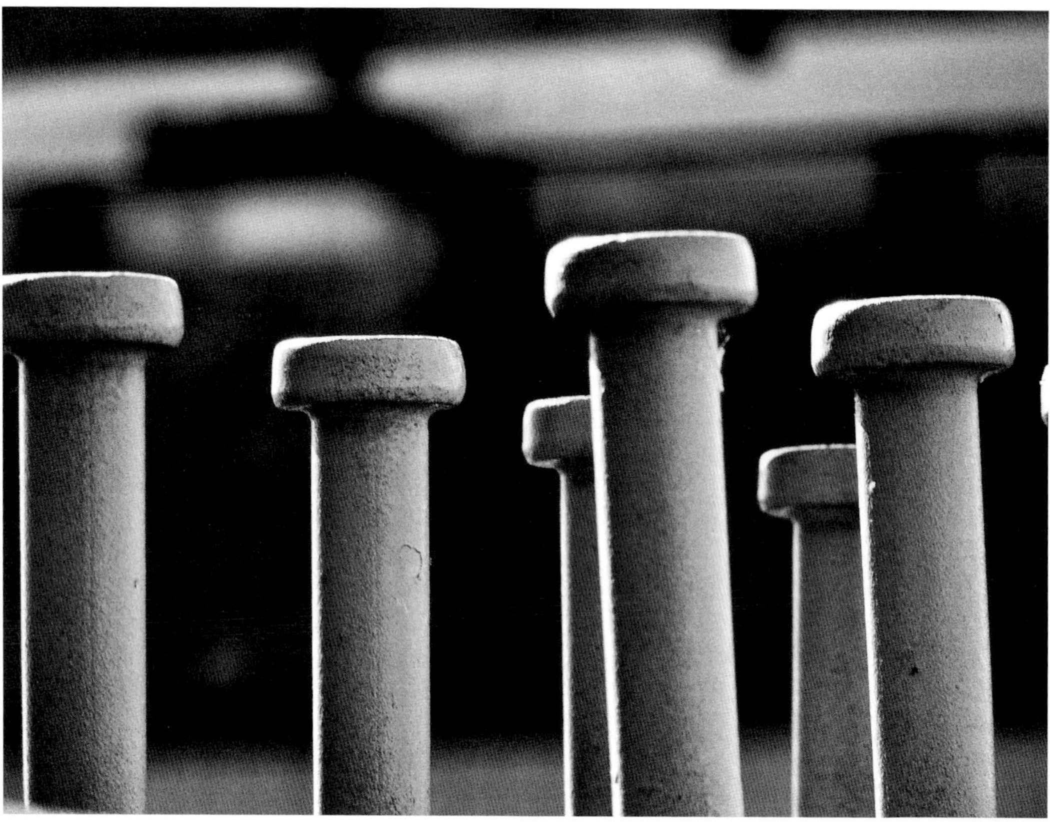

Aesthetics

While composition can be seen as the specific, aesthetics is the general. Aesthetics provides the overall context within which individual compositions are made. My favorite definition of aesthetics, as defined by scholars in the field, is "the critical reflection on art, culture, and nature." Let's examine this a little.

Applied art is when the work's primary function is something other than to be seen as a thing of beauty. Fine art is when the work serves no function beyond itself.

Art comes in two overall flavors, regardless of medium: *applied art* and *fine art*. Applied art is when the work's primary function is something other than to be seen as a thing of beauty. All advertising and marketing material falls into this category, as does issues-based or so-called humanitarian photography. Roughly speaking, if the art is selling something other than itself, it is applied. Fine art (or *pure* art) is when the work serves no function beyond itself. Fine art is no better nor is it of higher quality than applied art. In my experience, the labels bear no relationship to the *quality* of work.

Art and culture constantly interact and feed off of the other. The reason for splitting art into two classifications is to help us understand how aesthetics works. I would argue that the main interaction is between culture and applied art, with fine or pure art sitting off somewhere to the side of the process.

Photography is no different than any other art form in having both a pure and an applied side. We tend to differentiate by adding either *art* or *fine art* to the word *photography* to indicate the pure form and adding nothing if the work is applied. It is important to note that photography has a greater influence on culture

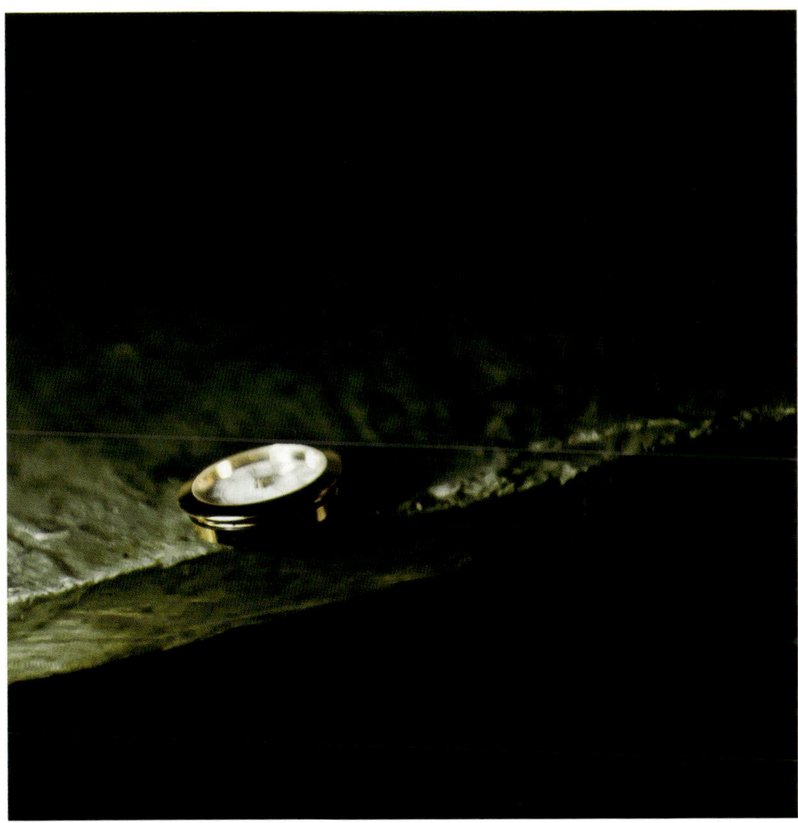

Time on the edge. This photograph is a conceptual reaction to tight deadlines. Concepts are an important part of aesthetics.

than all of the other applied arts combined. Likewise, culture influences photography more than it does any other art form. This is due to the instant nature of the medium. This was true in the decades leading up to digital technology, and even more the case now because with digital photography, the results are available for viewing a fraction of a second after the shutter-release button is pressed.

So applied photography and culture are now locked in this very tight feedback loop with a great deal of interdependency. The loop is, in fact, so established that it is all but impossible to know which leads and which follows. That is, does the culture determine photographs, or are photographs actually forcing the culture? Which side of the equation is driving modern aesthetics?

A few years ago I would have said that culture was the driving force and photography was basically doing as it was told—or, if you prefer, it was being led by the market—but that has changed over the past few years. This change is due to the massive increase in the number of people and, perhaps more important, the types of people, who use cameras as part of their daily lives, and the resultant change in photography from a conservative, reactionary force to a much more radical, exciting one.

Now the interaction is more equal, because those taking photos see themselves very much as a part of the culture rather than as an outsider looking in. The likely upshot of this blurring of lines or new dynamic relationship is that the evolution of aesthetics is experiencing acceleration. Changes that previously took years or decades to surface can now take weeks, or even days. Whether these changes are going to be significant, or whether they are superficial and self-canceling, has yet to be seen.

Fine art photography is largely but not completely separate from the dynamic that I've just laid out, but the world of fine art moves at a slower pace than pop culture and advertising imagery. While the world of applied photography is very broad and shallow, the fine arts side is much narrower, but it has depth.

Art and culture spring from a combination of nature and the thought processes and actions of human beings. Here, the use of the word *nature* with regard to aesthetics requires a short explanation. It does not mean nature in only the biological sense, but rather everything in the physical world; all matter including living things, natural nonliving things, and manmade things.

I first came across the definition of aesthetics used at the beginning of this section a couple of decades ago, yet it seems even more accurate now than it was then. Until recently, I felt the need to add an extra couple of words: Aesthetics is the critical reflection on art, culture, and nature *by the fine arts establishment*. My feeling about this has now changed and the qualifier can finally be dropped. Applied art is now more than worthy of the critical reflection required. There is also something very right about the dynamic as it now works—it is much more holistic, much more from the ground up.

The Difference Between Art and Design

Although some people now regard art and design as the same thing, I do not. I hold the traditional view that a work of art has no purpose outside of itself (pure art), whereas with design the aesthetics always serve another cause, usually, although not always, to sell something (applied art). The thing being sold may be anything from consumer goods to an idea. I will concede that on rare occasions what starts out as design can end up as art. This is not to say that I regard design as inferior to art in any way; they just serve different functions. In fact, I will go as far as to say that I am as likely to be drawn to a design piece as to an art piece.

Have you ever noticed how a pop song can sound wonderful at first, and then the song really grates after more than a few hearings? One possible reason for this is lack of depth. The song is all surface, with nothing left to explore after the initial hearing. I think a similar phenomenon exists in the visual arts, and it is potentially a huge trap for minimalist photography.

Today, there seems to be a fashion for simple, superficially minimalist images, and websites featuring such images abound. These images tend to be simple and often consist of a large flat area of either a primary color or tone and one to three objects of a complimentary hue or different tone. Initially these can be striking, but the impact does not last beyond the first minute or for subsequent viewings. There is simply no depth to these images; they are exercises in design—the art is missing. These types of images may be perfect for an advertising or marketing campaign. They seldom work well as art, though. Frame them and hang them on the wall, but they won't make someone feel the need to walk up to them and study them for a second time. The viewer will not be engaged. To truly engage the viewer, a photograph requires something more: it requires an additional quality. What exactly constitutes this quality is extremely hard to identify. The words I use are *tooth* or *bite,* because they imply something that holds the viewer and something that is not always comfortable—a counterpoint to the slickness that a photograph, especially a minimalist photograph, can easily fall into.

A tension has to be created within the frame, and an image that is too clean and too slick fails to create this tension. This is perhaps more

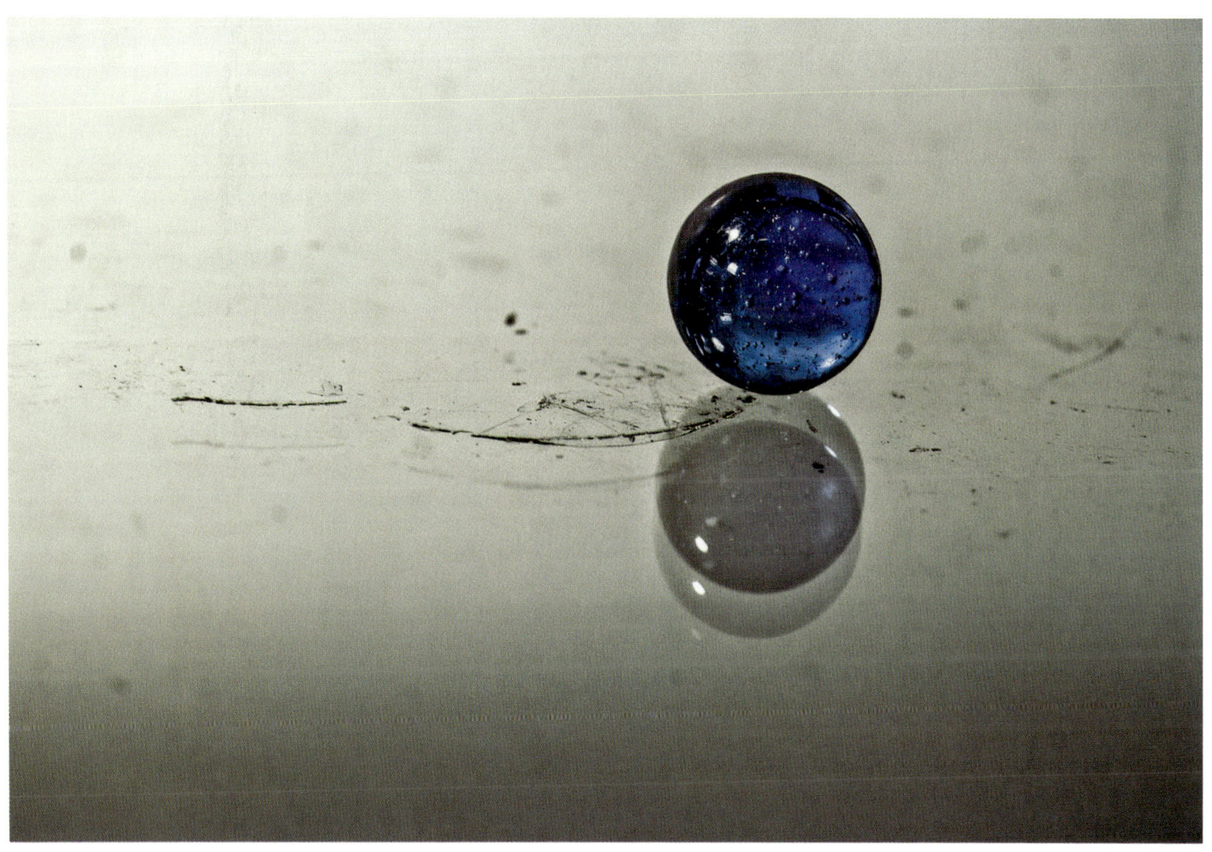

It is the imperfections that often make a shot interesting. Thinking that minimalism is about losing imperfections in an image is a common mistake.

easily understood by using music as an analogy. Without the occasional harsh-sounding note or chord, a musical piece will lack depth and sound thin. The discord provides the tension or bite. When there is only surface without depth, or to put it another way, style without substance, there is no possibility of a dialog between the artist and the viewer. There can be no dialog if everything is revealed within the first second.

Unfortunately, there is no pat answer as to exactly what can provide the necessary tension. If I were to make a suggestion, and you used that suggestion, it would be superficial—it would not come from you. I think it is possible to give you some ideas, though, with the caveat that these are just examples that have worked for me. Although imitation is the best form of flattery, I'd much rather see my ideas used as little more than jumping-off points for ideas of your own.

Although just about anything small on a pristine, white background can look minimal and appealing on first viewing, a scratch or some discoloration can provide the visual dissonance that will draw the viewer in and initiate a much deeper interaction. A perfectly slick minimalist photograph will often have objects that serve as visual points in an exact line, exactly one-third in and parallel to an edge, as per the rule of thirds. This may provide a pleasing design but offers little else. Shifting one of the objects off the line, however, creates a little tension and usually makes the image much stronger.

Another favorite approach of the design-based minimalists is the use of complementary colors. Typical examples are images of a ball on a plain background or a door in a building, and the common colors would be blue and its complimentary orange, or perhaps yellow and purple. With current image editing software, it is easy to change certain hues within an image, and shifting one of the colors a little, away from the exact complimentary, can create some dissonance. This is due to the brain expecting the exact complimentary, because most photographs of this type feature exact complimentary colors.

The subject of art and design and what defines them is a big one, and it is important for photographers to develop their own aesthetic points of view. You may disagree with me entirely and think this is all a matter of semantics, but the important thing is to form an opinion, preferably after reading about the subject. Good photographers have opinions on everything to do with aesthetics, and they tend to be every bit as passionate about them as the most vocal sports fans.

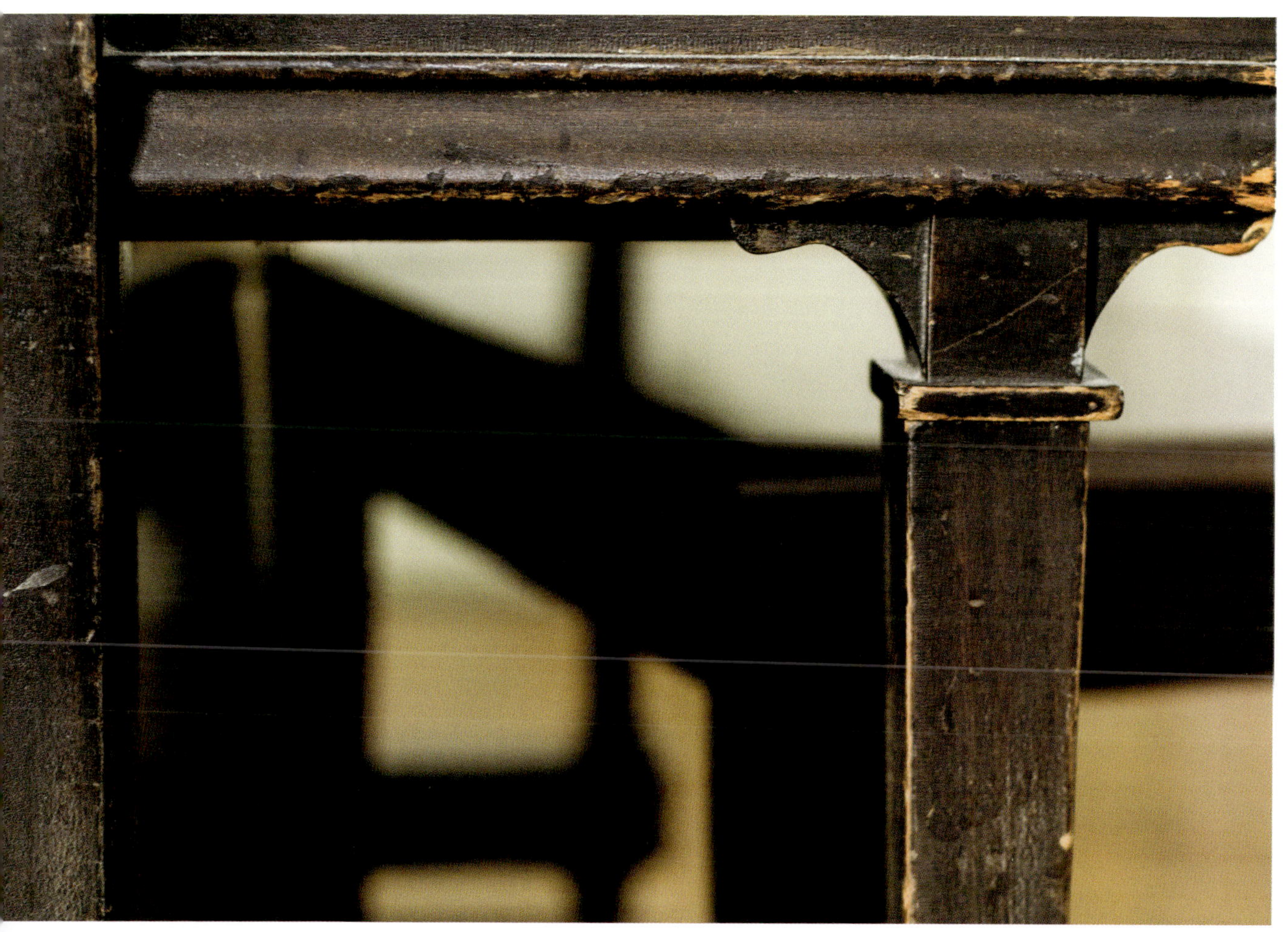

Piano and stool

An exercise I like to do from time to time is take an everyday object and work up a set of photographs, all showing different aspects of the object.

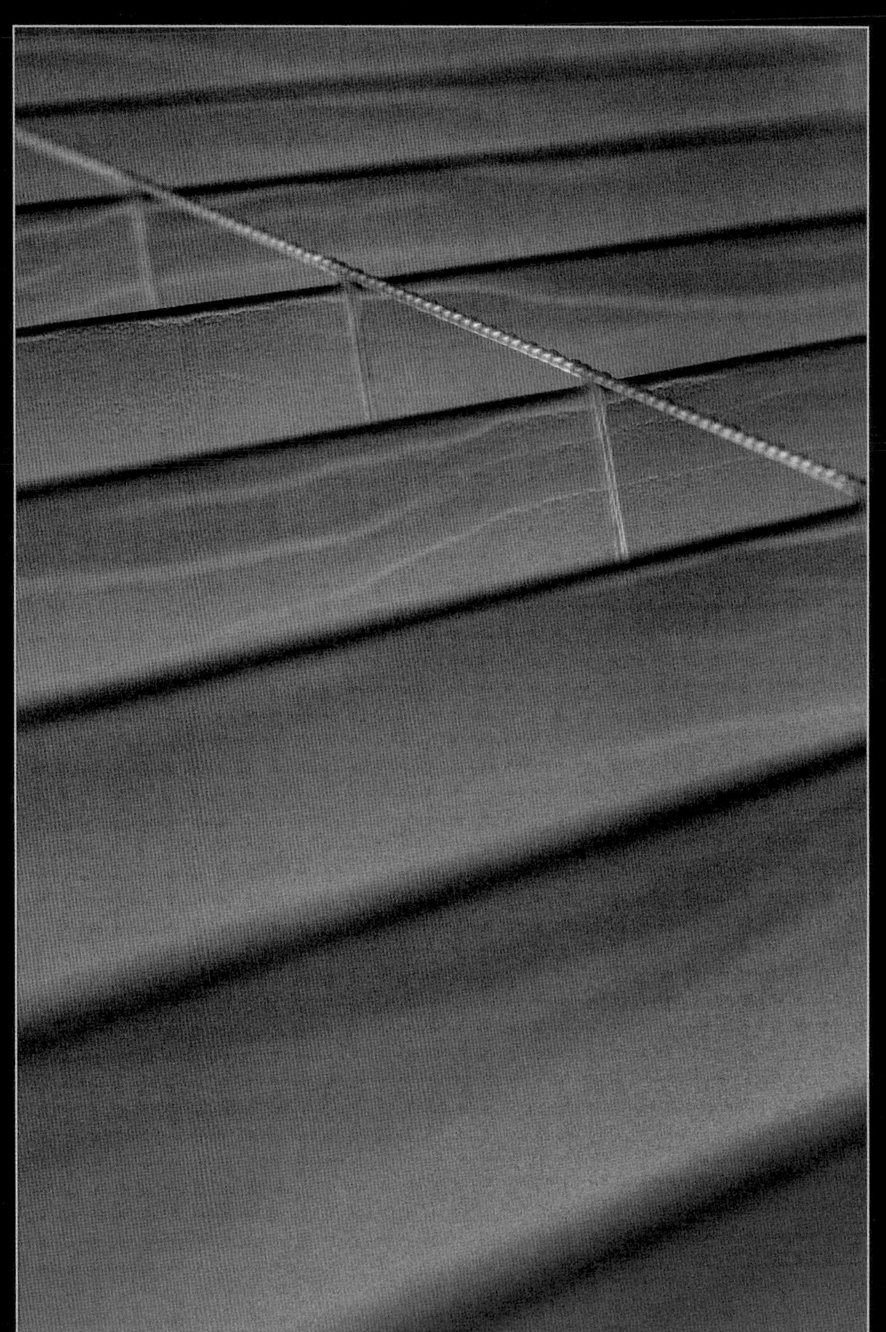

Abstract image created by photographing an everyday object from an unusual perspective

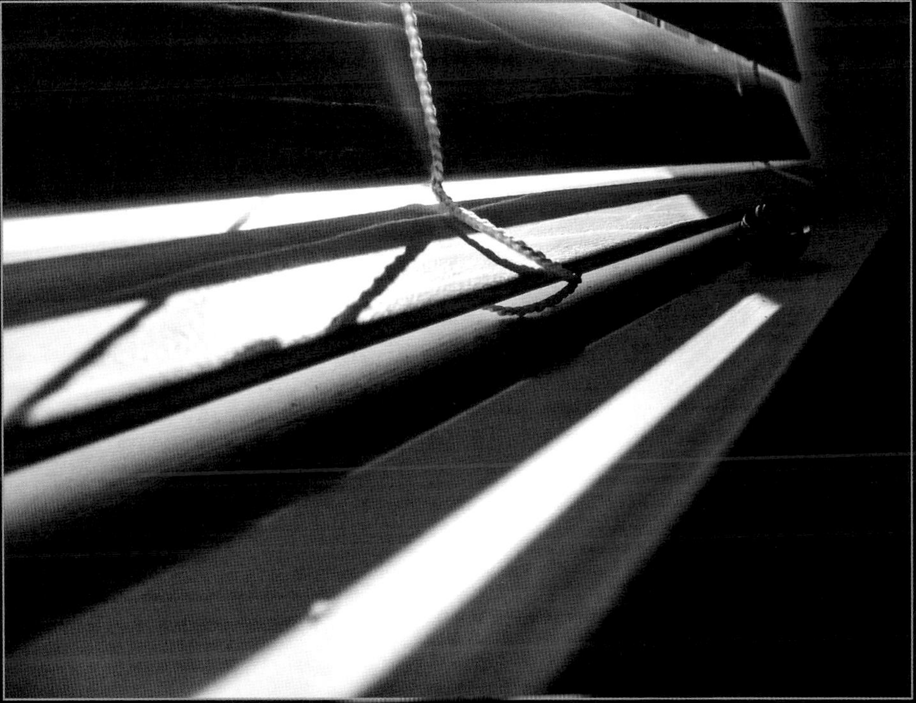

Leading lines and a ma

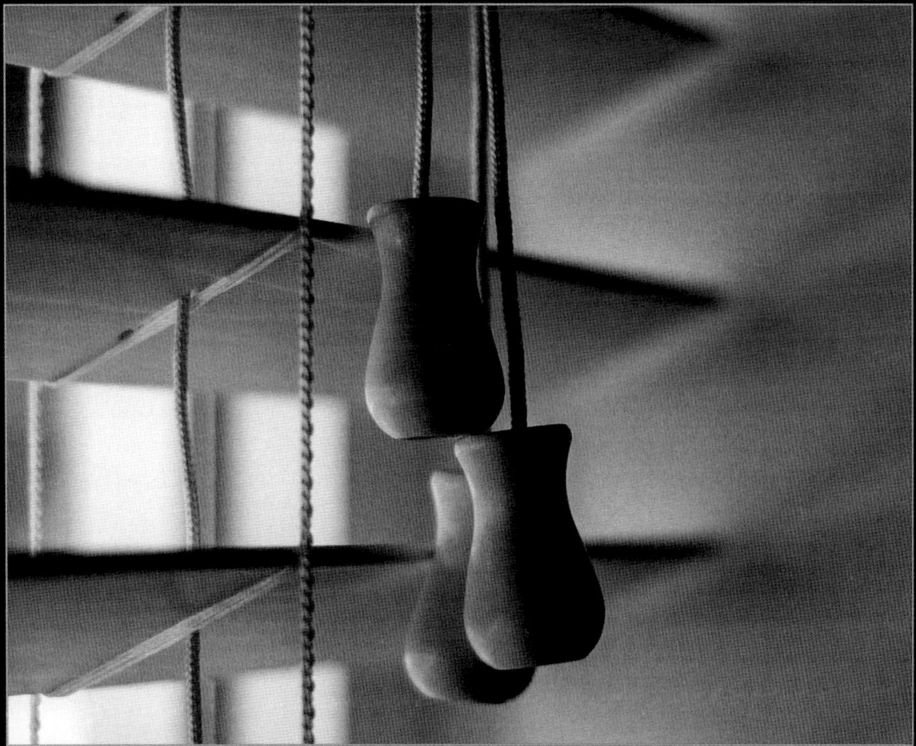

Open blinds and cords

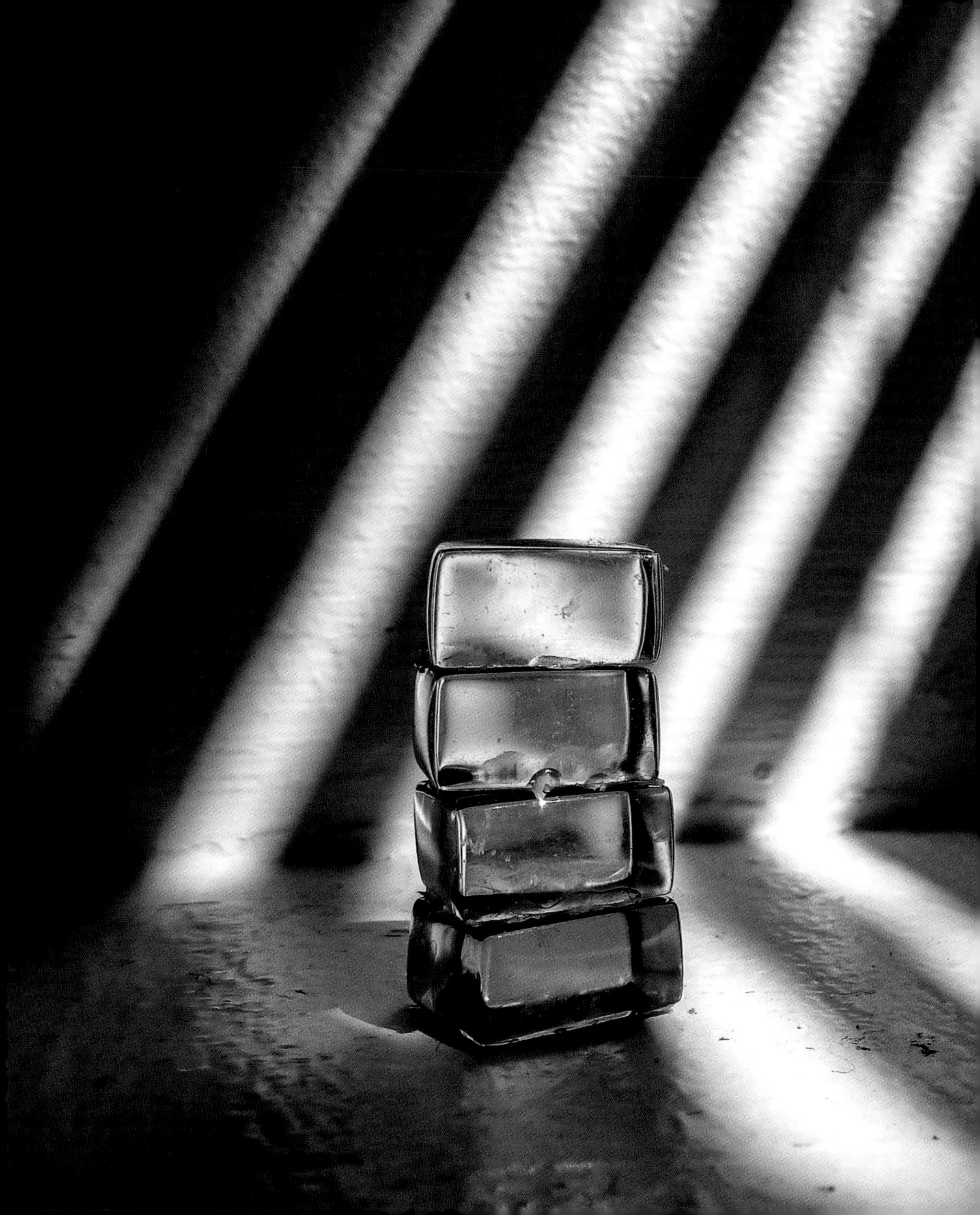

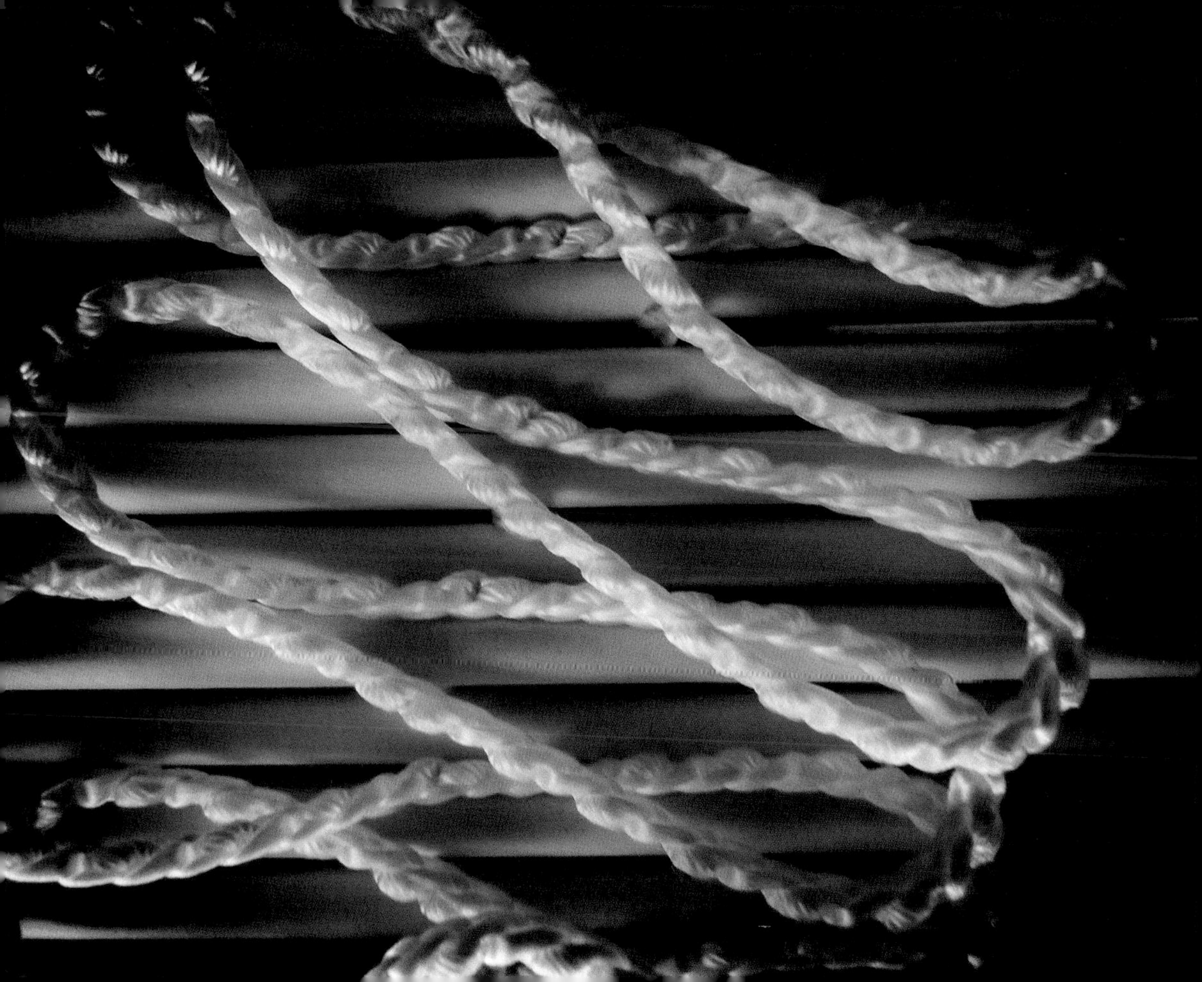

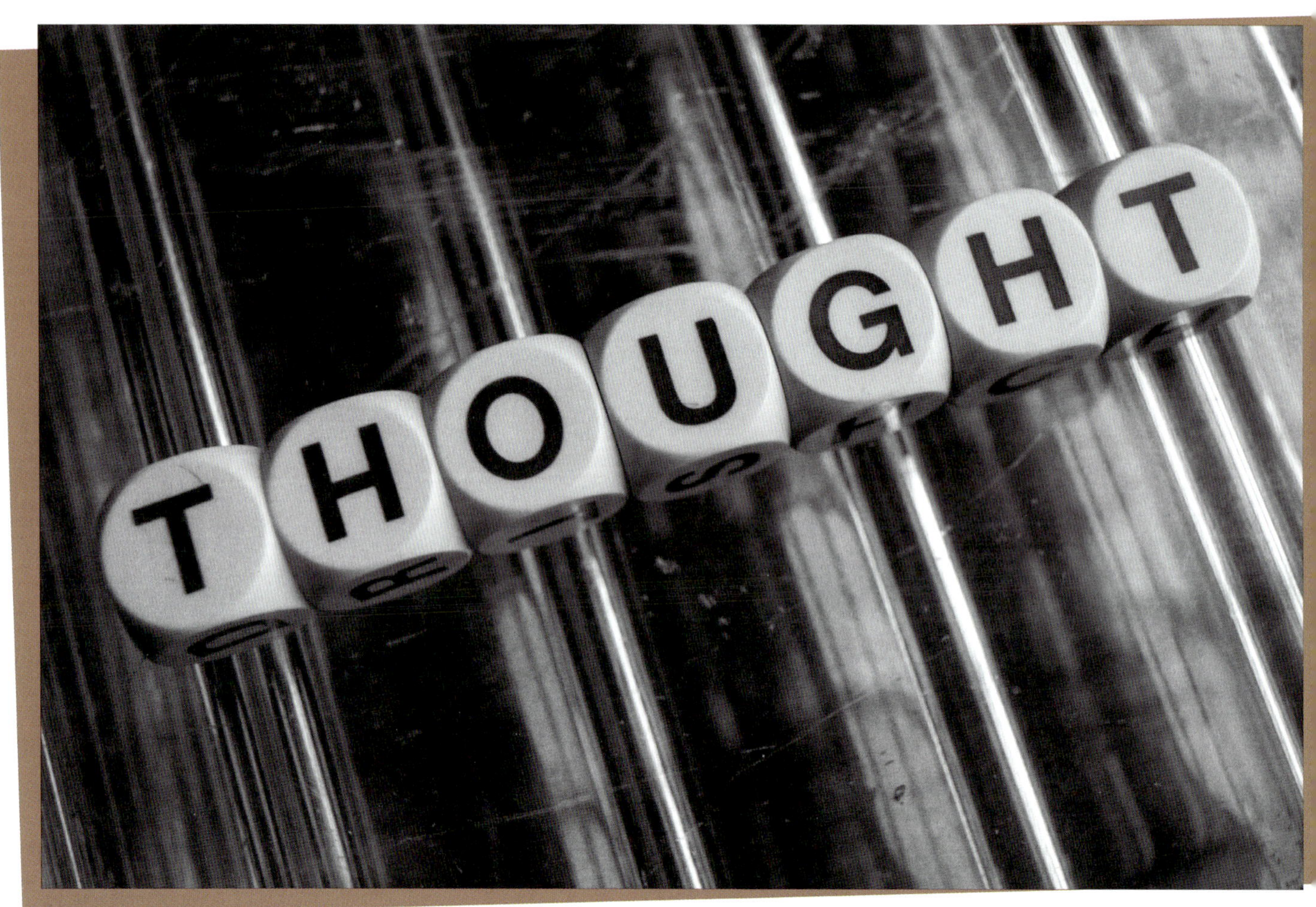
THOUGHT

Chapter 7 Photography Philosophy

The most significant moment in a photographer's development doesn't come with the mastering or understanding of light, composition, or any other technicality. It comes when he or she puts the camera down and asks why. There are thousands of good photographers out there, but few great ones. Asking why won't automatically make you a great photographer, but one thing is certain: it will make you a better photographer.

To test this idea, just go online and search for the name of any famous photographer from the past 100 or so years, and thousands of results containing their deepest thoughts, quotes, and other insights will come up in your search. To be a better photographer, read and listen to what other photographers think. It really is that simple.

The ideal approach is not to automatically absorb everything that every photographer says about the subject, but instead to read with a critical mind and then decide how you can incorporate their ideas into your own thinking. Of course, you may later reject another photographer's thinking, but the rejection should come with a solid reason that goes beyond the simplistic. You may also reject something after initially agreeing with it, which is a part of the ongoing process, a dialog between yourself and the photographers you admire, and maybe even a few you don't admire. One of the best ways to firm up our own understanding and position on any subject is to enter into a debate with someone who has an opposing but well-constructed point of view. This forces us to examine and shore up weaknesses in our own arguments.

Making Use of the Wisdom of Others

Now let's move out of the abstract and introduce some examples of famous photographers.

Ask any U.S.-based photographer to name just one photographer that he or she admires, and that person may respond with Ansel Adams, the American photographer most famous for his landscapes and dramatic tones. Adams was a strong advocate for something he called *Previsualization*. This process involved the photographer imagining as precisely as possible how they wanted the resulting print of the scene to look before putting an eye to the viewfinder. Adams argued that this allowed for the optimal aesthetic, intellectual, spiritual, and mechanical effects to be achieved. This approach obviously worked for him; however, that does not make it the only or even the best approach for other photographers, even though many photography teachers and writers treat anything said by Adams as gospel and therefore beyond question. We have a tendency to be a little too reverential toward our heroes when a critical and questioning eye may sometimes serve us better.

My personal take is that Previsualization is, generally speaking, a good thing and an important part of the photographic process, but it should not be the whole process. By taking Adams's approach, we entirely separate the camera and the photographer. This does not allow for the feedback loop made available with today's digital technology to be a critical part of the process. Now we can previsualize, take the shot, look at the shot on the LCD screen, and shoot an improved version all within a few seconds. Just about all photographers who work in digital use these extra steps to their advantage. This approach radically alters Adams's philosophy because the photograph is no longer conceived in one moment of perfection and shot in another moment of perfection. It is now a process, a feedback loop that can be repeated as often as a photographer sees fit.

I am the first to admit that being critical of Adams may seem presumptuous, but it is only by taking Adams's philosophy and applying my own thinking to it that I reached the conclusion that a great photograph is often an ongoing process of incremental improvements, and not a one-time perfect moment.

Another photography great, Henri Cartier-Bresson, was responsible for expanding on the idea of the decisive moment, first summed up by the 17th century Cardinal de Retz as follows:

"There is nothing in this world that does not have a decisive moment."

Cartier-Bresson applied this philosophy to his own photography and wrote the following:

"Photography is simultaneously and instantaneously the recognition of a fact and the rigorous organization of visually perceived forms that express and signify that fact."

Cartier-Bresson was a different type of photographer than Adams. Whereas Adams specialized in capturing the grandeur and timelessness of dramatic scenery, Cartier-Bresson all but invented street photography and is often considered the first photojournalist. Adams's approach to photography and capturing a moment was almost spiritual, but for Cartier-Bresson, the whole process was a little more prosaic and far less meditative. He believed that a perfect and instantaneous instinct for composition allied with perfect timing was the way to get the shot.

I don't believe there is a single hit-or-miss moment in any interaction, whether between clouds and a horizon or two people talking on the street. One question I can never answer is, exactly what time frame does an action encompass? Take a game of soccer, for example. Is the unit of action from the moment the striker kicks the ball toward the goal, the moment he pulls his leg back in preparation for the shot, or further back, when he starts running to collect the pass? Add to this that there can be any number of decisive moments within this scenario and it all becomes a bit abstract.

The real point here is not what I believe regarding the concept of the decisive moment, and believe me, I haven't even scratched the surface of my take on this particular element of photographic thought. Rather, it is that Cartier-Bresson's writing, and to a lesser extent Adams's writing, forced me to think about it *at all*. This may seem like fun musings for a rainy day, but it has had a real influence on my photography because it has profoundly affected the way I look for moments to take a shot. It has even changed my framing. If I'm covering sports, I often close in on the faces of the participants because, to use our soccer example, just as there are decisive moments that involve the whole body and the ball, there are decisive expressions that are not always in sync with the larger-scale action. Again, even though I disagree with Cartier-Bresson's viewpoint that there is just a single, decisive moment to an action, had I not read his thoughts on this topic, I may have never considered this particular relationship.

Some photographers go beyond aesthetics and write about the social and political aspects of the art. Some, like Paul Strand, have a foot firmly planted in both camps. He was an out-and-out modernist from an aesthetic point of view, yet his photography was largely driven by his politics and his conscience. To me, the shift from pictorialism to modernism in photography is all about the shift from the subject matter as taking precedence to the image itself as the important thing. From a modernist point of view, the subject matter is supposedly insignificant, and the more abstract compositional elements, such as line and tone, are everything. Of course, social and documentary photography places the subject back at the top of the visual hierarchy. An argument can be made that it is possible for a subject to be decided on and then a modernist approach to the mechanics and composition to be taken. But that doesn't quite ring true with me. To stress again, the important thing isn't whether or not I agree, it is that Strand and other modernist documentary photographers have forced me to do a lot of hard thinking on the exact relationship between the abstract elements—such as line, tone, and shape—and the subject matter of an image.

The whole purpose of discussing the philosophies of Adams, Cartier-Bresson, and Strand is to show that virtually anything you read can be a jumping-off point for deeper thought about the art form. You can read anything about a photographer's personal philosophy, and the moment you either agree, disagree, or consider a mixture of the two, your approach to your own photography will change.

Toward Minimalism via an Assessment of HDR

In addition to reading about great photographers, your visual philosophy can be formulated through considering the merits of various technical advancements. I will use an example from my own experience to further this point.

I have learned more about my own likes and dislikes by reading up on a genre of photography that I am not a great fan of: high dynamic range imaging, or as it is commonly known, HDR. I want to be clear that I am not anti-HDR—I just decided that it wasn't for me. Interestingly, it was through the writings of HDR proponents that I came to understand that what I first took as a superficial choice on my part actually had much deeper roots.

They key thing about HDR, at least for the purposes of this section, is that it increases the range of tones in the final image beyond what a digital sensor is normally capable of processing in a single capture. This allows for a tonal range that is closer to what the human eye perceives. This may sound great in theory, because anything that expands an artist's means of expression should be a good thing. I looked at a lot of HDR photographs before coming to the conclusion that it did not do anything for me. There were one or two examples I could admire on a technical level, but none gave me that feeling in the gut (instead of the brain) that comes from seeing a great work of art.

By nature, I am a tinkerer who likes experimenting with both the hardware and the software involved in making images. At the very least, I shouldn't have been HDR-phobic and should have been able to occasionally incorporate it into my workflow, but it just didn't happen. I wondered why this was the case, but it took me a long time to come up with the answer.

As I've discussed earlier in the book, photography is a reductionist art form. Unlike painting, where the artist starts with a blank canvas and then has to add everything, the photographer often starts with a visual jumble that needs the clutter sorted and removed before a strong image can emerge.

Fundamentally, the minimalist photographer seeks to remove information, but HDR seeks to add information, to make every pixel be all that it can be, so to speak. The working assumption with HDR is that the better and more accurate each individual pixel is, the better the overall image will be. The best photographers realize that a great image is not about individual pixels, it is about the whole image.

As an aside, I offer a few thoughts on the contentious debate that has been rumbling on for several years now, whether to make use of HDR or not. This, on the surface, is odd. Compared with many communities, we photographers tend to be a fairly non-contentious bunch. We may prefer Nikon over Canon or vice versa, or we may disagree about ideal lighting setups, but these discussions rarely rise above a level of friendly banter. Mention HDR, though, and normally sane people often seem to lose themselves.

Most non-photographers do not even know what HDR is, and wouldn't care if the technique had been applied to an image or not. It certainly doesn't change an image as much as converting from color to monochrome, for example, or adding noise for effect, yet these processing techniques rarely lead to rancor within the photography community. This still raises the question, then, of why photographers get so worked up over this subject. I think I have a possible answer.

The conclusion I reached is that the argument is not actually about HDR. HDR is symbolic of a deep divide within the photography community, and that divide has those who are predominately about the technology on one side, and those who come more from the general arts side on the other.

The most ardent supporters of HDR tend to enjoy the equipment side of photography for its own sake, rather than purely as a means to an end, and seem to place great stock in what type of camera and peripheral equipment is used for a given image. Conversely, those who do not use HDR are more likely to take the view that the human eye is the most important equipment, and hardware is far less important.

We non-HDR types have the desire to express something as best we can with the tools available, and will even happily accept the possibility that flaws in the equipment can actually bring us closer to our goal. The resurgence of the toy camera, whether obtained using the original equipment or by digital means, is a testament to this. Conversely, the HDR enthusiast is locked into the idea that the closer an image can be to technically perfect, the more worthy it is.

Thus, what started out as a minor curiosity, that is, the animosity in the HDR debate, led me to a greater understanding of things much more profound: the decision to lose visual information from an image, as opposed to emphasizing it, is not only valid, it is a critical part of a photographer's development; and, on a macro level, there is a schism developing between some fine-arts-based photographers and some technology-based photographers.

The overarching point here is that my attitudes toward photography have been shaped by means of a virtual dialog with other photographers, some famous and many not so famous. I see a point of view expressed and, rather than take it at face value and internalize it uncritically, I deconstruct and examine it. This is what a minimalist does; it is second nature. If you express an opinion to me about photography, I will compare it to my own knowledge and the knowledge of others, and then I'll decide whether it, or any part of it, has validity for me.

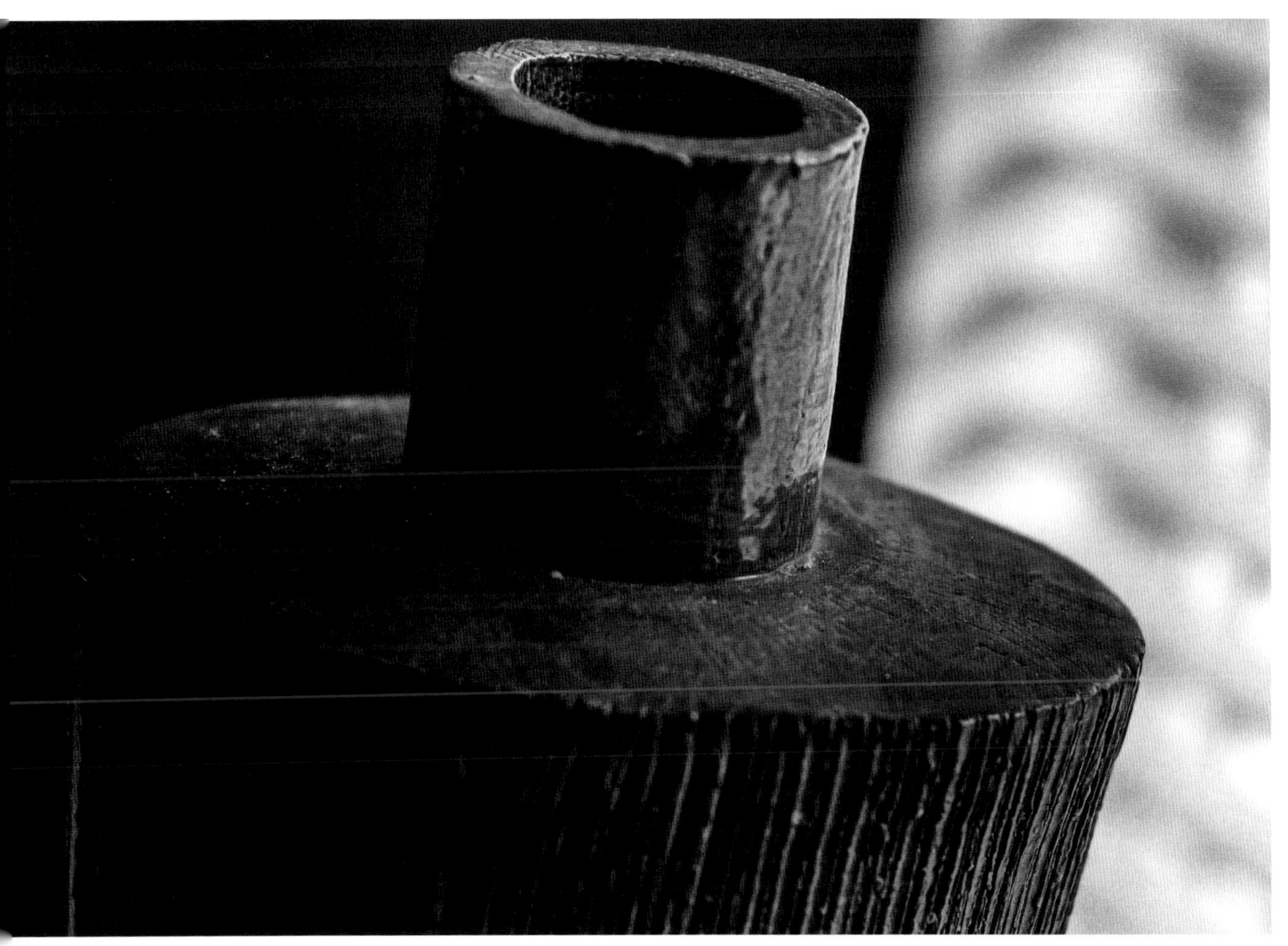

An example of the use of monochrome to emphasize tones and textures

Photographing an object away from its usual surroundings forces the viewer to look at it with a fresh eye. Here are three examples using a cherry without a cherry bowl or complimentary fruit anywhere in sight.

Reflections add interest to an image, especially if the object that does the reflecting has some interesting properties of its own. In this case, a large pink bowl with a mother-of-pearl type finish was used.

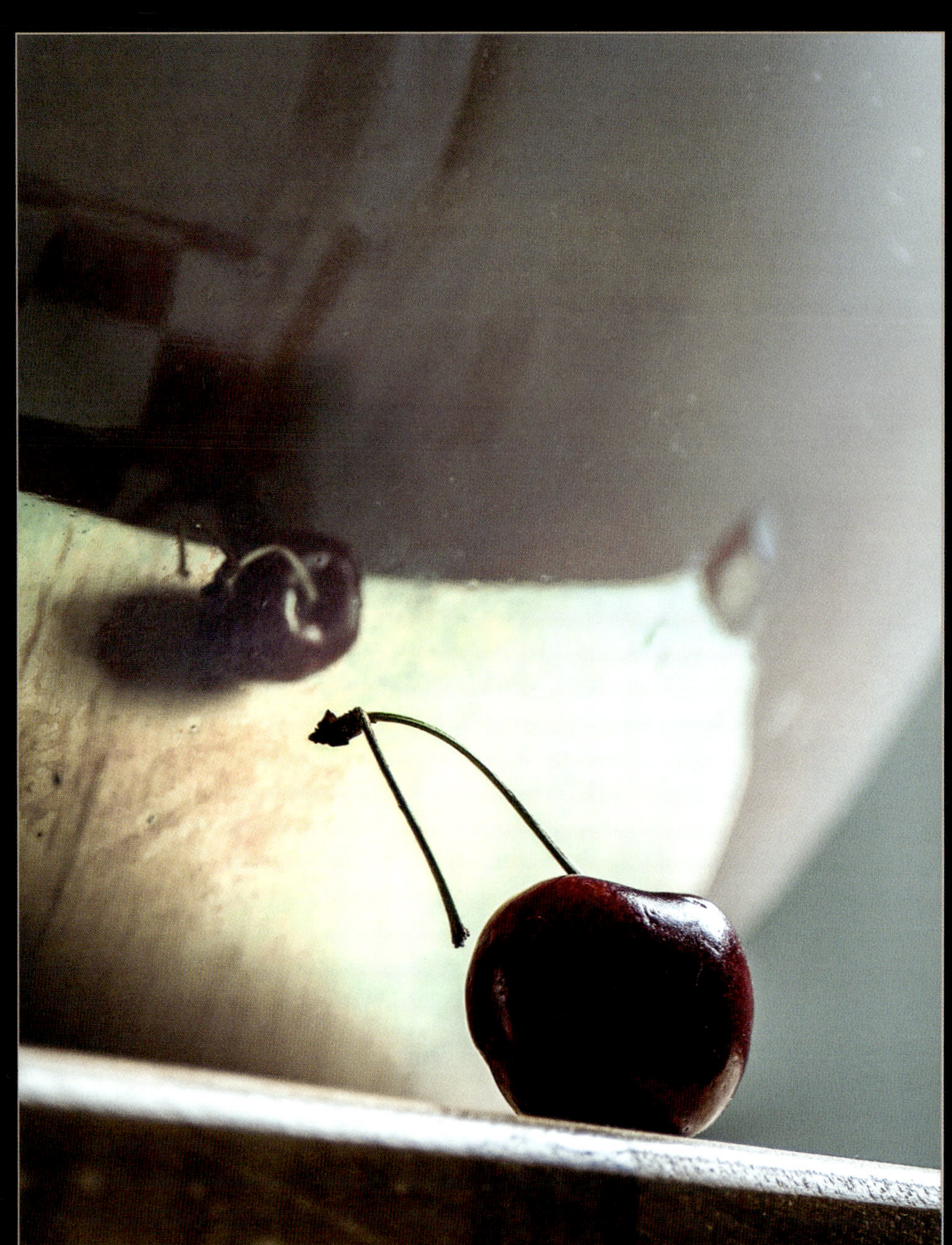

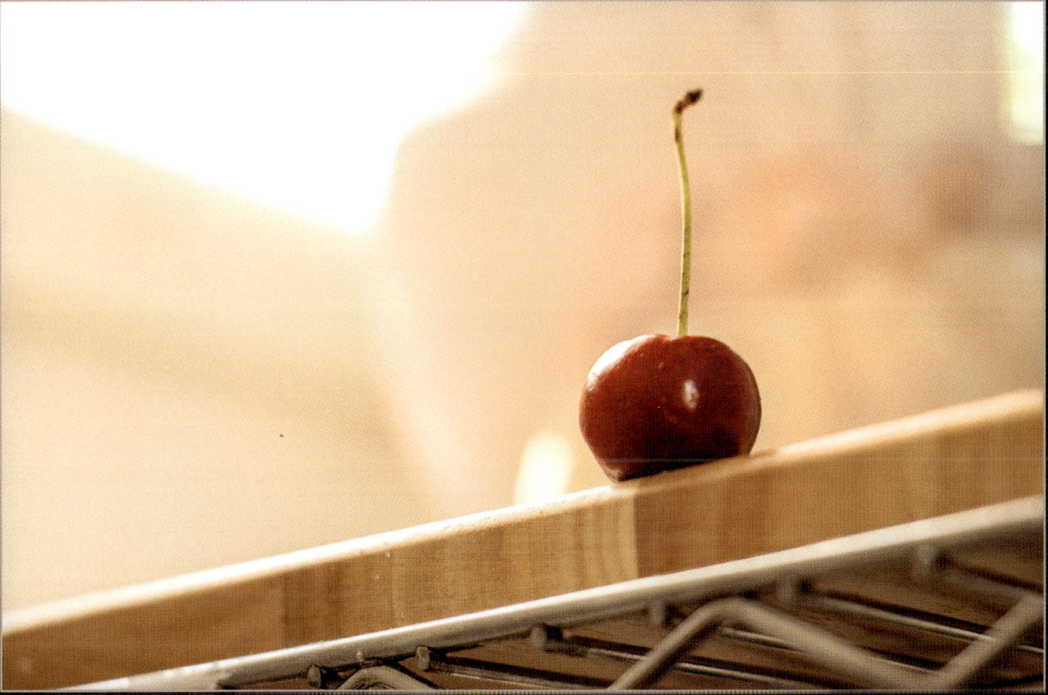

A simple composition, where the background echoes the properties of the cherry

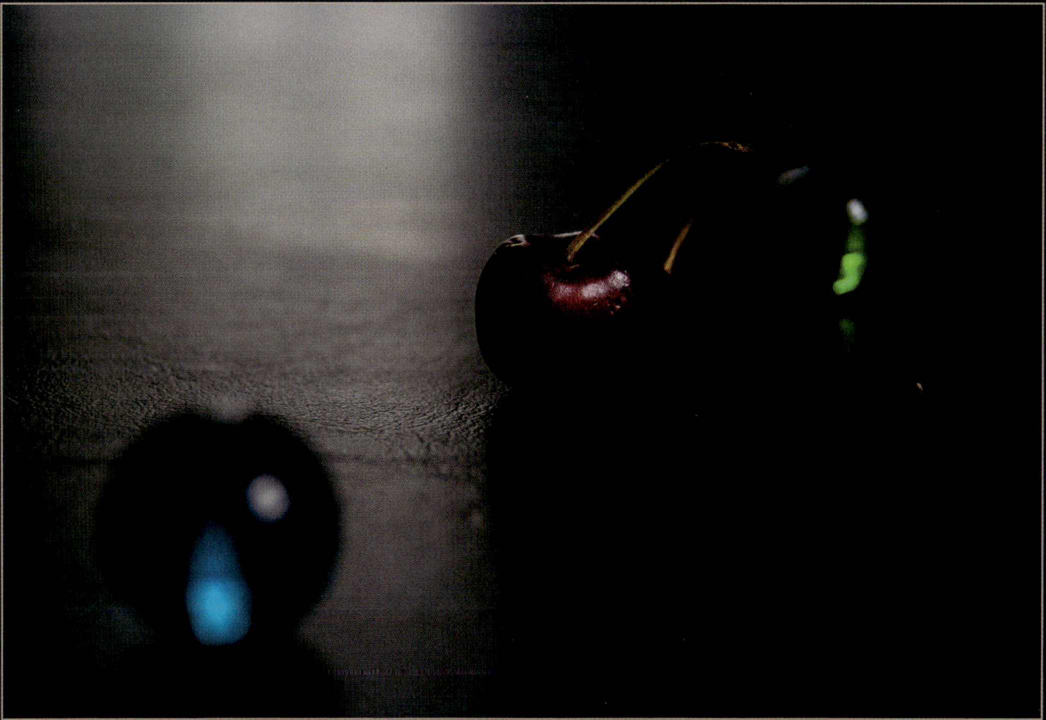

There are several supporting elements in this composition (including the window reflections), but they all have one job, and that is to compliment the cherry

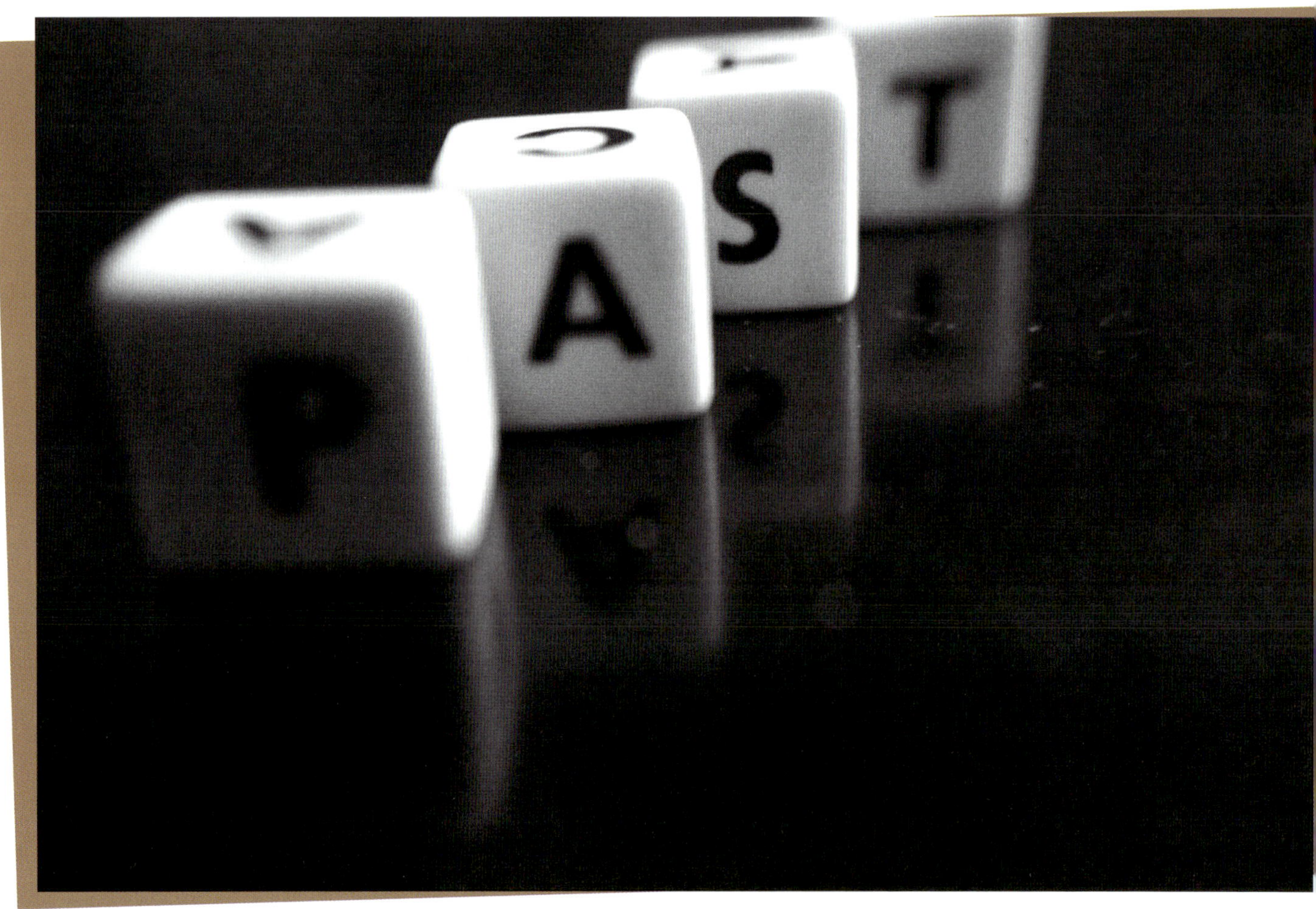
PAST

Chapter 8
A History of Photography

In this chapter, I look at the major innovations in photography using a timeline approach. This is followed by a look at the major aesthetic movements within photography, from the birth of pictorialism to postmodernism. I will conclude with a section on Alfred Stieglitz, who I feel was the most influential person in 20th century visual arts in the United States. Stieglitz was closely involved in the birth of both pictorialism and modernism and, as if this was not enough, he was responsible for bringing the work of the great painters Picasso, Matisse, and Cézanne to an American audience.

A Selective Timeline

The following is a whistle-stop tour through some of the milestones of photography's evolving technology. It is highly selective, and there are many omissions. It is not a technological discussion and does not describe the chemistry of different film types or the physics behind digital innovations. The intent is to show the context of various innovations in relationship to one another.

Early Advances

The roots of photography can be traced back to the fourth and fifth centuries BC, when the Greek philosopher Aristotle and the mathematician Euclid described a pinhole camera, and the sixth century AD, when Anthemius of Tralles used a *camera obscura* in his experiments. Even though these early forerunners of today's cameras were only capable of projecting an image, they were more than mathematical and scientific curiosities. The 18th century painter Canaletto was known to have used a camera obscura, and it is widely thought that Vermeer, the 17th century Dutch master, used one as well.

It wasn't until a means of fixing the image was developed, to make it portable and permanent, that photography really took off. This was the real beginning of photography as an artistic and social medium. In 1826, the French inventor, Joseph Nicéphore Niépce, produced the first permanent photograph on polished pewter. This means that photography, as we know it, has been in existence for a little less than two centuries.

Camera Obscura: a darkened enclosure having an aperture usually provided with a lens through which light from external objects enters to form an image of the objects on the opposite surface.
– Merriam-Webster

Niépce died in 1833 and left his notes to Louis Daguerre. In 1839 Daguerre announced a process that used silver on a copper plate, and the daguerreotype was born. During the Industrial Revolution, the daguerreotype satisfied a demand for portraits from the new middle class. This ready market helped to drive the technological development of photography.

Sometime prior to 1839, William Henry Fox Talbot discovered a different method using silver iodide to fix an image, but he didn't refine it to make the images readily available until after Daguerre announced his process. Around this time Talbot created the *calotype* process, the first method that involved a negative. This was significant because it was the first time that one exposure could produce any number of prints.

The word *calotype* comes from the Greek for *beautiful impression*.

The terms *negative* and *positive* were coined by the mathematician, astronomer, and experimental photographer John Herschel. He also came up with the word *photography*, without realizing it had already been used by Hercules Florence five years before, in 1834. Herschel was also responsible for the cyanotype process, which made blueprints possible, and he was the first to use a glass negative.

Glass plate and printing technology was refined throughout the 19th century until 1884 when George Eastman developed the first roll-film technology. This led directly to the film technology still used by photographers today.

Film Cameras

The Brownie box camera—introduced by Eastman's company, Eastman Kodak, in 1900—was as revolutionary in its day as the first consumer digital cameras were in ours. The device was a simple one, a box with a simple lens at one end, a roll of film at the other, and bare minimum controls. It cost $1 (equal to around $50 today when adjusted for inflation). The Brownie was the first consumer camera and was marketed as such, with the slogan "You push the button and we do the rest." The Brownie was responsible for the whole concept of the snapshot. For the first time, taking a photograph did not have to be a big production.

There were many different Brownie models manufactured over the years until the final one in 1962. Later versions of the Brownie had a doublet lens, facilitating smaller cameras due to the shorter distance between the lens and the film. Some models also allowed for the attachment of a flash unit.

Like all cameras at the time, the Brownie's exposed film surface was the same size as the intended print. The concept of using a smaller negative and then producing an enlarged positive originated around 1905, although it wasn't realized until 1913–1914. Oskar Barnack, the development manager at Leica, adapted a device that was used to take exposure samples of cinema film. Using the enlargement concept, he converted it to become the first 35mm stills camera. The 35mm standard, of course, is the one that survived from film to digital and is now the standard DSLR sensor size.

The landmark year of 1948 saw the first instant camera—the Polaroid Land Camera—hit the market. For those of us who are used to the instant world of digital, it is hard to imagine just how big this breakthrough was in its day. Named after its inventor, Edwin Land, the camera was manufactured by Polaroid. *Land* was dropped from the name in 1983, after the inventor retired. The first color Polaroid instant film became available in 1963.

The ability to instantly record a scene and see the results led to a number of new uses. Police and other investigators used instant cameras to produce unalterable images of crime scenes for evidence that could be developed, so to speak, in the presence of others. Professional photographers used them to get an instant check on lighting and other aspects of a scene. The cameras were also used on movie sets for visual note taking, which was especially useful with regard to continuity.

Obviously, the onset of digital photography had a big impact on the instant camera. In 2008 Polaroid shut down three film factories and laid off 450 workers. In 2012 the company released some digital cameras with built-in printers.

The instant camera is often wrongly referred to as an Instamatic, which is a different type of camera altogether. The Instamatic was a successful line of cameras that Kodak first brought to market in 1963. Convenience and low price were the main selling points. The film was contained in a cartridge, which also housed the exposure counter and film backing plate. This meant that the cameras themselves were cheap to manufacture. The Instamatic continued the Brownie's ethos of affordable and convenient snapshot photography.

In 1972 Kodak released the Pocket Instamatic, a small camera that used smaller film, called 110, than the original Instamatics. These cameras were popular well into the 1990s. The Pocket Instamatic's negatives were small, and the images could not be enlarged much without a serious degradation in quality.

The last country to sell Instamatics was the United States, where they remained on sale until 1988.

DSLRs

The first commercially available DSLR was the Kodak Digital Camera System (DCS) 100, released in May 1991. It was aimed squarely at the photojournalism market, and to this end it came with a separate portable digital storage unit that stored either 156 or 600 images on its 200-megabyte hard drive, depending on whether or not compression was used. There was also an external keyboard intended for captioning the photographs. The camera was capable of producing 1.3-megapixel images. Just shy of a thousand units were sold.

Kodak completely dominated the DSLR market in the early years, and Nikon didn't even begin to develop the D1, the camera that revolutionized the industry, until 1996. This was five years after the release of the DCS 100. Nikon had the advantage of being able to develop a camera from the ground up, unlike Kodak, which had basically built upon existing technologies and products.

The Nikon D1 solved several problems associated with DSLRs at the time, the major one being picture quality. The camera was advertised as having 2.7 megapixels, but it has since been revealed that there is more to this number than meets the eye. Each megapixel on the D1 is in fact composed of numerous photosites, and this explains the sensor's excellent signal to noise ratio and overall sensitivity.

It is fair to say that this is the camera that revolutionized the photography industry. It had the image quality and frame rate that made it a serious proposition for journalists and other demanding users. The other huge factor was price—Nikon's D1, at around $5,000, was much cheaper than any of Kodak's offerings. It also demonstrated that digital could actually rival film in quality.

Today, two companies, Nikon and Canon, dominate the DSLR market. They both produce a range of cameras that are aimed at the professional market as well as at amateurs. Professional cameras tend to be much more rugged and generally have higher specifications. The DSLRs at the consumer end of the market are capable of excellent pictures, though, and many professionals are on record as preferring their smaller size and lighter weight.

Digital Point-and-Shoot Cameras

Point-and-shoot cameras, like the Brownie and the Instamatic from the predigital era, get most photographers hooked. In many ways, digital compacts are even more seductive than their predecessors because they can do much more and produce photographs of a high enough quality to be used just about anywhere and for any purpose.

The 1996 release of the Canon PowerShot 600, with its half megapixel sensor, was the camera that started the ball rolling. Olympus and Casio also released digital compact cameras during the same year, and January 1997 saw the first Nikon in the category. Nikon's Coolpix brand is still in use today, as is Canon's PowerShot moniker.

Camera Phones

As much as DSLRs have changed professional and serious amateur photography, their impact was nothing like that of the camera phone. The camera phone changed everything because this was the development that meant people left the house with a camera whether they intended to or not.

The first camera phone, the Sharp J-SH04, was released in 2000 and cost $500. It took only three years for sales of this phone model to outpace sales of all stand-alone digital cameras combined, proving there was a demand for them. The majority of cell phones didn't come equipped with cameras until 2006.

The sensor size in camera phones increased quickly. The first 1-megapixel and 2-megapixel camera phones were introduced in 2003. In 2006 the first 10-megapixel camera phone was released. The increases in sensor size were driven largely by Samsung. By 2010 more than 81 percent of the world's mobile phones came equipped with a camera.

The camera phone that had the most impact was the iPhone from Apple. The original iPhone released in June 2007 came equipped with a 2-megapixel camera, and by 2011 the sensor had increased to 8 megapixels on the iPhone 4 S. The hardware is not the real story here, though. Apple set up a system whereby third parties could create software programs called apps (short for applications) for the iPhone. Apps were created for photo effects and filters, as well as online image storage, among other things. This ability to extend functionality beyond taking a picture and e-mailing it to someone, combined with the cachet of the Apple brand, made the iPhone a game-changing product.

Computers and the Internet

Computer software and the Internet have been just as influential in digital photography as have the cameras themselves. It is not really possible to use a digital camera without using a computer to store images and/or to download them to online storage spaces. Much has happened to enable this, from the software that comes with just about all cameras for uploading images to a computer hard drive to websites designed for storing and showing images.

The first version of the image-editing tool Photoshop was released by Adobe in 1990. This software, which has become the industry standard, was originally designed for manipulating images that were scanned into a computer. Photoshop really came into its own in version 3.0 with the introduction of its Layers function. Other image editors have come onto the market since then. Many of them are free, such as GIMP (originally designed to run on Linux systems but is now cross platform), or much lower in cost than Photoshop, such as Adobe's own Photoshop Elements, which is a pared-down version of Photoshop aimed at the amateur photographer market. Most cameras come with their own cataloging and editing software that is suitable for basic changes, but most photographers need more, which is where third-party software comes into its own.

Many companies now offer online storage for images, usually in the form of a website that allows the images to be organized by the photographer and viewed by others. The most popular of these is Flickr, which first saw the light of day in 2004 and was acquired by Yahoo! a year later. The website was originally set up as a forum with picture-embedding capabilities for an online game. The game was shelved, but Flickr was developed as a photo-sharing site. Flickr currently has more than 6 billion images on its servers, and the average daily upload volume during 2011 was 1.54 million images, or 1,070 per second!

An Aesthetic History

Broadly speaking, aesthetics can be defined as critical reflection on art, culture, and nature.

The thing about histories, especially for such subjective topics as art, is they are not true. People, especially artists, do not wake up one day with a master plan for the rest of their lives and then faithfully execute it until the moment they either retire or die. Rather, they start projects, finish some, shelve others, and change their minds often. Photographers contradict themselves a lot and are often capable of complete about-turns with regard to artistic philosophy and aesthetics. These changes of heart don't happen as a Hollywood movie would have us think—there is usually no grand moment with a date and time stamp—but rather it is a process that often involves two steps forward, one back, and three sideways. What I present here is not the complete aesthetic history of photography, but rather a history comprised of the elements that resonate with me.

Up until around 1890, nothing much of interest happened regarding photography aesthetics. It was all about the mechanics and simply recording what was in front of the camera. The photographers of the day presumably worked hard to get a satisfactory composition in terms of balance, but the priority was the recording itself, the capturing of the likeness of the people, the scene, or whatever else was in front of them.

Pictorialism

Toward the end of the 19th century, with the rise of a movement called pictorialism, photography became interesting beyond the technical. This movement introduced the photographer as more than a mere technician because he (and at the time it was usually a he) was expected to manipulate the image to get a more artistic result.

Some of the methods used were soft focus, alternative hues such as browns or blues, and visible brush strokes, all of which allowed the photographer to elicit an emotional response from the viewer. It is hard to imagine now just how much of a breakthrough this represented.

Pictorialism was at its peak from around 1880 until the beginning of the First World War. It was certainly still being promoted into the 1940s. I frequently make the argument that although the name *pictorialism* may have fallen into disuse, the underlying philosophy has never disappeared and is, in fact, as strong as ever. Pictorialism follows the lead set by painters, especially those such as the impressionists, and much photography still does this. Think of how many images use a narrow depth of field to blur the less important part of the image. This technique is firmly rooted in pictorialism, even though gelatin on the lens or some other strategy may have been used to achieve the end result.

It is interesting that the two main downturns in pictorialism, that is, the end of its major period and the time when the name itself ceased to be commonly used, coincided with the beginnings of the two world wars. At its heart pictorialism is a romantic movement. It is all about the photographer as an artist, imparting emotion to the viewer via the photograph, and I don't think it is a coincidence that something as cataclysmic as a world war made the soft lines and dreamlike blurs of pictorialism wrong for the time. A starker, more brutal aesthetic probably seemed more fitting.

Various groups were formed with the intent of promoting the pictorialist ethos. One such group was the photo-secessionists, formed by Alfred Stieglitz and F. Holland Day. Stieglitz is, arguably, the most influential artist of the 20th century, which I will further discuss later in this chapter. The biggest question regarding the photo-secessionists was what exactly they were seceding from. Pictorialism was already taking hold, and the group's stated aim that the photograph was the vehicle for the artist to achieve his subjective vision was exactly in line with pictorialism. But there is no doubt that this group did a lot to promote the idea of photographer as artist, which lies at the root of pictorialism.

The British counterpart to photo-secession was the Linked Ring, or to state its full title, Brotherhood of the Linked Ring, a group that seceded from the Royal Photographic Society. The Linked Ring was created by Henry Peach Robinson, George Davidson, and Henry Van der Weyde in 1892 to further the idea that photography was as much an art as a science. As an aside, there appears to have been a strong Masonic influence in this group because their logo was three rings chosen to represent the Masonic ideals of Good, True, and Beautiful.

It is important to note that although painting and photography have their separate histories, there has always been a cross-fertilization of techniques and ideas. Many photographers started out or at least trained as painters, and many painters took photographs. It has to be said, however, that the painters, including Manet, Degas, Gauguin, and Cézanne, seemed to use the camera as a means of recording and as a technical tool, rather than as a creative one.

Modernism

If there were a rule regarding artistic movements, it would be this: the bigger the movement, the bigger the movement that will rise up to present an intellectual and aesthetic challenge to it. Photography is no exception, and the modernism movement was the antithesis of pictorialism. Photographic modernism came about in the 1920s and was driven by what the photographers of the time termed *straight photography*. As can be discerned from the name, straight photography represented a rejection of all the manipulations of pictorialism. Traditional photogenic subjects gave way to industrial scenes, depictions of poverty, and still lifes that were unadorned and bare. Edward Weston, one of the major modernists, photographed his now famous peppers images. These peppers were not selected for their traditional beauty, and some even had maggots in them. Perhaps more important than the shift in subject matter was the shift in technique. The soft focus and other painterly techniques disappeared. The idea was to get the most objectively accurate shot possible.

A group that came to epitomize the straight photography ideal was Group f/64, co-founded by Willard Van Dyke, Edward Weston, Ansel Adams, and Imogen Cunningham. The group had only seven confirmed members, but there were a few others who exhibited with them. The name f/64 refers to a small aperture on a medium-format camera. The smaller the aperture, the greater the depth of field, and thus the more accurate the photograph. Group f/64 was established in opposition to pictorialism, and the name reflects this. There are different stories about how the name was actually chosen, but the logic is pretty much self-evident.

It is important to understand that many photographers who championed pictorialism made a smooth transition to modernity. In fact Stieglitz, the founder of the postsecessionists and one of the greatest proponents of pictorialism, was extremely influential in the modernist movement.

It is also important to note that movements do not always have a neat beginning and end. Just as many photographers are currently working with the pictorialist ethos, there are also many working in a modernist vein despite the fact that we are now supposedly living in the postmodern era. I look around at what photographers are currently working on and I see a mix of everything that went before, often in the work of a single photographer. This is exciting

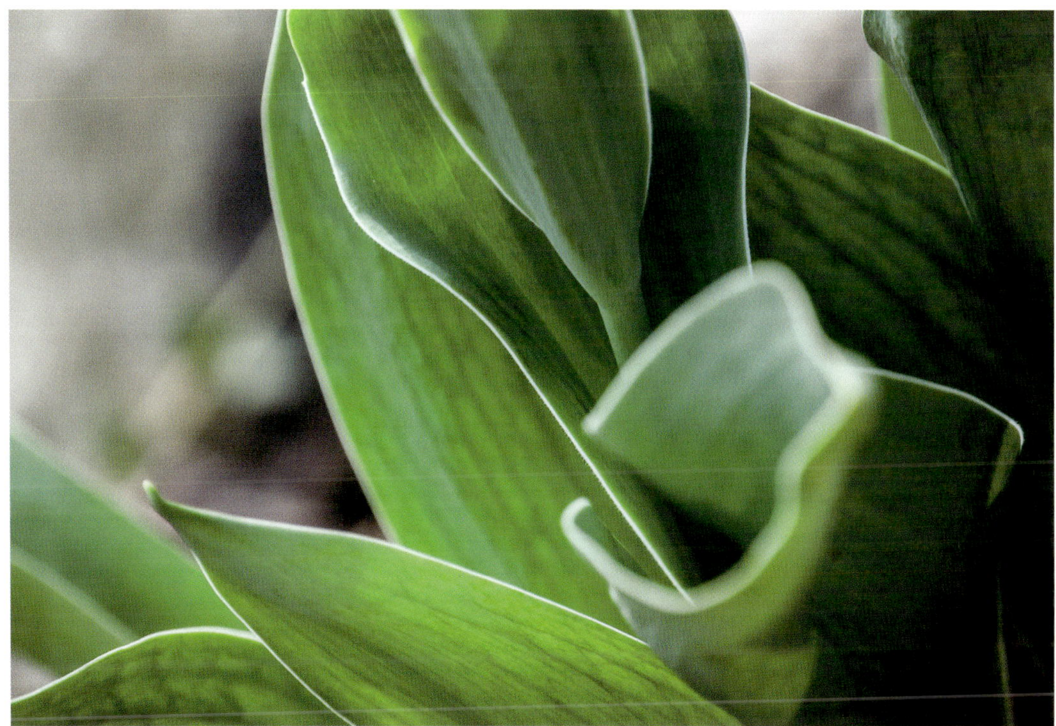

It is often easier to get a good photograph of part of a plant than the whole thing. The trick is to see it in terms of lines, tones, and hues as opposed to a complete living entity. Paul Strand, the pioneering modernist photographer, explored this idea.

and makes the current situation volatile and unpredictable, which is a good thing. Too many histories try to make things linear when they aren't. There is often a need for simplification to get an idea across, but the dangers of pigeonholing have to be taken into account.

The major artistic movement to come after modernism was, predictably, postmodernism, simply translated to *after modernism,* and this is where things get complicated. As with all major art movements, postmodernism was and is largely a reaction against what went before, which, in the case of photography, was the objective—the detached, science-based approach that worked toward a single version of reality.

Postmodernism

Modernism was a minimalist photographic philosophy in many ways—the photograph was to be as close to an objective reality as possible. Of course, the photographer could choose and frame the subject or scene, but after that his or her duty was to ensure as faithful a reproduction as possible. Postmodernism, by contrast, is off in the other direction, denying the existence of a single unifying reality. It is a philosophy of relative truths, where each individual's reality is unique and is based on personal experience. Of course this means the photographer is no longer a detached modernist observer but is now front and center, the focal point of the action, in many ways like a pictorialist on steroids. Whereas pictorialists had the freedom to manipulate the surface elements of a photograph, postmodernists have carte blanche to do absolutely anything as long as they are being true to something in themselves. It is often said that pictorialism was about what was being photographed, modernism was about the photograph, and postmodernism is all about the photographer.

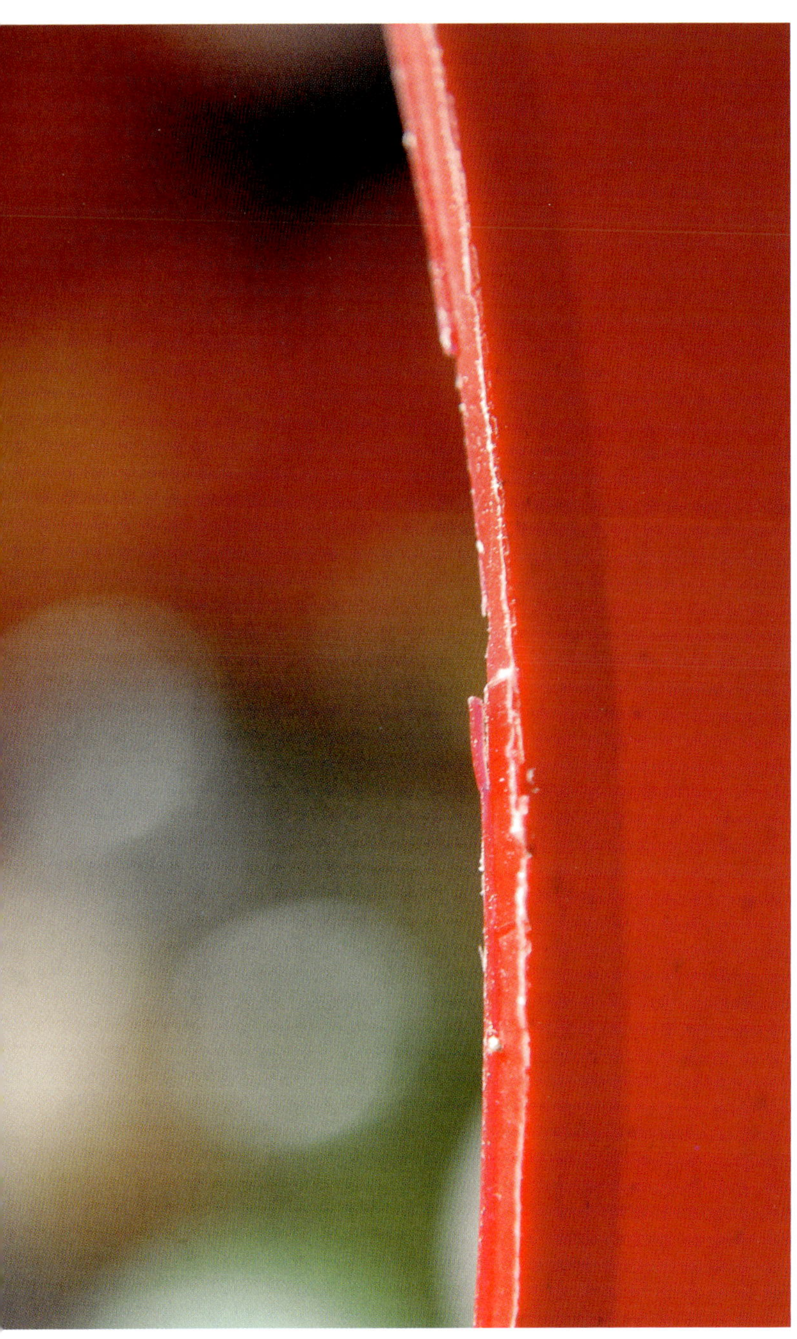

In terms of composition, many photographs taken today are similar to those shot a hundred years ago, while others are firmly rooted in the here and now

This may sound trite, but there is more than a little truth in it.

This headlong dive into subjectivity does present a problem, though. It is never easy to write a history of anything at the best of times, but the fragmentation represented by postmodernism makes it all but impossible. The modernist photographers may have had their differences, but the commonality, the belief in an objective condition, makes a cohesive account possible. Up until the 1920s the aesthetic history of photography could just about be represented by a straight line, but with the advent of postmodernism that changed and the linear model no longer works. A better way to view it is as a central hub with lots of spokes.

Alfred Stieglitz

Alfred Stieglitz was an accomplished photographer in his own right, but his major contribution to photography was as a promoter. It is fair to say that he had more to do with photography being accepted as a legitimate art form than any other person. He also played a prominent part in determining the direction of photography, from the founding of the photo-secessionist pictorialist group, to modernism, through his promotion of the work of Strand and Weston, among others. The foundation of aesthetic minimalism in photography can be traced directly back to this shift from the painterly approach of the pictorialists to the much harder reductionism of the modernists.

Stieglitz promoted photography through several galleries in New York and in the major photography journals for which he was responsible. He was a perfectionist who was obsessed by his mission to promote photography and photographers. He worked himself to the point of exhaustion several times during his life, often fulfilling two or even three roles that on their own would constitute full-time work. Whether he was driven more by a passion for the arts or by a passion to establish his own place in history is up for debate, but there is no doubt that he did more to raise the stature of photography than anyone else.

At the age of 20, Stieglitz moved to Germany for six years, and it was during this time that both his first writings and first photographs were published. His piece "A Word or Two About Amateur Photography in Germany" appeared in the British *Amateur Photographer* magazine, and his photography later won in the magazine's competitions.

At the behest of his father, Stieglitz reluctantly returned to the United States in 1890. Three years later he became the coeditor of *American Amateur Photographer*. He was hands-on, writing most of the reviews and articles. This further enhanced the reputation that Stieglitz had started to build in Europe. The Linked Ring, the prestigious London-based pictorialist group, elected Stieglitz as a member. This gave him the impetus to push on with his own ambition, which was to put photography on par with the other visual arts.

Stieglitz used his leverage to force a merging of the two major but moribund New York photography organizations, the Society of Amateur Photographers and the New York Camera Club. The merged organizations became the Camera Club of New York. Stieglitz created the magazine *Camera Notes,* which was an outgrowth from the club newsletter, and it was generally regarded as the best photography publication in the world at the time. Paradoxically, Stieglitz limited his coverage in the magazine to only a few of the most well-established photographers, despite his claims to want to push the boundaries so that photography could take its rightful place as a true visual art; the resulting conflicts with the staff took its toll on his health. After four years, he eventually resigned from the magazine because of the internal politics.

While he was recuperating, Stieglitz was urged by a fellow photographer to put on an exhibition to be judged solely by photographers, as opposed to painters and other types of artists as was the norm. Stieglitz was invited by the National Arts Club to put together such a show and was granted complete artistic control. The exhibition that opened in March 1902 was a public and critical success. This show marked the start of the photo-secessionist movement. The exact reason for the timing is not certain; some accounts indicate that it was a political move by Stieglitz to give the impression of support for his opposition to the New York Camera Club, but others give a more benign interpretation. Stieglitz was greatly influenced by a show in Munich several years earlier, where the artists involved called themselves the Secessionists. The idea of seceding from something, whether artistic or political, always resonated with Stieglitz. The show did mark his final and complete break from the New York Camera Club. More importantly, though, this show represents the point in history where photography became an art form in its own right.

From today's vantage point the idea of pictorialism as something revolutionary may seem a little odd. The shift from the ultrastrict Victorian photographic conventions to an atmosphere in which photographers were free to manipulate the medium to project their own vision was, however, every bit as revolutionary as the later shift from pictorialism to modernism. The secession was not purely an aesthetic one; it was a revolt against entrenched views and power structures within the art and photography worlds.

After another bout of exhaustion and a trip to Europe, Stieglitz set up the Little Galleries with his photographer friend Edward Steichen. After a few photography shows, a painter, Pamela Colman Smith, approached Stieglitz, and he put on a show of her watercolors and prints along with the more usual work of photographers. The show was a great success, and it

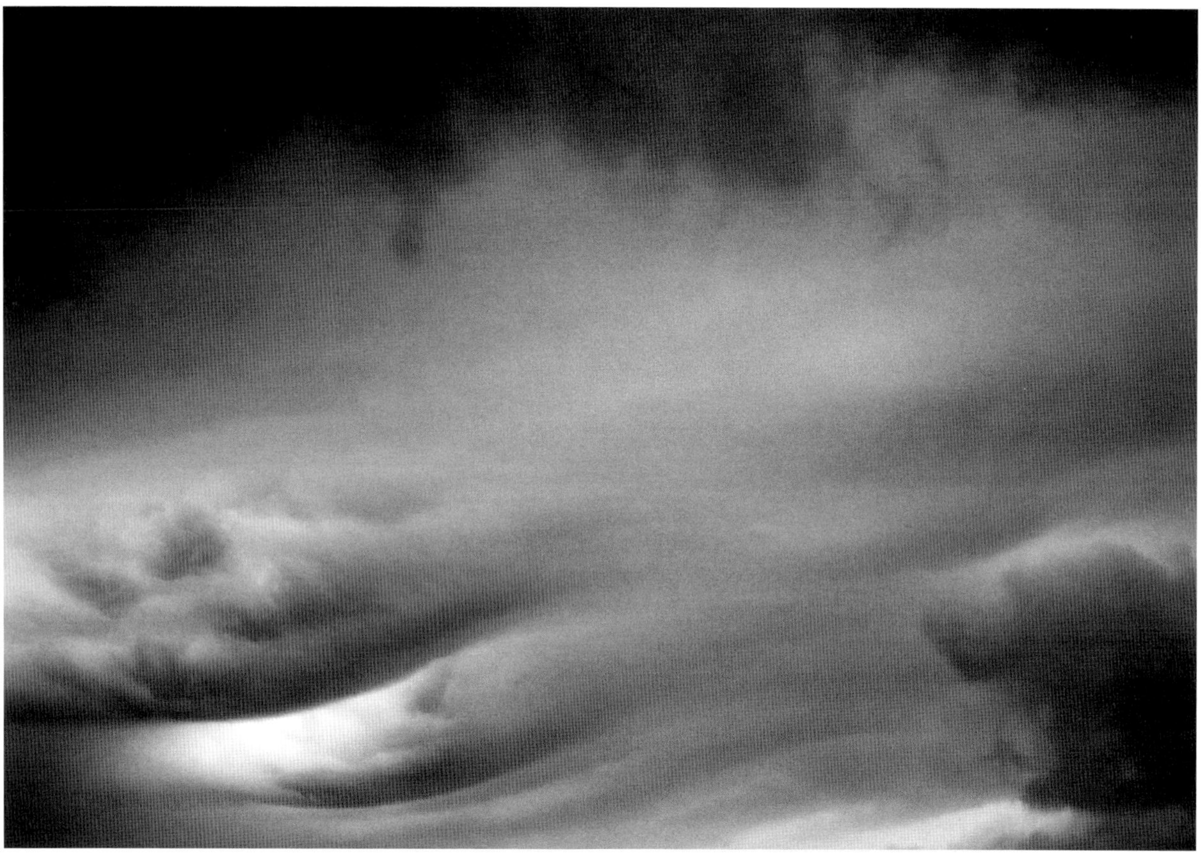

Photographing clouds can be surprisingly addictive!

marked the point in time when Stieglitz pivoted from being a promoter of photography to a promoter of visual modern art in general.

The Little Galleries closed due to lack of money, but was reopened a short time later under the new name 291. It was now no longer primarily a photography gallery but one that sought to break down the barriers between all art forms. Stieglitz was driven by a desire to show different art forms by different artists and from different regions side by side. He wanted the public to be able to compare and contrast different mediums and practitioners without having to consider a meaningless hierarchy based on the medium used. Stieglitz was responsible for introducing Americans to many of the great European artists, including Picasso, Matisse, and Cézanne. He also exhibited work by relatively unknown American artists and photographers.

In 1915 Stieglitz was introduced to the photography of Paul Strand, which was different from that of the pictorialists. The subject matter was everyday and the compositions were stark. They were what the camera saw, with no artistic embellishments. The beauty of these images came from the lines, tones, and shapes. It was reductionist photography, capturing only what was essential and doing away with the decorative and incidental. This was modernism and the beginning of minimalist photography. Stieglitz put on a major exhibition of Strand's work at

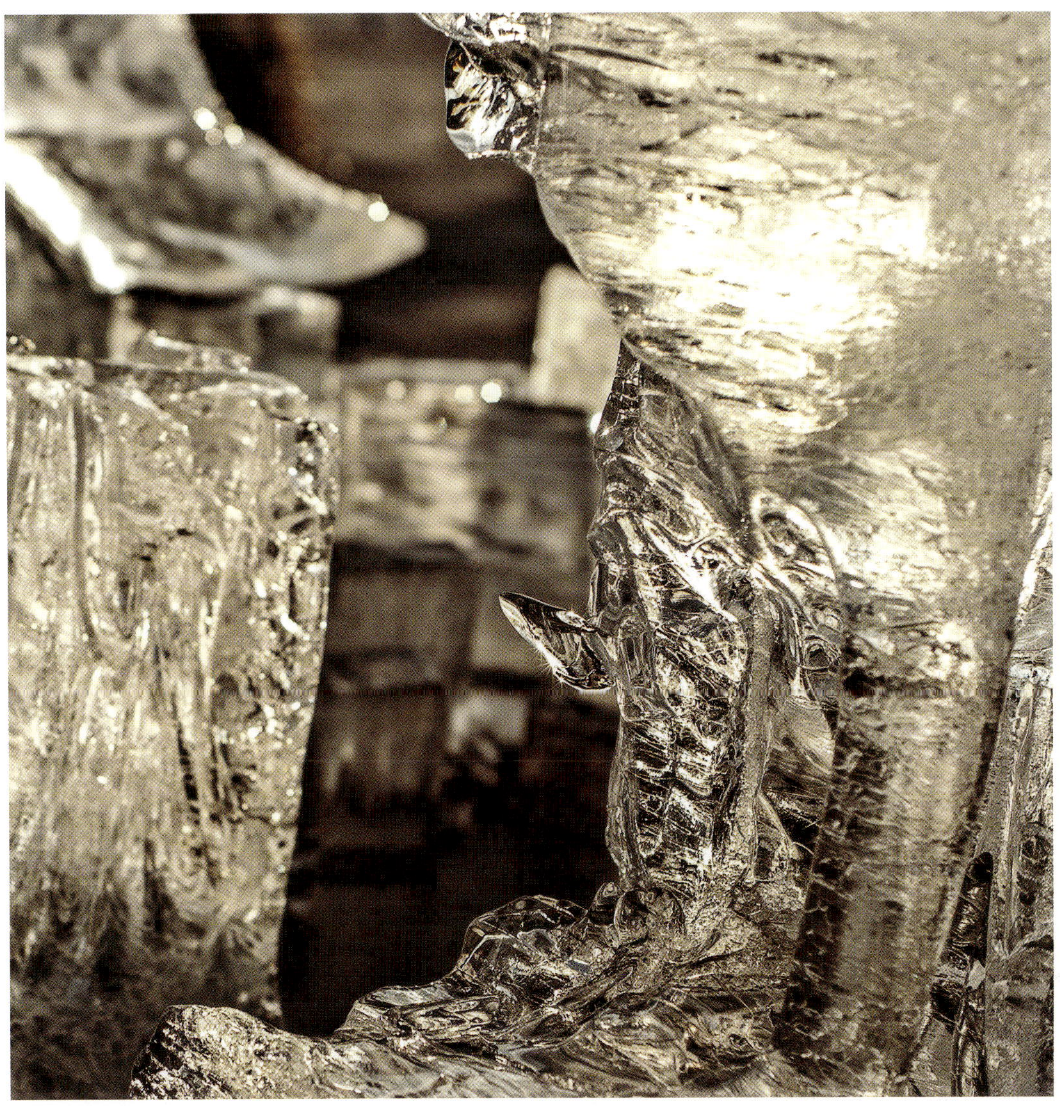

Stieglitz used clouds because they forced him to make the image. The same principle works with other subjects. This scene is comprised of several large blocks of melting ice and, as a photographer, I could make of it what I wanted to.

291 and devoted most of the last issue of *Camera Work*, the magazine he created after resigning from *Camera Notes*, to Strand's photography.

It was at this time that Stieglitz embarked on his relationship with the painter Georgia O'Keeffe. From 1918 to 1925 he photographed her obsessively. Many of these photographs were closeups of various parts of O'Keeffe's body, including the famous ones of her hands. These images are both modernist and minimalist. Everything in the images is essential and nothing is decorative, yet Stieglitz manages to catch the essence of O'Keeffe in these deceptively simple images.

Stieglitz's next major project was equally significant—he decided to photograph clouds. He described several reasons for embarking on this undertaking, including a desire to show that his success with photography was not due to his choices of subject matter, and to find out for himself what he had learned in his time as a photographer. Stieglitz spent 12 years taking

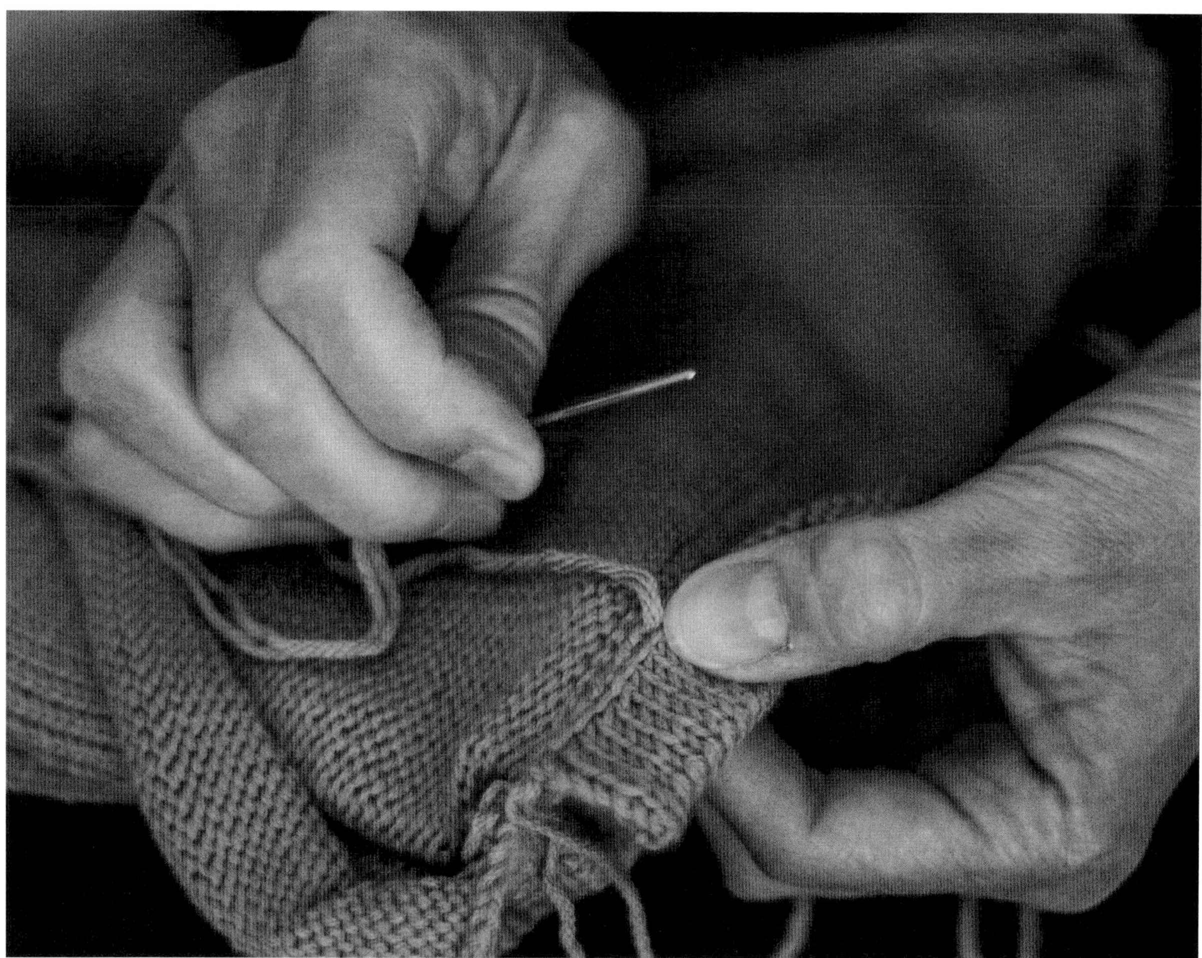

Zeroing in on a body part gives an image strength. As Stieglitz realized, emotion and intensity is not conveyed just in the face.

hundreds of photographs of clouds, and these images are recognized as the first intentionally abstract photographs ever taken.

Stieglitz represents a great study in the importance of context, in the importance of the bigger picture. Here was a photographer who was not only passionately concerned about the state of photography, but also its relationship to the other visual arts. This constant questioning made him a more complete photographer, but more important it moved photography, and visual arts in general, forward.

If your own photography ever ceases to excite you, spend some time reading works about and by photographers that you admire, especially the ones who changed history. Knowing our place, or desired place, in the grand scheme of things is important. It gives us direction and gives our photography purpose.

Further Reading

Peterson, Christian A. 1997. After the Photo-Secession: American Pictorial Photography, 1910–1955. New York: W. W. Norton & Company.

Whelan, Richard. 1997. *Alfred Stieglitz: A Biography*. Cambridge, MA: Da Capo Press.

Nothing defines modern photography more than highly saturated images featuring a prime color.

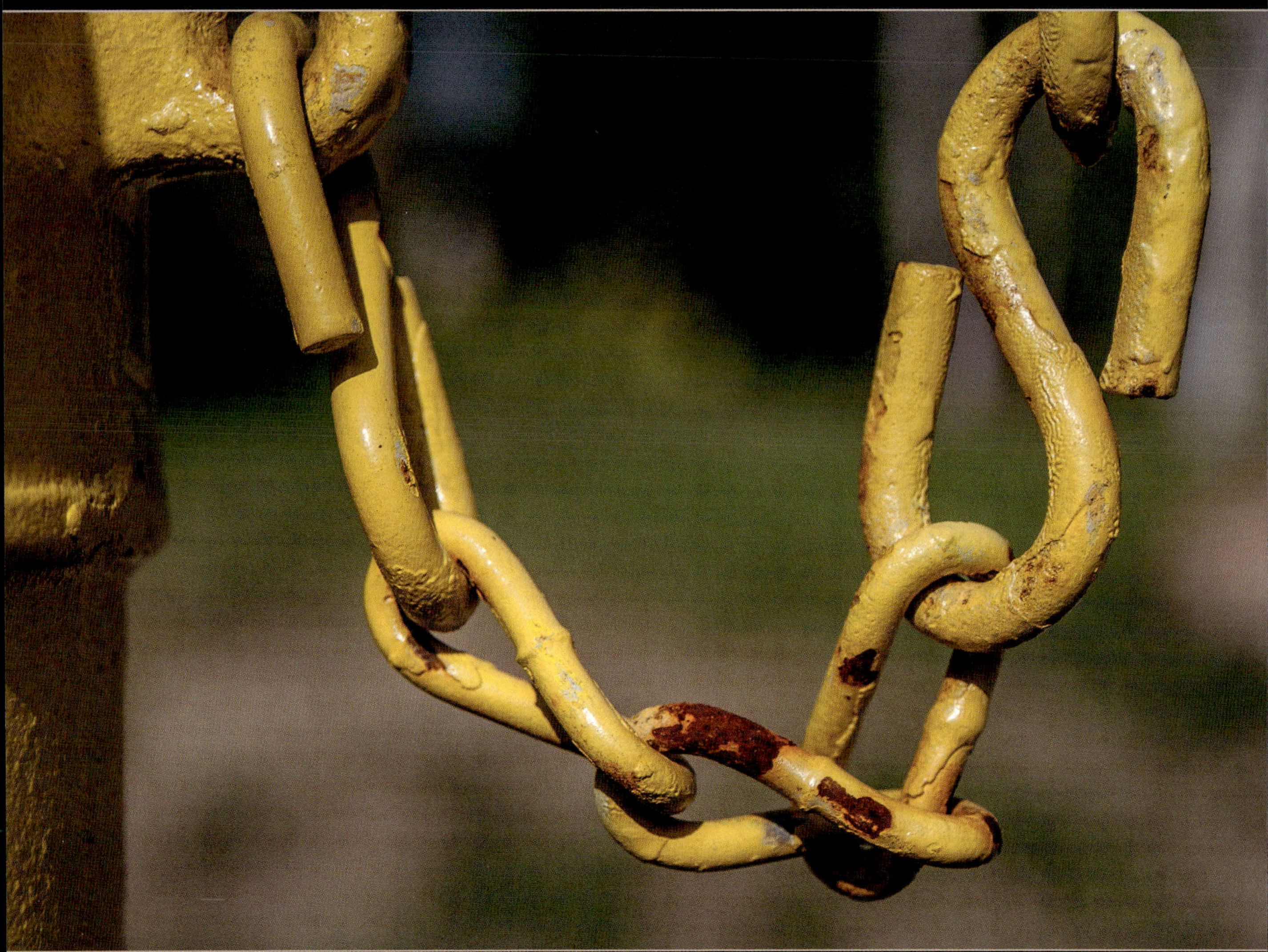

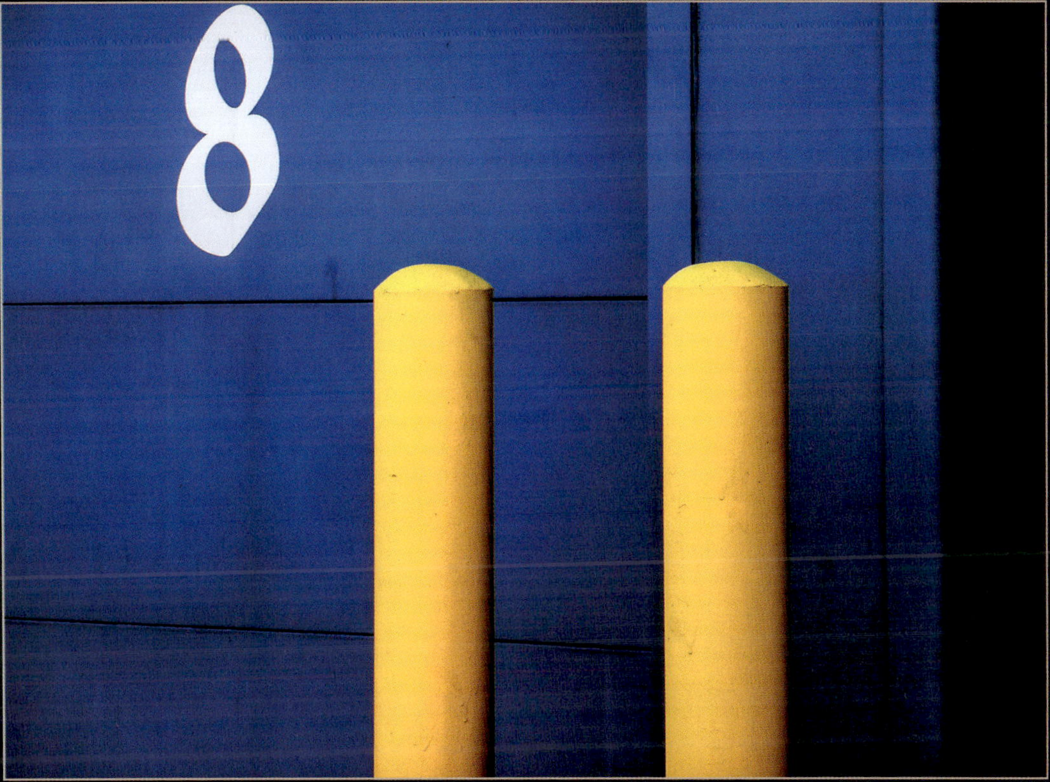

Numbers or text can add interest to an image. The 8 and the interplay of yellow and blue are the major factors here.

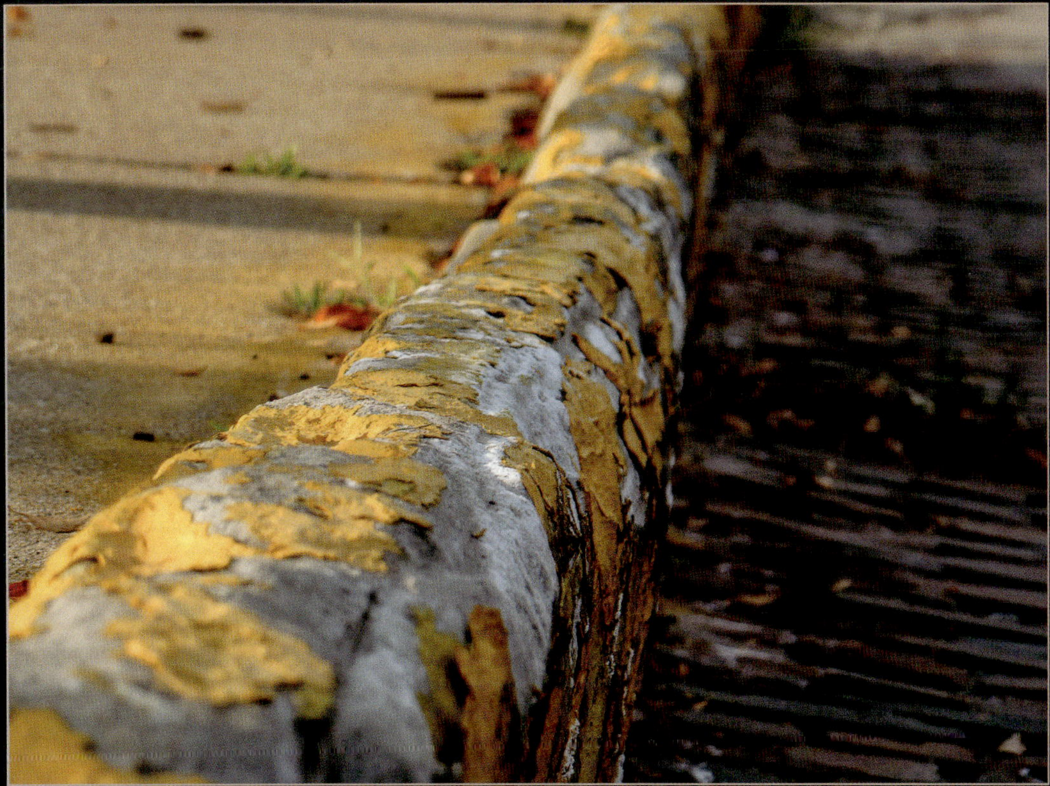

Paint peeling from a curb

A weed and a painted curb

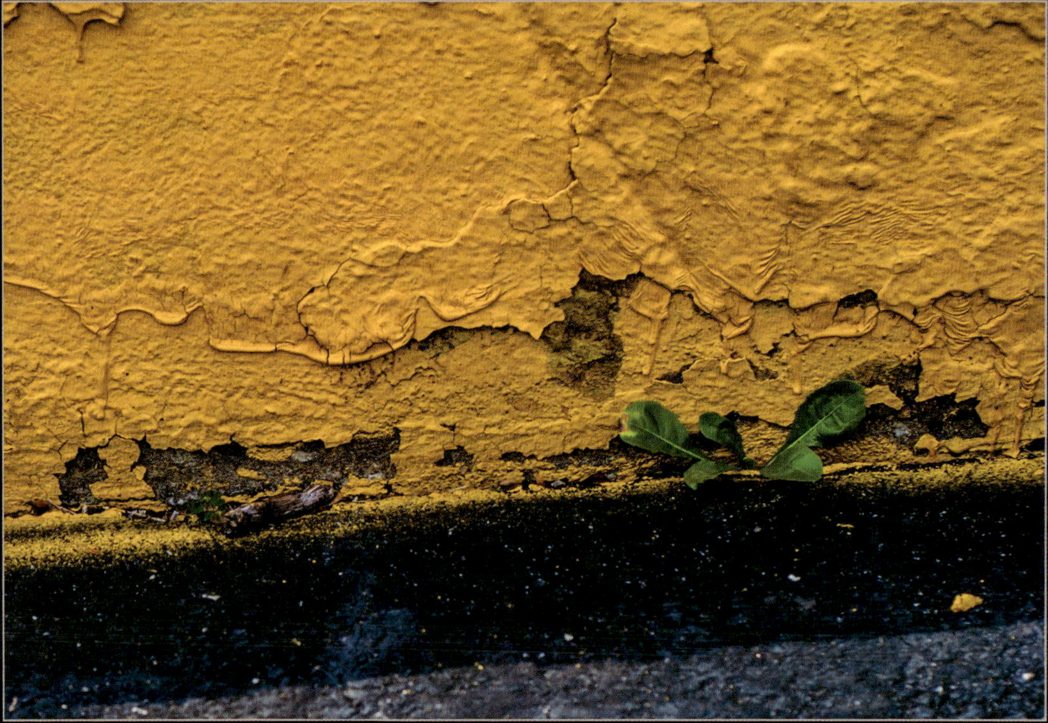

This way

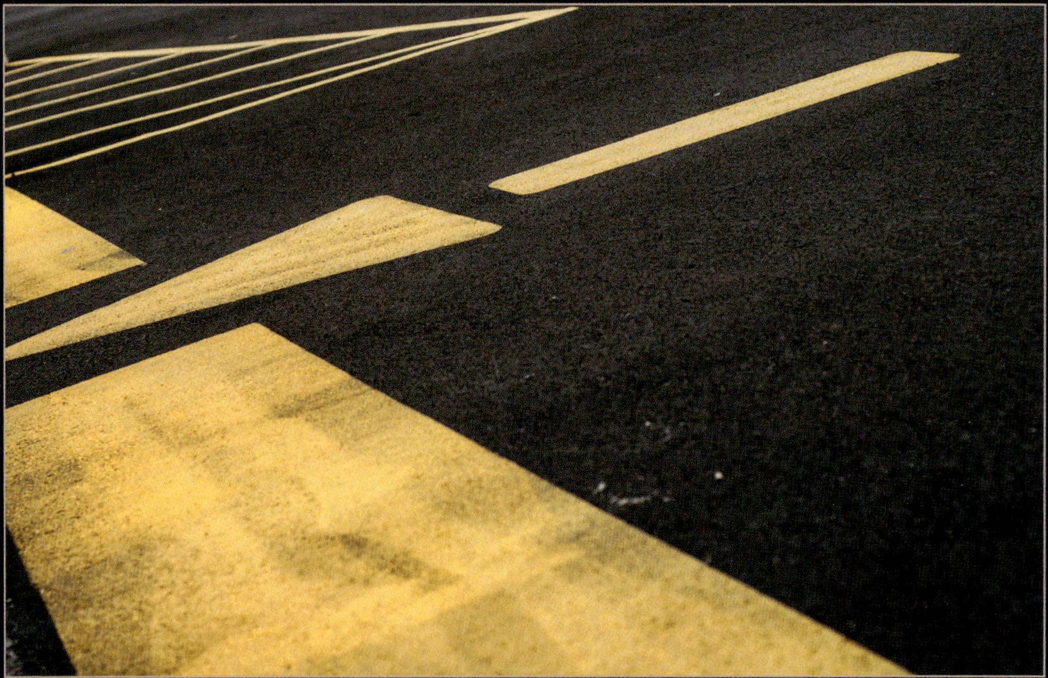

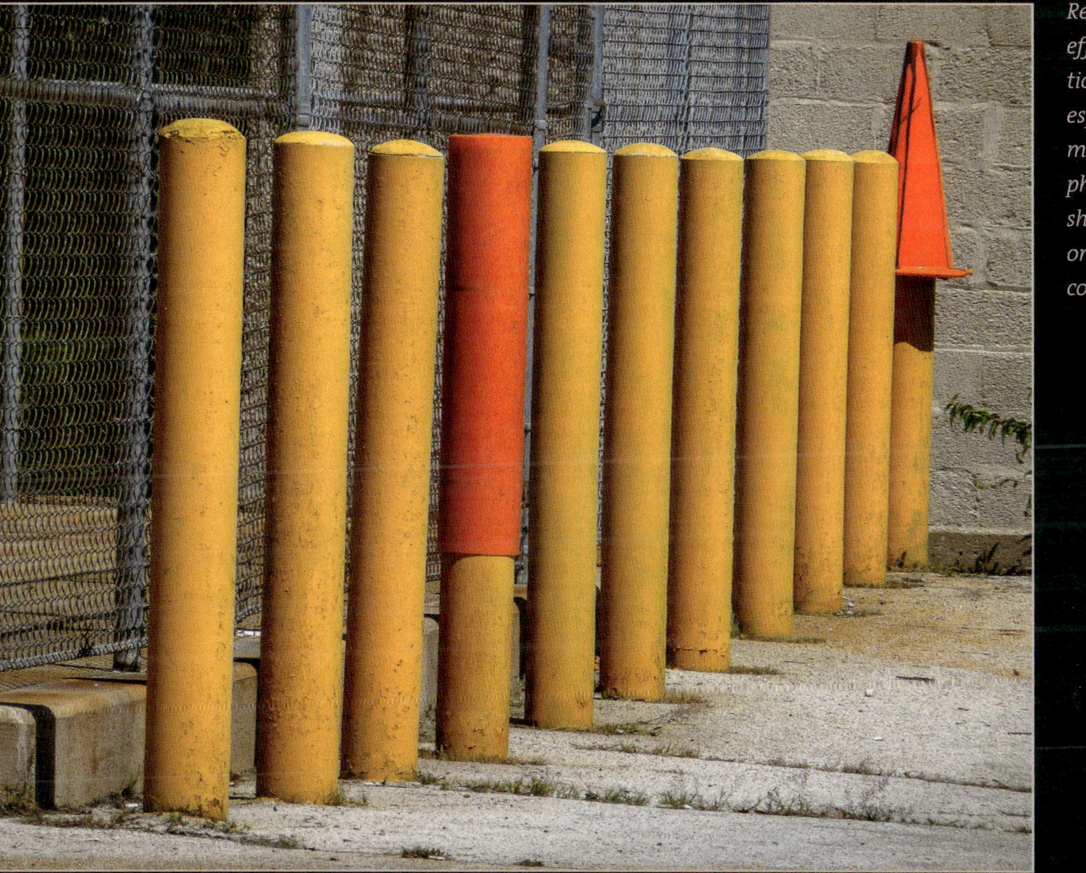

Repetition is an effective compositional element, especially in minimalist photography. The relationship between the orange pole and th cone adds interest

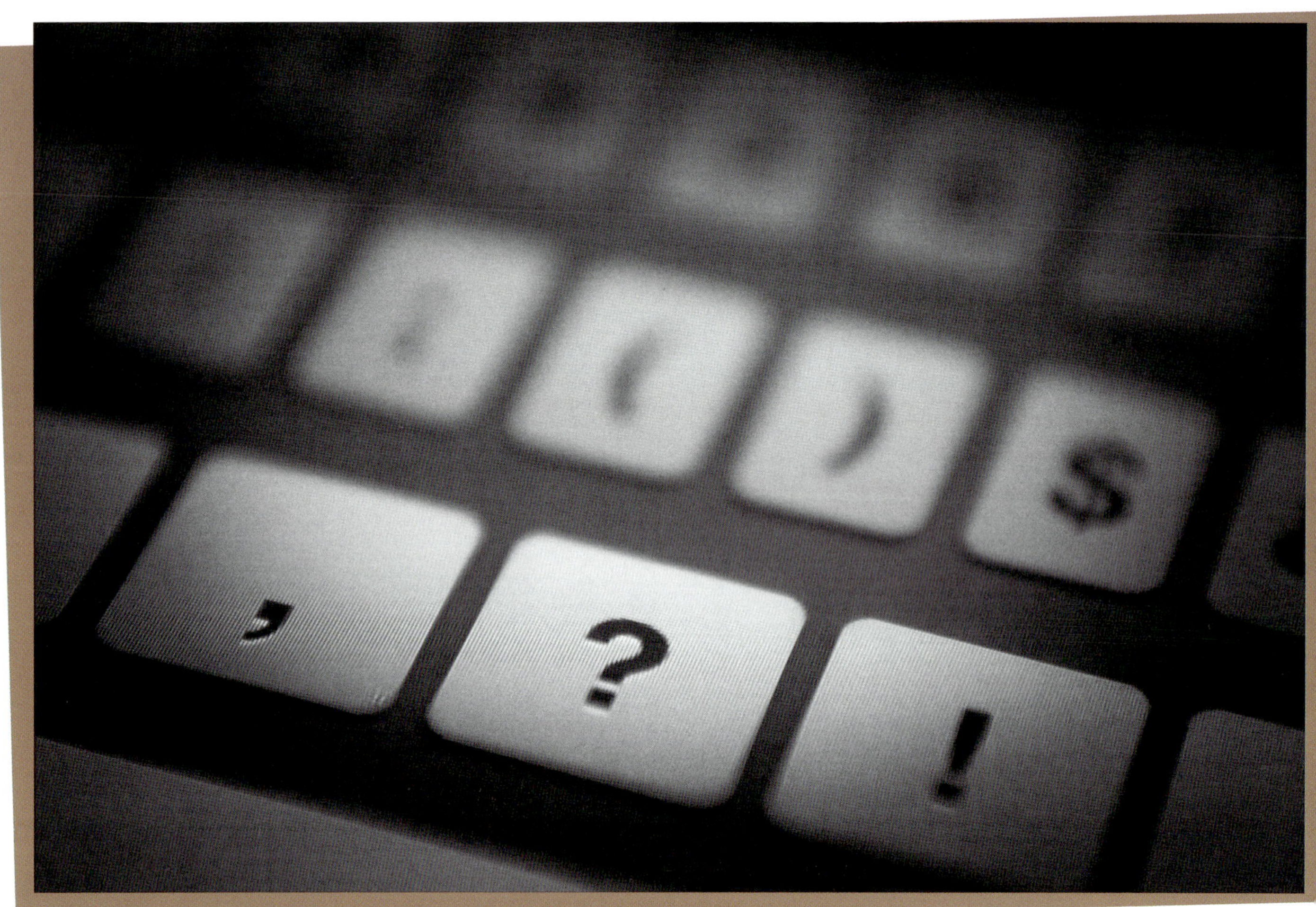

Chapter 9
What Next?

Photography is progressing at an ever-accelerating rate and this appears to be the pattern for the immediate future. All aspects of photography—equipment, technology, distribution, and aesthetics—are being, and will continue to be, affected.

Change

Change comes in two basic types. The first and most common type is the incremental kind, where refinements are made to existing ideas and technologies. An improvement in sensor sensitivity and technology that enables point-and-shoots to have greater zoom capability are a few examples of incremental change. The second and more rare type of change is when something happens that changes things at a fundamental level—a change that makes *everything* different.

Ask someone what the biggest change in photography has been over the past few decades, and it is a fair bet that the answer will be the transition from analog to digital. The move from analog to digital was a truly fundamental change, but maybe not for the reasons most people think. In terms of technology it was a big change, but it didn't change the fundamentals of *photography*. Light is still gathered on a surface to create a permanent version of reality. The fundamental change was a *socioeconomic* one. In a nutshell, we suddenly had free film, and this really did change everything. The initial investment may have become higher, but the ongoing costs had, in effect, been reduced to almost zero. This lowering of the economic bar of entry into photography has produced fundamental changes, and it is those changes that will form the basis for the rest of this chapter.

The Facebook Effect

I don't think anyone predicted just where the invention of digital photography was going to lead. What started out in many photographers' minds as a bit of a gimmick made photography affordable for the masses. Photographs can be taken without film and developed without a darkroom. Now, for an initial outlay of less than $200, which will buy a good compact camera, most anyone can not only shoot good-quality images but can also do their own post-production on a computer that was originally purchased to pay bills or browse the Internet.

Another important change made possible by going digital is much smaller cameras. This meant that cameras could be a secondary part of another device. Adding a camera to a cell phone may seem like an obvious thing to do, but the person who first thought to do this probably impacted photography more than Cartier-Bresson and Adams combined. Ironically, this anonymous innovator may not have even been a photographer. With cameras built into their cell phones, people who previously did not consider themselves photographers on any level now always have a camera on their person.

This image, as well as the images on the following four pages, were edited with Pixlr-o-matic, one of an increasing number of retro-style editors. Available effects include intense color saturation, simulated light leaks, textures, and many more.

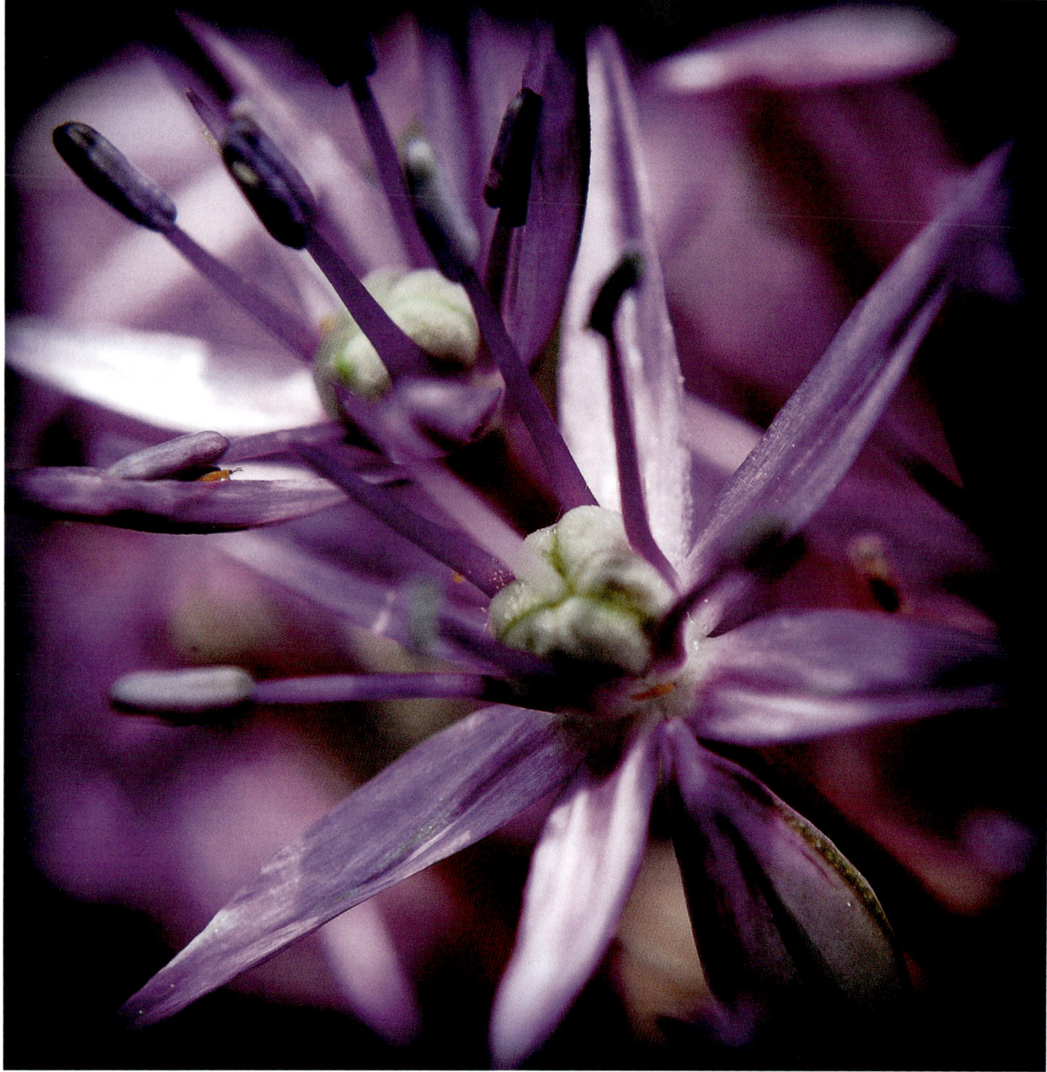

Initially, the whole cell phone camera idea seemed to be little more than a gimmick. The image quality was low; the images could be e-mailed to friends or stored on a personal computer, but for what? This is where Facebook and other social networking websites come into the picture, so to speak. With the advent of these sites, people could share their pictures with the world, and they could also look at the images of others. Millions of images suddenly entered the public realm and, more importantly, the public consciousness. Over time digital camera technology improved, especially the small-scale camera equipment, and today we have smart phones, such as the iPhone, with cameras that can compete in quality with midrange point-and-shoots. Now everyone is a photographer.

You may think this social aspect is all very interesting but has little impact on the professional end of the photography market. This is not the case. Until digital cameras first appeared, and even for the first few years after,

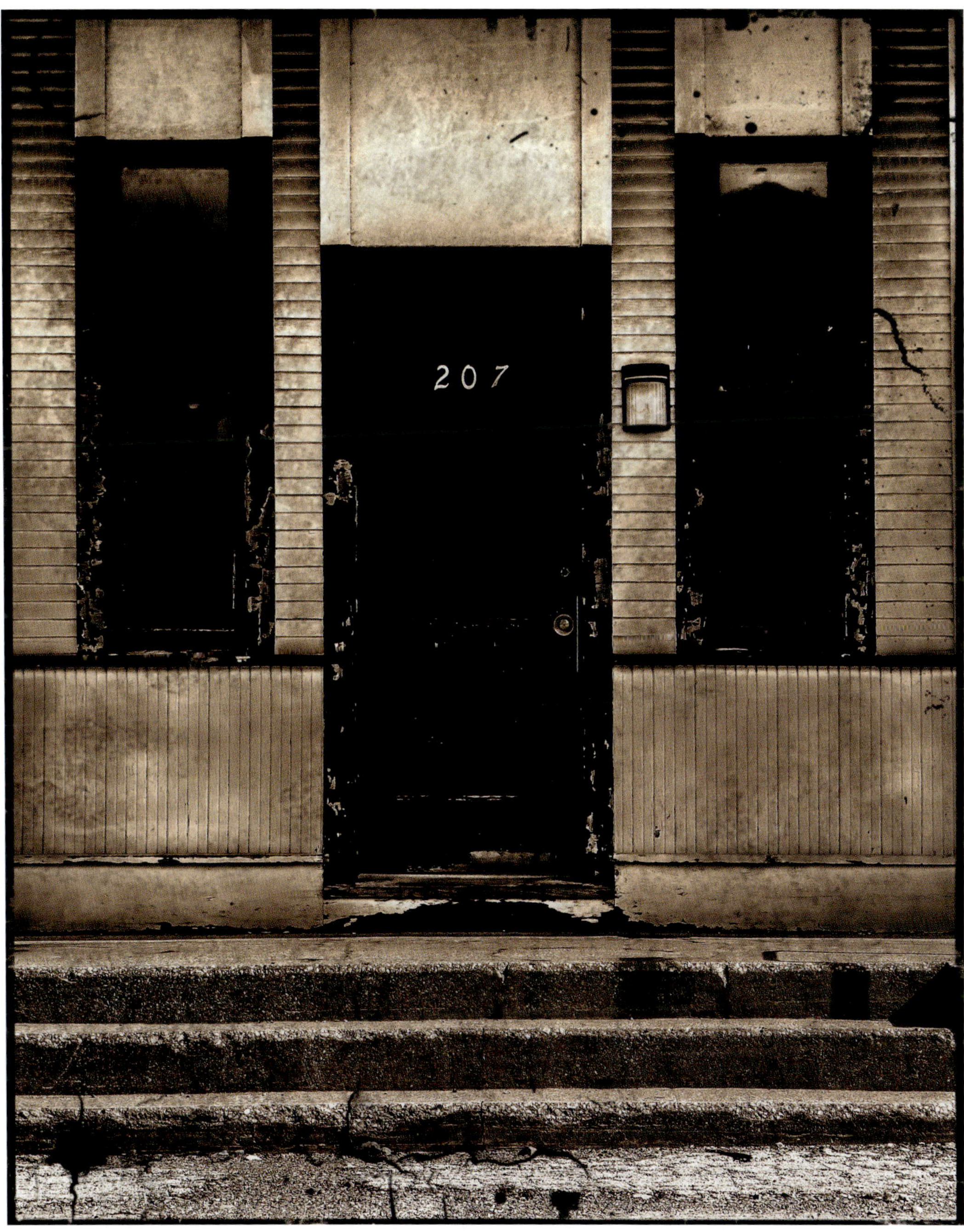

the whole photography aesthetic was driven by very few photographers and picture editors. It was a top–down process. These gatekeepers determined everything from what images were appearing on billboards and in magazines to what articles were being written and published for hobbyists and amateurs. Experimentation was extremely limited and, with a very few

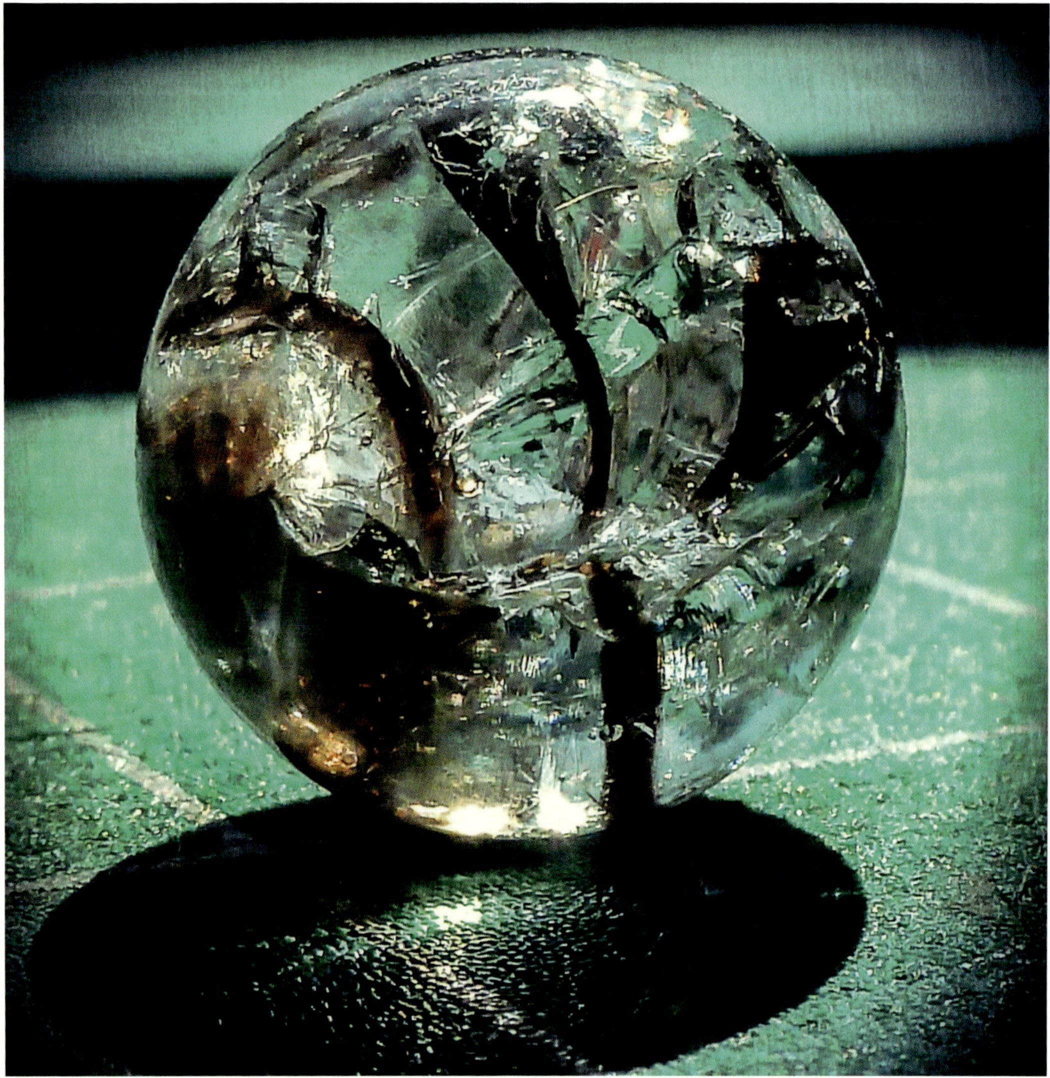

honorable and brave exceptions, photography was artistically stagnant.

Now a wonderful anarchy has come to photography, where it is permissible to attempt just about anything. Of course not everything works, but the days of being ridiculed for trying something different seem to be over. Photography is no longer the conservative profession and pastime that it once was. The net effect of the freedom to experiment is a lowering of the bar of entry into the field. This has turned photography on its head, and rather than being an occupation controlled by a very few elite photographers and editors, it has become one where those at the bottom and in the middle of the pyramid are the true driving force. The original leaders now have to struggle to keep up.

This newfound democracy may be the new normal; perhaps another group will eventually rise and dominate, or the old guard may return under a different guise. History teaches us that the most likely outcome is a mix of these. I think

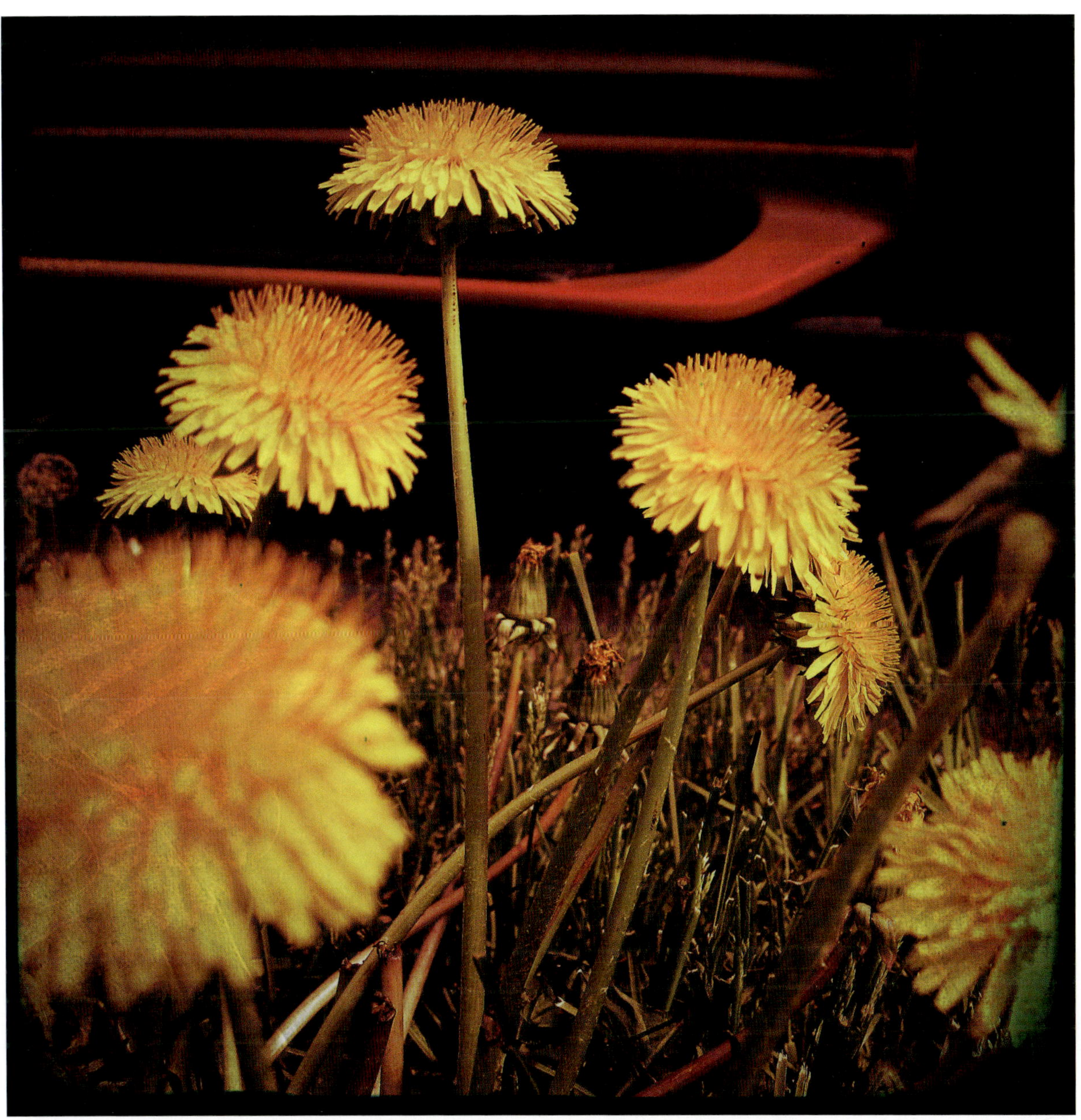

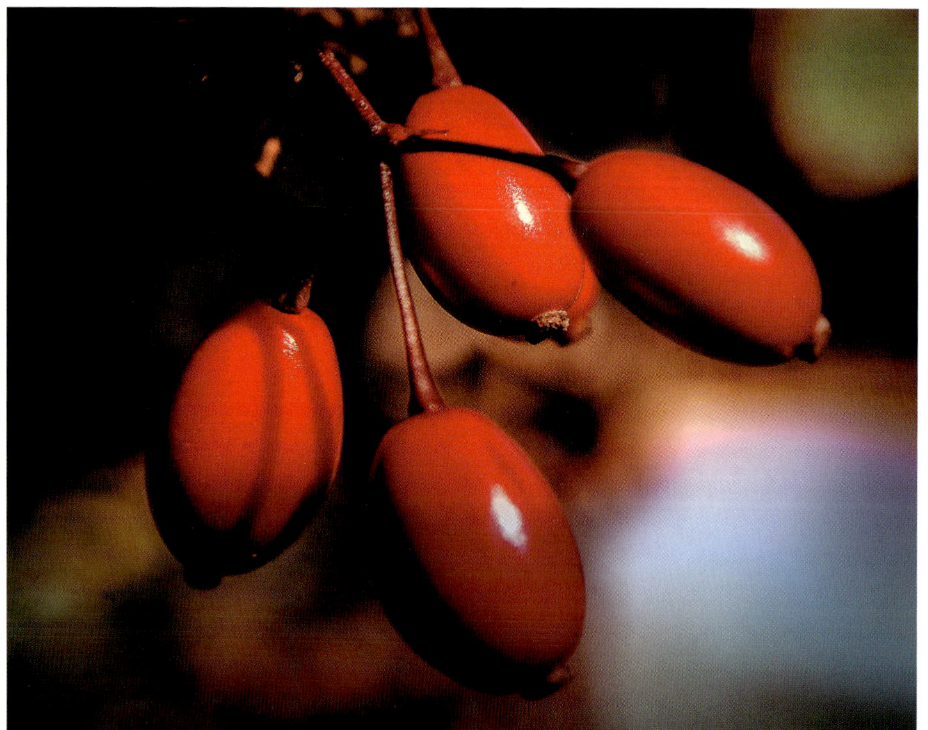

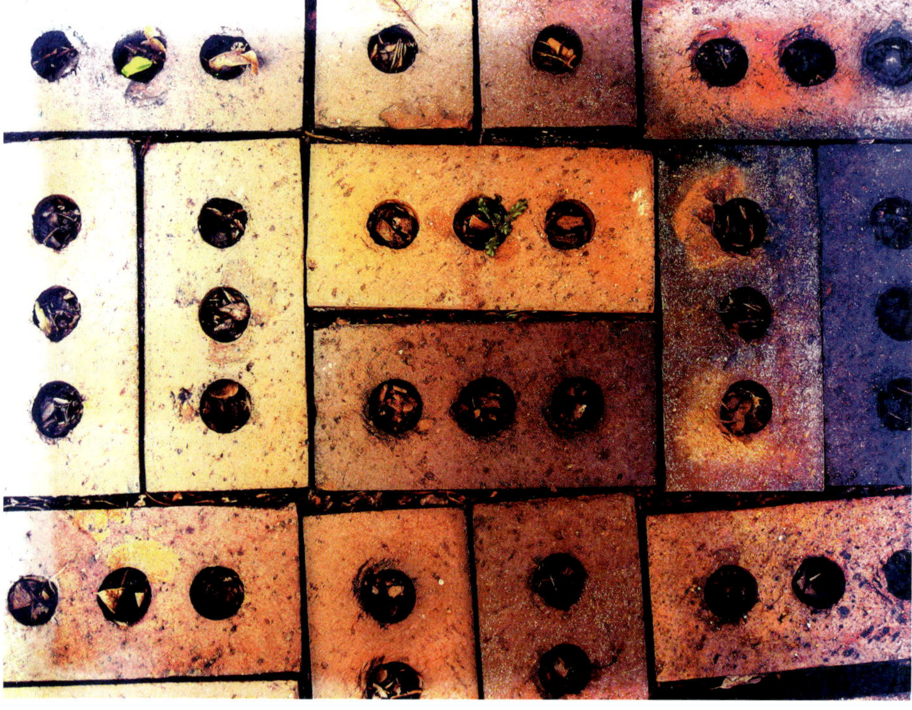

photography will be better off the longer the current state of happy chaos remains—there will be more variety, and it will be harder to tame it, neuter it, make it thoroughly predictable, and reduce it to mere commodity.

Who Will Be the New Gatekeepers?

The old days of half a dozen leading photographers and editors controlling everything—either directly by their acceptance or rejection of others' work or indirectly through their juniors in the industry who took their word and philosophy as gospel—are not likely to return, at least not in the same way.

I do believe that some of the most influential figures in photography will again rise to the top and, intentionally or not, position themselves as the gatekeepers and self-appointed arbiters of good taste. The photography industry will rush to sign up these individuals for huge sums of money, giving them even more power, and the currently fluid situation will begin to stabilize yet again. The glimmer of light this time around is that some good people will understand the dangers of stagnation, fight to be the influencers themselves, and push a philosophy that encourages experimentation and risk taking as opposed to playing it safe and imitating others. Some of the current high-profile personalities seem to be very different than their predecessors, insomuch as they really do seem to value change and encourage the pushing of the envelope. Unfortunately, there are also some who want to cast their own particular approaches in stone and promote said approaches as the only true way to photography nirvana.

How These Changes Will Affect You

Nothing is ever certain in this world, but I would bet a fair amount of money that things will never return to the way they were before. Changes in style and what is considered photographically acceptable will no longer be driven from the top down. Just about anyone can afford to both take photographs and, even more importantly, publish them for zero cost and almost zero effort. There are now literally thousands of photographers who can publish an image online knowing that hundreds, if not thousands, of people will see that image within seconds of it being uploaded.

The really exciting thing is that anyone can become one of those photographers by building up a following on one of the social networks. Providing there is something in the work that appeals to others, it will happen. Also, bear in mind that not everyone has to *like* what you are doing; as long as some people do, that is enough. My own photo publishing criteria is simple: I post work on the principle that if something about a particular shot interests me, then it will probably interest someone else. The shot itself doesn't have to be a masterpiece or even all that good, as long as there is something about it that may be of interest to someone else. The question that goes through my mind when selecting an image is: If someone else were to publish this, is there anything I would find useful in it?

This approach is very much the antithesis of the conventional wisdom that says to only post your best work online. I think the new approach, which is much more akin to a scrapbook or sketch pad than a traditional portfolio, keeps things fresh and enables a dialog between the photographer and the people who view the photographs. This is far more useful than handing down a carefully crafted precious jewel of an image that has only one function: to show the world what a great photographer you are.

The shift from the portfolio approach to the conversational approach encapsulates the biggest change of the past decade. The photographer, regardless of expertise, is now a part of an ongoing dialog both with other photographers and with the public at large; the days of splendid isolation are over, probably for good. This flexibility has created another interesting dynamic: the roles of student and teacher are now much more interchangeable. The old way, where photographic wisdom was passed down the hierarchy, appears to be over. In the current climate, an experienced photographer can and, more importantly, should learn from novices. I often learn more from those new to photography than I do from those who have been around longer. Someone new to the arena simply doesn't have the same baggage as someone who has been around for a long time (including me), and the self-censorship is much less in evidence. A new photographer is most likely to help me see something in a new way.

The Future

Some predictions can be made with a fair degree of confidence while others would be far less certain. The online revolution and the downward trend in camera prices will almost certainly continue the democratization process that photography is currently undergoing. The impact of other innovations, such as cameras capable of recording real depth information could have a profound impact on photography or they could just be a passing fad.

The End of the Decisive Moment?

Thanks to continuing technological improvements, we could be on the verge of something very new. History has shown us that digital storage space and processing power increases rapidly over time. At the turn of this century, $800 would buy a 3.3-megapixel camera with a 16-megabyte memory card. The megapixel count has since risen steadily, with the lowest now coming in at around 10 megapixels and costing around $100. But the real leaps have been made in storage space. Memory cards are now up in the 32 gigabyte range, which represents an increase of two thousand times the capacity. They are also drastically cheaper. And they keep on getting cheaper while the capacity levels continue to increase.

Until now, this ongoing increase has had an incremental impact because the benefits were limited to not having to swap cards out so often and a financial savings. Memory cards are now becoming large enough to store high-quality video from which still images may be extracted that are of equal quality to a traditionally shot still image.

Most photographers are aware of Cartier-Bresson's decisive moment concept: everything has an exactly right moment, and the photographer's task is to become skilled enough to instinctively press the shutter-release button at that exact moment. Now, consider that at some point in the near future, video formats will be developed for 10-plus-megapixel uncompressed formats that operate at extremely high frame rates. When this happens, *each second* of video footage will yield at least two-dozen high-quality photographs.

The question is, how will photographers respond to this development? Will they still try to capture the decisive moment, or will they shoot video and then select the best frame either in-camera or later on the computer? If the decisive moment approach is lost, the photographer will, in effect, become a photo editor whose role at the time of shooting is limited to framing and checking settings. The real work will be done after the fact on a computer.

This will be a dramatic change, but there has been a trend in this direction for some time now. In the days of film most photographers handed the film roll to someone else to develop it; but even if they had their own darkroom, the changes they could make to the images were limited. As digital has taken hold, photographers have had to become familiar with so-called lightroom techniques that mimic darkroom processes and enable more creative possibilities.

An interesting new product, the Lytro camera, captures light in such a way that the depth of field can be chosen *after* the photograph is taken. This means that all the information required to allow any depth to be rendered in focus is stored. Currently this camera is targeted at the consumer market, claiming ease of use as a selling point. It is not hard to imagine a higher-spec version that could be used to produce professional-quality images. It all comes down to available storage. This device again reduces the number of decisions a photographer has to make at the time of shooting. All you have to do is point the device in the right direction and press the button—all decisions about exactly what should be in focus can be made after the fact. There is nothing to indicate that increases in storage space, coupled with huge decreases in the price of storage, will not continue apace. If the current trend continues, it could result in a thousand fold increase over the next 12 years and would give us around 16 terabytes of storage. With this amount of storage available, it is possible that future cameras will be able to combine the very high-quality video approach and the Lytro three-dimensional space approach. This would allow for just about every decision to be made at the editing stage. It would also make video editing very interesting, but that discussion is beyond the scope of this book.

The Online World

Until a couple of decades ago, the only way for fine art photographers to get their work before a wider audience was to have it published in a book or to exhibit it somewhere. Commercial photographers had to secure work through advertising or editorial channels. Either way, they required the approval of at least one other person before their images could be seen by anyone other than those who they could physically show their work to.

Of course this has now all changed. Work can be published on the Internet by anyone with a reasonably fast connection to social networking sites such as Flickr, Facebook, and more recently (and it has to be said, more photographer friendly) Google+. Just putting the images up

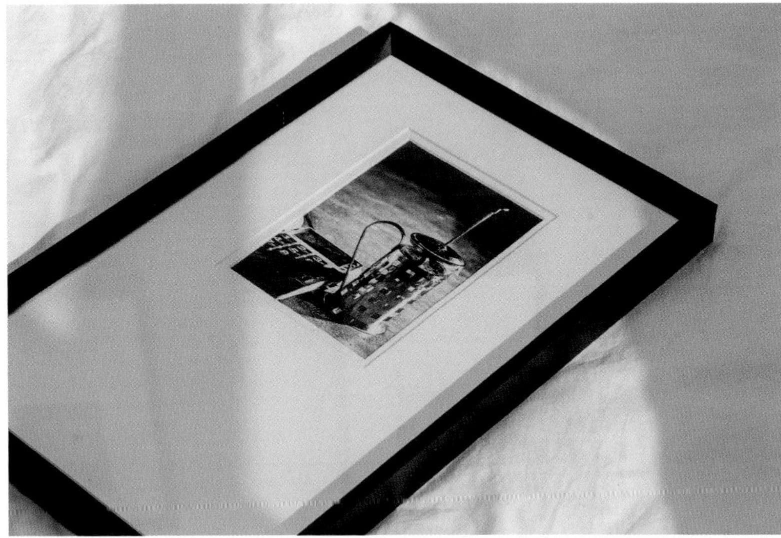

Will on-screen viewing force print production to go the way of the dinosaur?

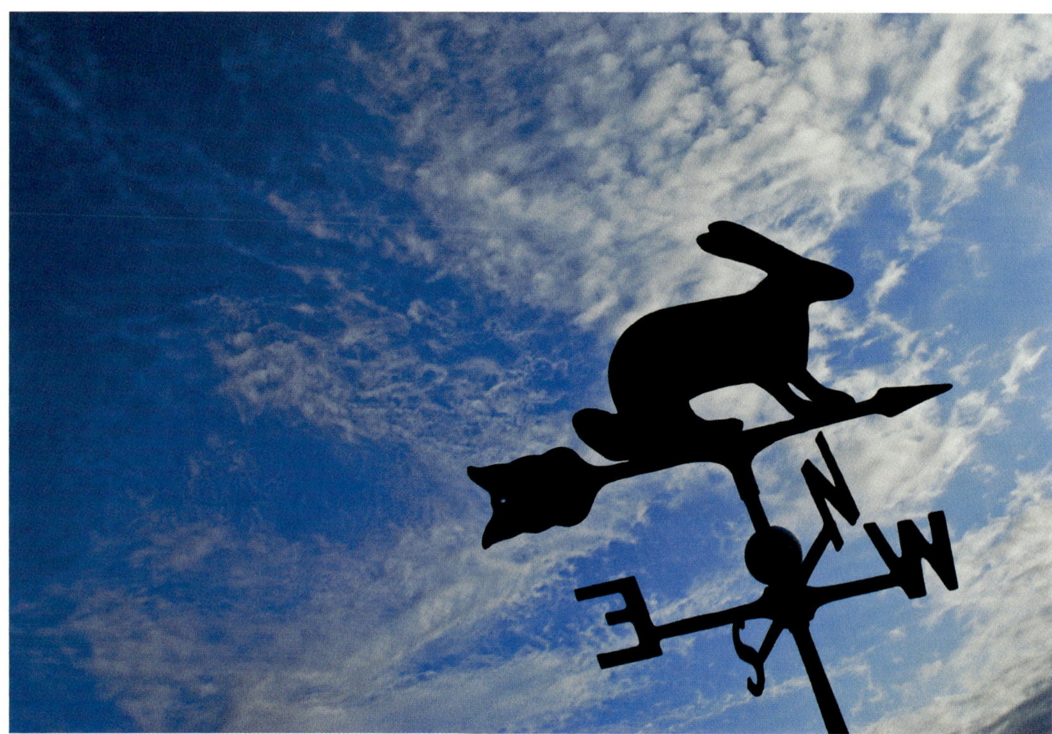

Which direction now?

on these sites isn't enough on its own to build a following, but the sites make it relatively easy to attract an audience.

Many photographers also have their own websites because this gives them control over things such as layout and functionality. Building a professional-looking website used to be beyond those who couldn't afford to hire a web developer or devote hours to learning the very complicated skill set required. Over the years this task has been greatly simplified by the success of various so-called platforms, but the one that really stands out is WordPress. It enables just about anyone to build and manage a first-rate website.

Of course, the online world may not be primarily about marketing for every photographer. The opportunity to communicate with other photographers and to share work easily at any time is almost unlimited. This speaks to something I have noticed over the past few years that I can see becoming even more pronounced, and that is the speed at which photographers develop and mature. The time between first picking up a camera and becoming extremely competent has been massively reduced. Whether this accelerated learning process causes photographers to mature faster as artists is open to debate. I suspect that still happens at its own pace. There is no doubt regarding technique, though. The ability to take limitless shots for free, view thousands of photographs by other photographers, and get feedback from others who share an interest accelerates the learning curve exponentially.

The Biggest Change of All

For the first time in history, photography is a meritocracy. The time has now arrived when people can buy a camera for less than $100, take as many photographs as they like, develop them on their own computer, and then publish them to a place where they can and will be seen by others. If a photographer wants to push boundaries and do something different, there is nothing to stop them—there is no gatekeeper to say no or to preach caution.

Contrast this with how things used to be. The camera may have cost about the same, but taking a lot of photographs was prohibitively expensive unless someone else was paying for the developing, and to have a future someone had to see and approve your work before you could reach a wider audience. This meant that the system was geared toward maintaining the status quo, and consequently the conservative visual approach was likely to be the most successful one.

The new world of photography is still in its early days, and it will be interesting to see how it develops. There are forces at play such as the old guard that wants to put photography back in its box, to make it safe and predictable. I suspect that will no longer be possible, thanks to the thousands of people picking up and experimenting with a camera who now have the means to flourish.

In short, there has never been a better time to be a photographer.

Gallery 9: The Hot Dog Diner

A common scene can be treated in different ways.

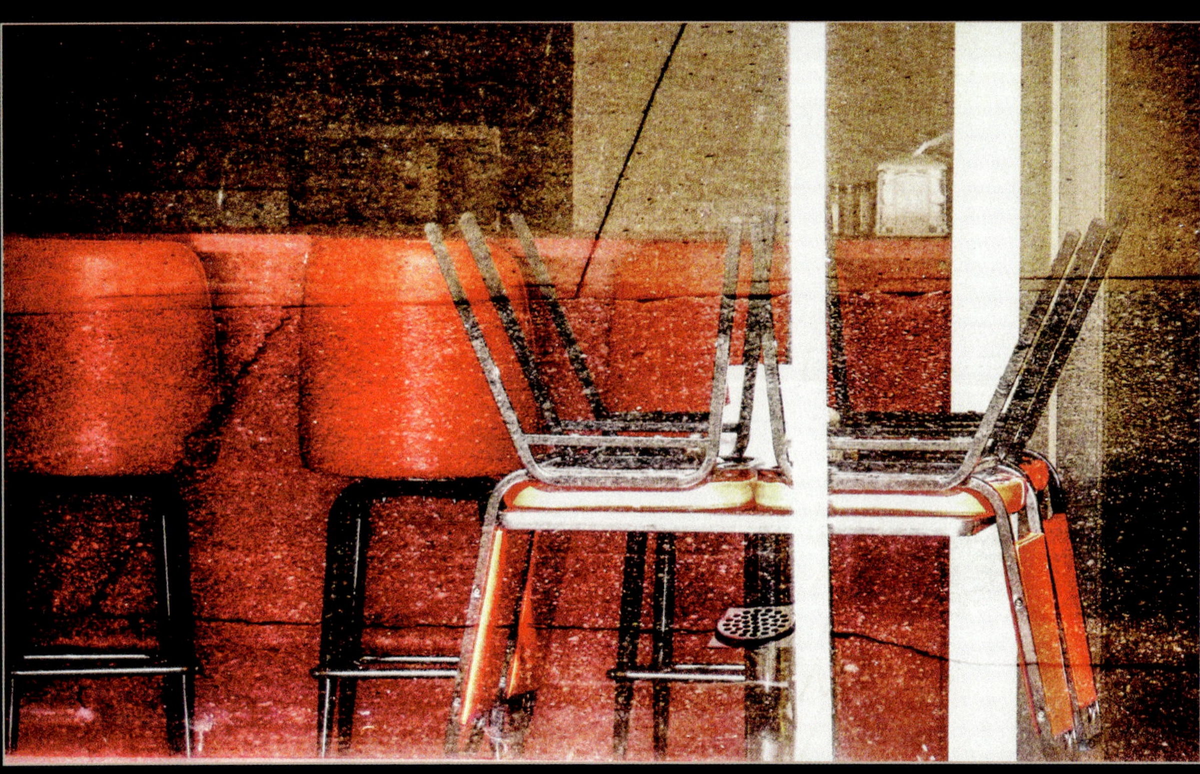

A different treatment of a hot dog diner

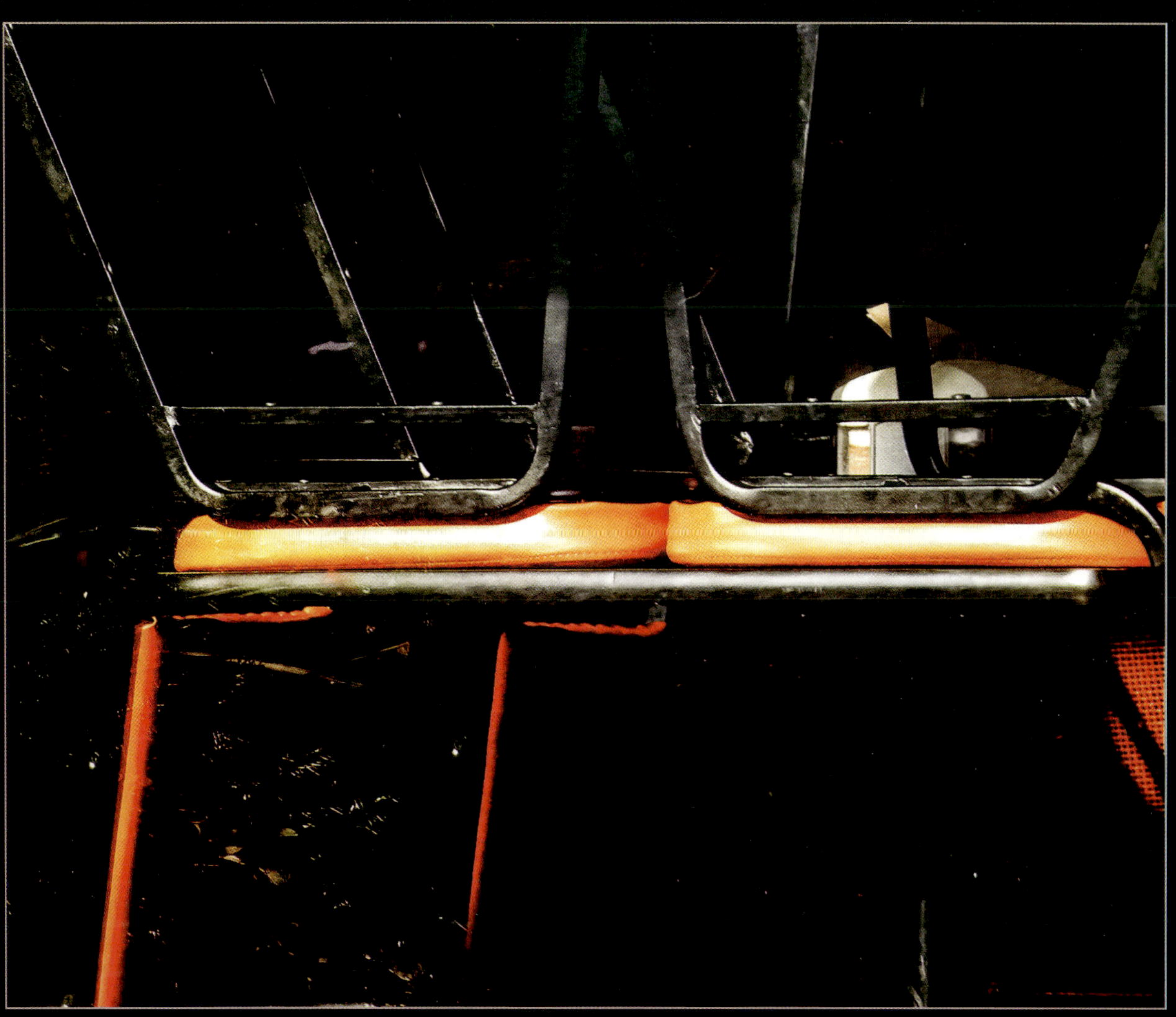

A hot dog diner, edited for an imperfect retro feel

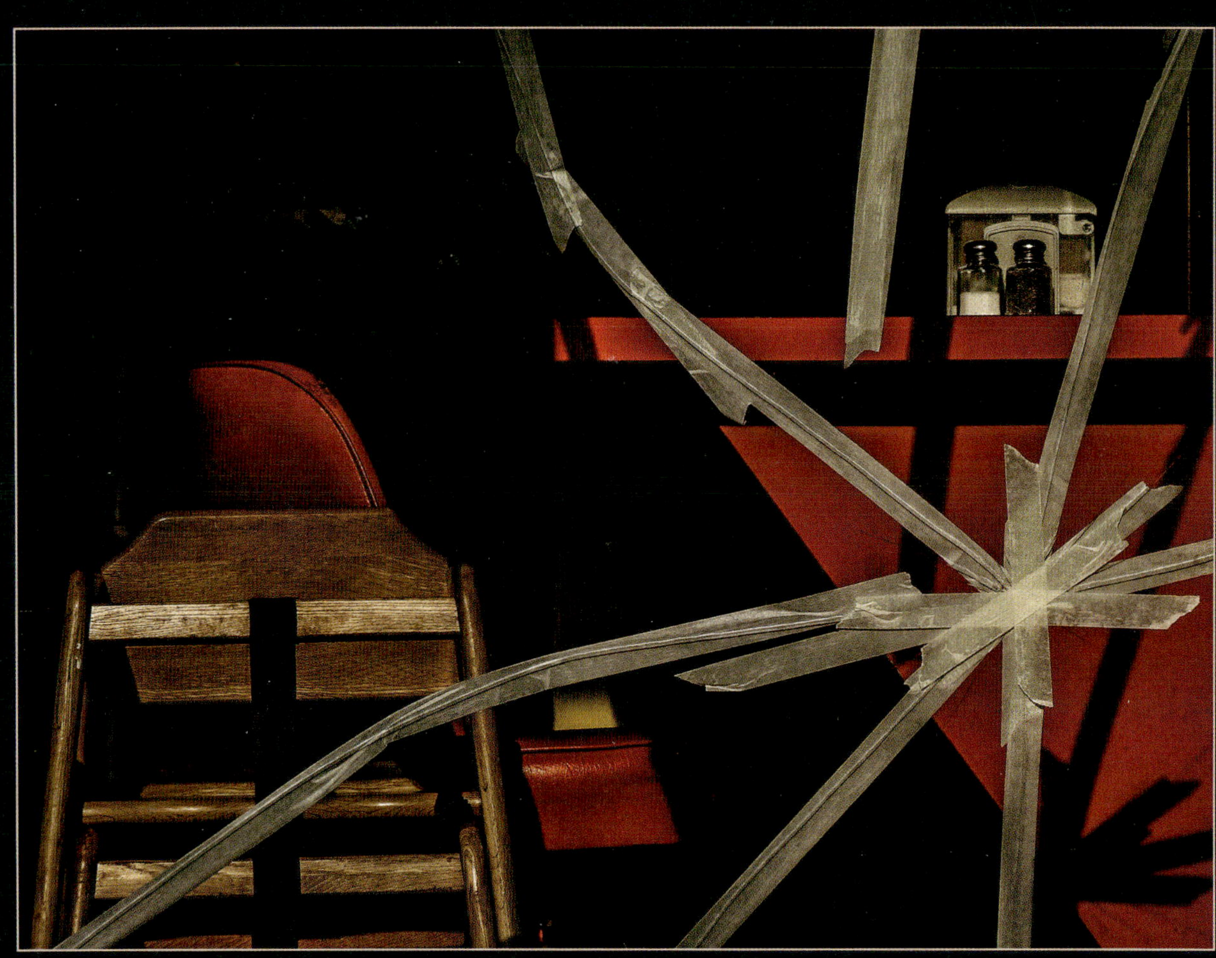

Broken window. The tape made for an interesting layer over the initial composition.